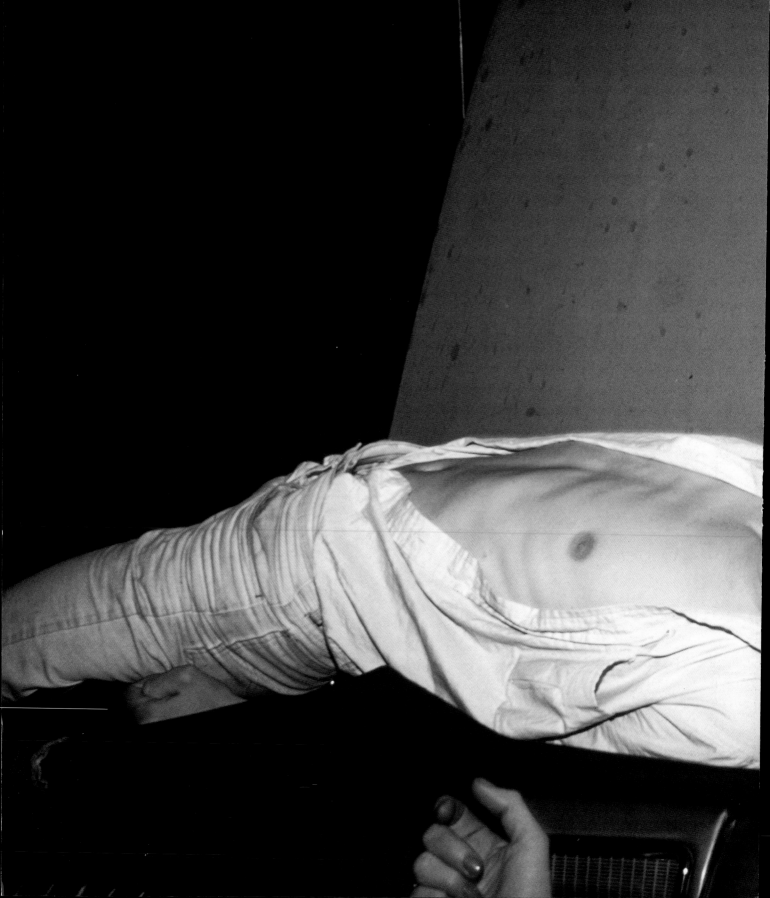

GERMAINE GREER THE BOY

with 206 illustrations, 177 in colour

Thames & Hudson

p. 1 Pinturicchio, *Portrait of a Boy*, 1480–85;
pp. 2–3 Nan Goldin, *French Chris on Carhood, NYC*, 1979; pp. 4–5 Francesco Albani, *Salmacis and Hermaphroditus, c.* 1633

First published in the United Kingdom
in 2003 by Thames & Hudson Ltd,
181A High Holborn, London WC1V 7QX

www.thamesandhudson.com

British Library Cataloguing-in-Publication Data
A catalogue record for this book is available
from the British Library

ISBN 0-500-23809-X

Printed and bound in Singapore by
C. S. Graphics

Contents

Proem

This is a book about male beauty. There are some who think the expression 'male beauty' oxymoronic, even perverse. Students of English as a foreign language are taught that it is incorrect in English to use the word 'beautiful' for a male. Good-looking males should be described as 'handsome'. Handsomeness is not an aesthetic quality so much as a moral quality; handsome is as handsome does. The substitution of the word 'handsome' for 'beautiful' when referring to a male is the linguistic sign of an implicit understanding that it is wrong, demeaning even, to appreciate men for their looks. The feminist campaign against the failure of the phallocracy to appreciate women for anything else has rendered even more difficult the acknowledgment that many males are beautiful, at least for a part of their lives, and that some are staggeringly, even supernaturally beautiful.

Most people have accepted without question that women are treated as sex objects, viewed principally as body, with a primary duty to attract male attention. Though this is clearly true, it is also true that women are at the same time programmed for failure in their duty of attraction, because boys do it better. This is not good news for men, because a boy is a boy for only a very brief space. He has to be old enough to be capable of sexual response but not yet old enough to shave. This window of opportunity is not only narrow, it is mostly illegal. The male human is beautiful when his cheeks are still smooth, his body hairless, his head full-maned, his eyes clear, his manner shy and his belly flat. On a black-figure kylix in the Fitzwilliam Museum in Cambridge, showing a back view of just such a boy standing in a tub and stooping to wash himself, is written το παιδος, το παιδος ιννε καλος, 'the boy, the boy is beautiful'. Artists straight and gay have always known this, at least until the nineteenth century. Women too have known it and know it still. Girls and grandmothers are both susceptible to the short-lived charm of boys, women who are looking for a father for their children less so.

In 1978 a boy called Markus took off his clothes and stood holding them as he was photographed by Will McBride, in a corner of what appears to be an outhouse at McBride's Tuscan property at Casoli in Camaiore. The boy's body is fetishized by the optical distortion; the focus of interest is not his slightly averted face, or even his elongated torso and arms, but his penis.

David, the naked warrior of I Samuel xvii, provides the perfect pretext for the public boy nude. The pose used by Antonin Mercié in 1872 allows the sexy contrapposto to be interpreted as entirely unselfconscious. His young tough is simply propping one foot on Goliath's face, so that he can concentrate on sliding the giant's huge sword into its scabbard. The observer being nowhere acknowledged, decorum is preserved.

The erotic interests of girls and older women are seldom acknowledged by the mainstream culture, which allows itself to presume that images of the most outrageous flirtatiousness will pass unnoticed. When the exhibition 'Exposed: The Victorian Nude' opened at Tate Britain in November 2001, every news-paper sported pictures of the back view of Frederic Leighton's *The Sluggard*, selecting the angle that pushed the youth's bronze buttocks into the viewer's face in a manner that would have been considered pornographic if the subject had been female, but the guardians of public morality noticed nothing. The figure of St Peter that stands in the pediment of the West Portal of Winchester Cathedral is young and stark naked but neither tourists nor parishioners stop to look up at him; on the steps of the Slade School of Fine Art students walk unseeing between replicas of Roman copies of classical ephebes; workers pass in and out of Broadcasting House without lifting their eyes to the façade to admire the naked figure of Ariel sculpted in loving detail by Eric Gill.

There may be a historical explanation for such blindness. It has been assumed that the great Greek sculptors created their ideal types of boy figures because the Greeks were pederasts. This is as absurd as to assume that artists paint still lifes because they want to have sex with shellfish and dead game or because they are hungry. The concealment of Greek women's bodies from public display actually suggests that it is they who were the primary stimulus to sexual activity, which is not normally carried out in public; this concealment is part and parcel of the visual culture that demands the under-emphasis of male genitalia in all classical representations of the nude. Sex is off-stage, which is the root-meaning of 'obscene'. The ubiquity of boy figures in Ancient Greece tells rather of a universal joy and pride in their visibility, a pride which the Romans had no difficulty in perpetuating through literally hundreds of replicas of the best-known types. This tendency continues to our own day, when reproductions of sculpted boy effigies have been commercially reproduced in all sizes and media, the most obvious being Michelangelo's *David*. To this could be added such perennial favourites as the Idolino, the Spinario, the Belvedere Apollo, Gilbert's *Perseus Arming*, Leighton's *The Sluggard*, Hamo Thornycroft's *Teucer* and Antonin Mercié's *David with the Head of Goliath*, of which replicas in bronze and marble were to be seen in thousands of drawing-rooms. Nineteenth-century patriarchs could allow such images to be exhibited in public and enjoyed in private only by refusing to admit that decent women had either eyes to see or an erotic agenda of their own. Women who did react, of course, were fair game.

Only since the nineteenth century has it been assumed that the ideal figure that is the subject of figurative painting and sculpture is female. This assumption has to some extent skewed the history of art because female subjects were favoured over males by the great nineteenth-century collectors who went on to found public museums and art galleries. This skewedness still affects the art market, where figure paintings of females attract higher prices than paintings of male subjects regardless of painterly quality or merit. It was not until the nineteenth century that male artists got to study any female body by paying female models to take off their clothes and pose nude for them. The great masters before them had made do with boys, their own apprentices or professional models, to model female personages for them. They drew the boys nude and then, to make Madonnas of them, blurred their contours and covered them in heavy drapery. Female nudes were modifications of the young male, with added breasts and subtracted genitals, sometimes with bone and sinew extracted as well, until they were as sexless and uninteresting as blow-up dolls. Their pearly inertness was more likely to signify Truth or Divine Love or Religion or Europe than the object of physical desire. As icons of the ideal, female nudes were more convincing if they were less real, with discreet embonpoint, small breasts, no body hair and no body openings whatsoever.

The female nude is physically constrained. She is never to be seen playing, lolling on steps or sitting astride a wall or on horseback, or fighting and slaying the Python or the Minotaur or the Chimaera, or sleeping arms and legs akimbo, or lying dead on the seashore or on the battlefield. Thousands of male nudes are to be seen in all these situations and most of them are beardless. In any artwork before the nineteenth century a boy is more likely to be entirely naked than any other figure; indeed he is sometimes the only naked figure, every other being fully clothed. His body is as it were public; modesty is not required of him. In the poor world to this day, a group of stark naked boys playing in a stream or by a fire hydrant is a common sight, and not something staged for the benefit of paedophiles. The nakedness of boys is celebratory rather than revelatory. When painters begin to position wisps of ribbon over a boy's penis, or hide his groin with an artfully positioned scabbard or spray of foliage, they temper our delight with guilt. This is not to say that the image of the boy is not erotically charged; when the boy sports wings and is called Eros he is understood to be lust itself. When the winged boy is called Gabriel or Raphael, the eroticism is less obvious but still potent. When the angel of the

No attempt was made to confer an identity on the Hellenistic bronze figure of a boy unearthed in Pesaro in 1530. It was dubbed, simply, the Idolino.

Caravaggio painted *St John the Baptist* in 1602 for
Ciriaco Mattei, as a name-day present for his son Giovanni
Battista. The boy himself may have been depicted as John
the Baptist; Giovanni de' Medici was by Bronzino before
him and later James, Duke of Monmouth, by Sir Peter Lely.
The substitution of a ram for the usual lamb and the boy's
rather knowing grin as he hugs the animal are difficult
to explain in any context.

lord spoke to Mary he was after all performing a miracle of love. Human beings can only understand divine love through the medium of human love, and love of all kinds is made manifest in the figure of the boy.

As women joined the viewing public of institutionalized art towards the end of the eighteenth century, both masculinity and sensuality drained away from depictions of the male nude. After women won their struggle to be admitted to the life class, they too could draw full-length academies and paint nudes. The few who then went on to work as professional painters of the figure chose to paint female nudes rather than males. Though studies of the nude male were deemed a necessary preliminary for any subject involving figures, the young male nude as an embodiment of ideal beauty all but disappeared from straight iconography. As a female painter's subject, the boy, insofar as he exists at all, is a girl. There are exceptions to this rule but they are few indeed.

At the end of the twentieth century guilty panic about paedophilia completed the criminalization of awareness of the desires and the charms of boys. A nude boy called Eros presides over London from his pedestal in Piccadilly Circus but we do not see him. Beneath him rent boys ply their miserable trade. Where once boys were considered 'made for love and loved of all' they are now considered attractive only to a perverted taste. The rest of us avert our eyes. Yet, not so far away, on giant billboards dotted about the city, can be seen seductive photographs, much more than life-size, of a ravishing boy. Naked to the waist, he sits on a sofa with his knees apart and arms spread wide, as if waiting for someone to jump on him. The fly of his jeans is unzipped just far enough to reveal the designer name woven into the waistband of his underpants. Market researchers know what they are doing; they know that the buyers of most men's underpants are women. Men's fragrances too are sold to women, which is why the representative image is so often a pouting boy wearing nothing but lipgloss.

Part of the purpose of this book is to advance women's reclamation of their capacity for and right to visual pleasure. The nineteenth century denied women any active interest in sex, which was only to be found in degenerate types. By the end of the twentieth century female appetite for sexual stimulus had been recognized and platoons of male strippers mobilized to take commercial advantage of it. That healthy appetite should now be refined by taste. If we but lift our eyes to the beautiful images of young men that stand all about us, there is a world of complex and civilized pleasure to be had. Delight in the boy can only be sharpened by the pathos and irony of his condition of becomingness. What we see in life is gone before we have had time to appreciate it. It is only in art that the compellingly evanescent charm of boyhood can be preserved against the ravages of time.

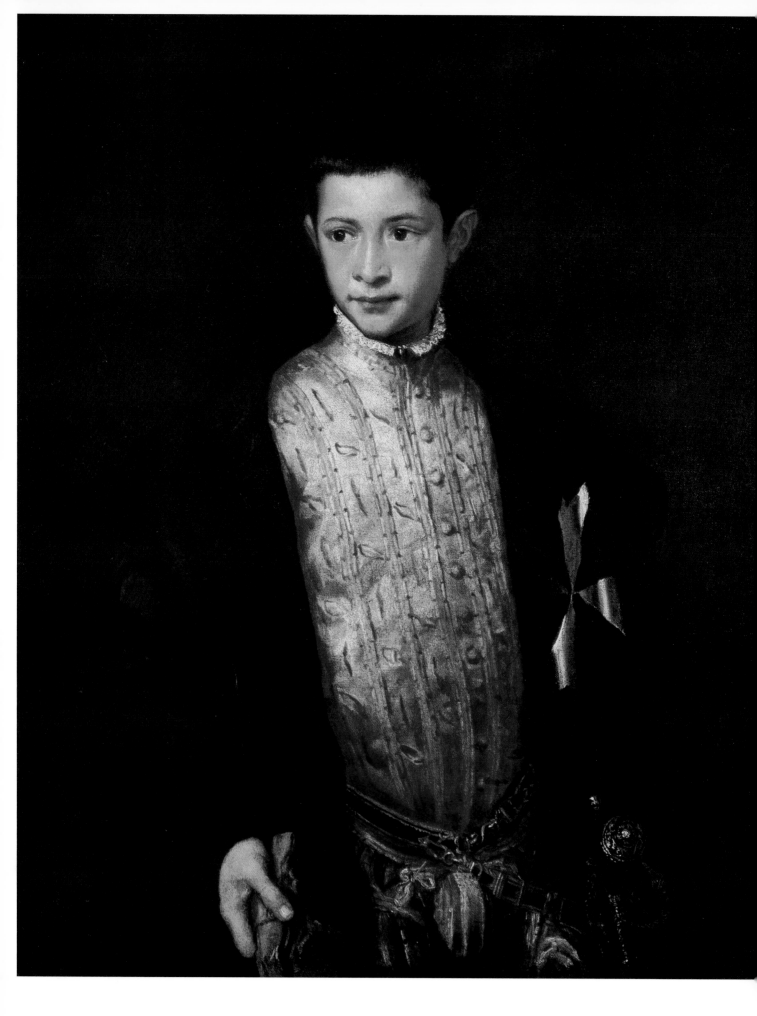

chapter 1

What is a Boy?

Titian painted twelve-year-old Ranuccio Farnese in 1542 for his mother, the Duchess of Parma. The strange contrast of the boy's small, shy face with the man-sized mantle that slides off his shoulders, and the incongruity of the sword, codpiece and the muscular hand holding a glove cannot simply be explained by the possibility that Ranuccio may have been present only when Titian was painting the head. He stands in his shimmering doublet on the brink of darkness, his brilliance doomed to be eclipsed in the formality of life as a celibate prince of the church.

A boy is a male person who is no longer a child but not yet a man. Boyhood may be long, beginning as soon as a male baby is weaned and not ending until he is permitted to assume the insignia of manhood, which may be as much as fifteen or even twenty years later. Boyhood may be telescoped, as when a boy-child is removed from the debilitating society of women, immediately dressed in male clothing and required to imitate the behaviour of grown men. Then, behaviour considered childish or, worse, girlish, such as weeping or showing fear, will be severely discouraged, even punished. In some societies the unmanly boy will find himself called a girl; in others his unmanliness will not only be indulged but will entitle him to special privileges.

Whether boyhood be a crash course or a long and gradual induction, the outcome should be manhood. In some cultures the production of a decent moustache may be sufficient to raise a boy to the dignity of manhood; in other societies males are considered boys until they have found themselves wives and married them; and in others even this will not be enough to admit a boy as an equal in the society of grown men, if he has not slain his lion single-handed or beaten his penis flat between two stones. In no human society is someone who considers himself a man happy to be treated as a boy. Though the criteria that distinguish the men from the boys may differ, the distinction is universal.

The rites of passage from boyhood to manhood may be as simple and painless as shaving the boy's head, dressing him in a saffron robe and sending him to live as a monk for a year, as is done in some Buddhist societies. Other cultures require a series of painful and dangerous rituals that enact the destruction of the boy before he can be reborn as a man. The Barabeg of East Africa inflict a series of deep cuts across the boy's forehead that lay bare the bone. The Native American Luiseños of southern California stake the initiate out on an anthill. The Poro of Sierra Leone first circumcise the boy, then

Above Edward, Prince of Wales, son and heir of Henry VIII by his third wife, Jane Seymour, was painted by Holbein the Younger in *c.* 1539 as a New Year's present for his father in 1540.

push him face down on the ground and cut deep gashes in his back with a razor; these are said to be the marks made by the fangs of the Poro spirit who eats up the boy so that the man may live. At puberty the Masai boy is circumcised; for eight to twelve months thereafter he must wear white face paint and dress in black. He is then ready to become a *moran* and join his age-set living in the bush, raiding settlements for cattle to build up their herds. Before he can be accepted as a man, the *moran* must kill a lion single-handed. As a *moran* he is encouraged to bedizen himself with beads and other ornaments; he may wear his hair long and elaborately braided or modelled into fantastic shapes with red ochre.

In Britain it is still the practice in some purlieux of the middle class to send boys far away from home to schools which are even now reluctant to give up the routine canings and birchings required 'to make men of them'. Poorer boys used to be indentured or sent to sea or into the army or set to unskilled work. What masters did to their men, the men did to the boys and the older boys to the younger boys. Military service segregated boys, alienated them from their families and often subjected them to painful rituals. The Boy Scout movement claimed to be able to make 'big men out of little boys' virtually overnight. A Cub Scout was a miniature version of a Scout, already at the age of eight uniformed, clean-cut and manly, and unafraid of the dark. Instead of dancing and singing and dressing up, as is a teenaged boy's prerogative, the uniformed Boy Scout would be tramping about the wilderness, demonstrating hardy self-reliance – and purity.

For centuries European mothers wept when their sons were breeched and their hair shorn; indeed, many mothers would keep their boys in the long skirts of infancy for as long as they could. Portraits of the same date showing male children of the same age may show them either as elfin creatures with floating curls and muslin skirts or as tough mini-men in breeches. Among the most moving of the mini-man portraits must be those of the orphan boy-king Edward VI. In the portrait painted by Holbein the Younger when Edward was less than two years old, he wears the skirts of infancy but is imposingly hatted and holds up his baby hand in a gesture of authority. At the time of his accession, though he was only nine years old, and thin, pale and sickly, he is shown clad as a man in stiff padded doublet and hose with jutting codpiece, under a heavy fur-lined surtout, standing with a poniard in his hand, his shoulders open and thrown back in the bluff pose typical of his father. The portraits show not a boy but a king, for whom boyhood was not an option.

A wife had been chosen for him when he was only six years old and he was confidently expected to be married by the time he was twelve. Another unfinished portrait sketch showing Edward in profile was probably meant for a betrothal portrait. In this he does seem a delicate boy, almost as fragile as the rose he holds in his hand.

It was not only boy-kings who were catapulted into manhood. Titian's 1542 portrait of twelve-year-old Ranuccio Farnese shows him with all the attributes of adulthood; his curls have been shorn and he is buttoned into a tight doublet, equipped with sword and codpiece, with the heavy mantle of the Knights of Malta balancing on his narrow shoulders. The portrait was commissioned for his mother on the occasion of the boy's leaving his home in Parma to take up residence in Venice, where he had been appointed prior of the Venetian chapter of the Order of the Knights of Malta as the first step in the career of a celibate prince of the church. (Three years later he would be made patriarch of Constantinople.) It is Titian's genius to show that Ranuccio's face is not just that of a boy, but of a small boy, with sticky-out ears, a mouth that is set but tremulous, and the suggestion of shadows under his eyes. In 1555 when Ranuccio's nephew Alessandro was ten, Girolamo Bedoli painted him 'vestito da Marte' in full armour over scarlet breeches and hose, complete with codpiece, sitting on a globe and being embraced by a vast kneeling female, also in armour, representing the adoring city of Parma. Both pictures, Titian's moving masterpiece and Bedoli's extravaganza, were painted for the boys' mothers. Ranuccio's mother, who was Gerolama Orsini when she married Pier Luigi Farnese in 1519, twenty-six years before he became Duke of Parma, seems to have been a very different person from Alessandro's mother, Margaret of Austria, bastard daughter of Emperor Charles V; she almost certainly directed Bedoli to pose her son the way he did. We know very little about women as patrons, and even less about the extent to which they influenced the artists whose work was intended for their apartments, but it seems probable that when it comes to the portraiture of their sons, mothers' attitudes would be crucial.

The condition of boyhood being so variously understood, we should not be surprised to find contradictions in the concept of the male's life-career. The ages of man could be and were numbered in different ways, by analogy with the Trinity, the seasons of the year, the ages of the world, the days of the week, the months of the year or the signs of the Zodiac. The simplest division is into three; boy, man and old man, beardless, bearded and long-bearded. As a pictorial topos the ages of man are often also group portraits. Giorgione's *Three Ages of Man* presents, besides the mature man and an older man, a sweet-faced boy gazing at a piece of music. The three ages are here presented as a consort, with the old man as the bass, the boy as the treble and the man instructing the boy as the tenor. In *Cyropedia*, an idealized account of the manly boyhood of Cyrus the Elder in Ancient Persia, Xenophon describes the public square as divided into four sections, one for boys, one for youths, one for grown men and the last for men too old for military service. Valentin de

Opposite Eight-year-old Alessandro Farnese, Ranuccio's nephew, was togged up in scarlet tights and shining armour in 1555 for a portrait to be painted by Girolamo Bedoli for his mother, who was the bastard daughter of the Emperor Charles V. It was her burning ambition rather than his that resulted in the curious image of an unresponsive boy having his steel collar felt by a vast metal-clad female.

Boulogne follows this four-part division; small boy, youth, man, old man correspond to spring, summer, autumn and winter. The small boy plays with a cage; the older boy makes music. An interesting sub-group in the four-age scheme personifies one of the ages as female. Of these Titian's is the best known and the most intriguing. The first stage of a man's life is shown in the little heap of amorini, the last in the distant figure of the old man contemplating a skull. In the foreground of the picture, resting as it were against the picture frame, sits a naked man. His body is tanned and weathered, his face hairy and he appears preoccupied or distracted. He does not respond to the fully dressed young woman crowned with flowers who lies along his naked thigh, holding two flutes as if suggesting that they play together. Boyhood is here the missing term, emblematized not in a boy portrait, as in Giorgione's *Three Ages of Man*, but in the personification of Flora; the flute is the attribute of Theocritus's amorous shepherd, and the man's time of playing is past.

The five-age scheme was constructed in analogy with the five ages of the world: the Golden Age under Saturn, Silver under Jupiter, Brazen under Neptune, Heroic under Mars and Iron under Pluto. Two of the five

were devoted to immaturity, divided into childhood and youth. The mediaeval six-age version divided youth into three sections: infantia, puerilia and adolescentia. The predominance of youth in all these schemata reflects the demographic structure of early modern society, which had many times more young people than there were mature or old. The division of life into seven ages summarized by Jacques in Shakespeare's *As You Like It* also gives three of the seven to youth. After infancy come the two phases of boyhood, before and after puberty:

> … the whining schoolboy with his satchel
> And shining morning face, creeping like snail
> Unwillingly to school. And then the lover,
> Sighing like furnace, with a woful ballad
> Made to his mistress' eyebrow.

The soldier follows, 'bearded like the pard'. According to Jacques, then, the time for love in the life-career of a male is the time between leaving school, at twelve or fourteen, and qualifying for military service at twenty-one. During this time a boy might have been a scholar in the Inns of Court or the Universities, or an apprentice, or a squire, or a footpage. In all these walks of

Above In the picture painted by Titian *c.* 1513 and usually called *The Three Ages of Man*, manhood, as distinct from childhood and old age, is expressed as a couple of lovers, perhaps Daphnis and Chloe. The position of the pipe in the woman's left hand has even been interpreted as an indication that they have had sex. It is more rewarding to read this picture as a vanitas; the old man with the two skulls is an obvious memento mori and the female figure too may be an allegorical representation of a time of life rather than a personage.

life a boy was expected to behave in an irrepressible manner, whether as a wit or a womanizer, a toper, a rioter or an extravagant dresser. In Shakespeare's time gangs of working-class apprentices regularly terrorized the city with their hooliganism, middle-class gallants brought uproar into the playhouses and young noblemen were a law unto themselves. Just so Prince Hal, son of Henry IV, 'the nimble-footed madcap prince of Wales', Falstaff's 'sweet wag' and 'tender lambkin' whose 'chin is not yet fledge', spends his youth in 'riot and dishonour', enjoying his boy's preference for good fellowship among 'gallants, lads, hearts of gold'. When he drinks deep with the staff at the tavern where he lodges they tell him that he is 'a Corinthian, a lad of mettle, a good boy' … and that when he is king he shall 'command all the good lads in Eastcheap'. His boyhood ends when he proceeds to Jacques's fourth age and kills Hotspur in single combat, no more sweet-faced Prince Hal but ferocious Harry Monmouth.

Just as Harry annihilates Hal, every male who survives boyhood must agree to annihilate the boy in him and confine himself to the narrower scope available to him in patriarchal society. This takes discipline and self-repression,

summarized by Wordsworth in 1807 as 'shades of the prison-house' closing on the growing boy. The boy who survives to become a man must learn to husband his energy, to walk and talk with caution and deliberation, and to take his place on the ladder of authority. As Mary Douglas wrote in *Purity and Danger*, 'Danger lies in transitional states, simply because transition is neither one state nor the next, it is indefinable. The person who must pass from one to another is himself in danger and emanates that danger to others. The danger is controlled by ritual which precisely separates him from his old status, segregates him for a time, and then publicly declares his entry to his new status.'

Boys are volatile, unpredictable and vulnerable. A male teenager is more likely to attempt suicide than not, more likely than anyone else to write off a motor vehicle, almost certain to experiment with drug experiences of one kind or another, and at greater risk of committing and/or suffering an act of violence than any grown man or female. His vulnerability is made more acute by his own recklessness and spontaneity.

Adolescence is not a moment but a process. A male child becomes a boy when it starts but may not yet be a man when it finishes. It begins as soon as he becomes aware of sexual feelings, which happens for some male children very early and for others relatively late. Sperm begins to be present in boys' urine when they are eight or nine, but awareness of sexual feelings is mediated by other factors. R. W. Connell divides the maturation of the male into six phases: the first is infancy, no body hair and testes of one to two cubic centimetres in volume; adolescence begins with the appearance of downy pubic hair and a doubling in the size of the testes, and proceeds by degrees with changes in pubic hair and testicular volume, to hair in armpits and testicles of up to sixteen cubic centimetres in volume. These four stages take about five years and the process is not over then. For many boys traumatic events signal real as distinct from schematic stages in the adolescence process: the first wet dream, the breaking of the voice, the first shave. Body hair can increase steadily for many years after adolescence is officially over. Masturbation is agreed to begin at eleven or twelve, but there is little systematic evidence.

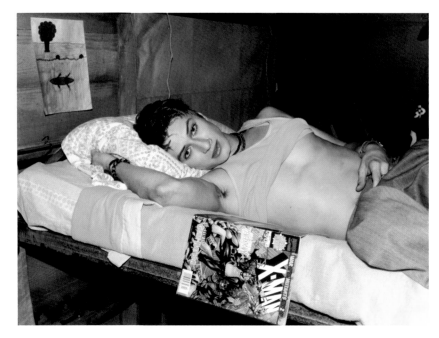

Above Collier Schorr, born in New York in 1963, has been photographing adolescents assuming the insignia of various masculinities since 1987. Her photographs emphasize the vulnerability of very young men, especially amid brutal surroundings, as for example in the military. There is no knowing how consciously the male odalisque in a photograph from *Cast of Happy Campers*, 2001, assumed the pose of Michelangelo's *Dying Slave* (see p. 109).

According to Daniel Levinson, who like Xenophon's Ancient Persians, favours a four-part seasonal division of the life of man, puberty happens at twelve or thirteen plus or minus two years, which is to say, anywhere between ten and fifteen. He further hedges his bets by marking seventeen as the beginning of early adulthood, and twenty-two as the end of adolescence.

An adult male who remains slim and lovely and keeps the hair on his head rather than growing it on his face and body may play a boy's role for as long as it is congenial. In the Renaissance young men who kept their hair long and luxuriant and their faces clean-shaven could prolong boyhood well into their twenties, while they explored the roles of scholar and lover. Raphael, 'a very amorous man with a great fondness for women', according to Vasari, chose to put himself into his fresco of The School of Athens, 'with a youthful head, an air of great modesty, and a gracious and attractive manner … wearing a black cap', portraying himself effectively as a boy though he must have been in his mid-twenties. Raphael's portrait of the banker and connoisseur Bindo Altoviti as a young man shows him turning away, looking back at the viewer over his right shoulder as if bidding farewell, in a similar attitude to Raphael's own in the self-portrait. The crisp golden hairs sprouting on Altoviti's cheeks signal the end of boyhood. He holds one hand softly pressed to his breast-bone as if feeling a pang at his heart, a gesture familiar to us from other portraits of young men, of which the best known is Giorgione's in the Szépmüvészeti Museum in Budapest, painted in about 1510. The young man in Giorgione's picture rests his elbow on a stone ledge, on which is fixed a tiny circular plaque showing the three faces of the allegory of prudence, another representation of the ages of man.

Such portraits are depictions not of identity but of allegorized stages in lives that were understood to involve transformations. All of them are distinguished by a distinctly elegiac mood. Among the attributes that are on the verge of extinction is youthful narcissism; the young men are carefully dressed, their hair curled and brushed out into floating clouds, their caps jauntily cocked. Add to this the suggestivity of the half-removed glove that appears again and again in portraits by Titian and his older and younger contemporaries, and it will be seen that these are pictures of a moment that is already past. Titian's *Man in a Red Cap* is pale and languid, his dark eyes abstracted and mournful, his red cap the same as the one worn by the young lutenist in Titian's arcadian *Concert Champêtre* (*c.* 1509) in the Louvre. The hair that gushes from under the cap is rich and dark against the luminously

Above The proper pursuits of boyhood are love, music and poetry; many Renaissance portraits of unmarried males show them following all three. In *Portrait of a Young Man* of 1590 by Alessandro Allori, the fealty to Apollo of a now unidentifiable young man is indicated by the figurine behind him. His sober dress is not only appropriate to melancholy and scholarly pursuits but also reveals the youthful slenderness of his physique.

Below left and right The Rembrandt self-portrait on the left, from the Mauritshuis, is typical of the images used by portrait-painters to recommend themselves to future patrons. The sitter is shown in the best possible light, as young, handsome and confident. A later version of the same composition shows us a more tremulous and apparently older figure, whose image has not had the glamorizing treatment.

Opposite In the conventional self-portrait the artist depicts himself with turned head studying his own image as if in a mirror placed beside him in order to transfer it to a canvas placed in front of him. Dürer first shows himself at 13 as he can hardly have seen himself, in half-profile, then twice at 21 or so, his features distorted by the intensity of his self-contemplation, and then in a magnificently Apollonian aggrandizing version, which may depict him as a bridegroom, though what he bends in his finger is not the usual rose but a prickly sprig of sea holly.

pale skin of his neck. The richly furred lappets of his loose coat could easily slide from his shoulders as, in a strangely Onanistic gesture, he draws into view the bulbous pommel of his sword, which is crowned with a single pearl of light. The split in the neat-skin glove on the hand that clasps the sword exposes a contrasting lozenge of bare flesh.

Portraits of young men are usually commissioned by their betters, by their parents, either for themselves or to serve as betrothal presents, or by their patrons and/or lovers. We can only wonder whom Titian's deeply and subtly erotic image was destined for. More decorous portraits of noble young men show them as lovers of beauty, with ancient cameos in their hands and figurines of Apollo standing by to signify their fealty to poetry and music. Others have slender index fingers inserted in slim volumes indicating their passion for poetry or for a mistress to whom they have written poetry. These gorgeous boys could continue showing their tight buttocks and long legs in clinging hose until the hair on their head thinned. Then they adopted the citizen's hat and gown and let their beards grow.

Hundreds of painters have left portraits of themselves when young. Dürer drew himself as a rather adenoidal youth of thirteen, as a tormented twenty-one-year-old, and as a serene young god at the age of twenty-two, still almost as beardless as Apollo. Rembrandt charted the loss of his looks with brutal frankness. In the Nuremberg self-portrait dated *c.* 1629 apparently simply from the apparent age of the sitter which is assumed to be twenty-three, his lips are rosy, his hair shimmery and he gazes serenely at the viewer with the cockiness of a not-yet-man. In the Uffizi portrait the face is foreshortened and the technique drier but in other respects, the literalness of the rendition of the mantle and its chain, the pernicketty detail of the shirt appearing over a similar metal collar, it seems an early work of the same period as the

Nuremberg portrait. In the Munich self-portrait both the rosiness and the composure are gone, though the shirt seems to be the same shirt as in the Nuremberg portrait. It is as if Rembrandt had revisited the cocky portrait and deliberately distorted it to produce a truer version that replaces the phony self-assurance of the aggrandizing portrait with genuine inner turmoil.

The self-portraits of Anthony Van Dyck too offer a fascinating opportunity to trace his progress from boy to man. The earliest shows him at the age of fourteen or so, when he was training in the studio of Rubens, plump cheeked and pouting, much as he is in a portrait painted at the same time by his master. As his majority approached, he painted three self-portraits; in each the face is turned slightly to the right, with the eyes looking out directly at the viewer. In the finest of these, he wears a suit of lustrous black satin, knotted at the breast by a simple bow. The skin of his sweet face and long slender hands is a warmer version of the white of the lawn shirt that froths through the opening of his doublet and the slashings in the sleeves. Though the face has thinned down the cheeks still bear the bloom of youth, and the brow under the clustering auburn curls is smooth and unlined. The brown eyes rest upon the viewer with a hesitancy that is almost coquettish, a suggestion that is borne out by the slight parting of the young man's rosy lips. Though Van Dyck was probably in his early twenties and shaving fairly regularly, he shows himself with peach-smooth cheeks. In other words, the boy he is painting has already ceased to exist. This portrait is a pictorial document of passage, a farewell to youthful extravagance and self-obsession.

Young men's arrogant consciousness of their own fugitive beauty crystallizes in the well-known cautionary tale of Narcissus. When Ovid's story opens Narcissus is sixteen years old, has been wooed by many a man and maid, and has coldly spurned them all. The goddess Nemesis hears the prayer of one of his rejected lovers and grants that Narcissus too might love without hope. Narcissus, hot from hunting, finds himself by a still, grass-fringed pool in a cool and shady thicket and lies down to drink from it.

> While he seeks to slake his thirst, another thirst springs up, and
> while he drinks he is smitten by the sight of the beautiful form he
> sees. He loves an insubstantial hope and thinks that substance which
> is only shadow.... Unwittingly he desires himself; he praises and
> is himself what he praises; and while he seeks is sought; equally
> he kindles love and burns with love.

Above Anthony Van Dyck, *Lord John and Lord Bernard Stuart*, 1637. Van Dyck accentuates the glamour of two sons of the third Duke of Lennox, 17-year-old Lord John to the left and 16-year-old Lord Bernard to the right. Their indolent postures and haughty expressions are the same as those used by catwalk mannequins today. The high stacked heels of their soft leather boots add to their already improbable height and slenderness.

Opposite As the face in the self-portrait by Van Dyck that is usually dated 1621 is clearly derived from a self-portrait painted when he was in his teens, it must be a portrait of the artist as a dazzling young man painted when he was far more accomplished as an artist but no longer so young or so beautiful. Nostalgia is more prevalent in portraiture than is usually recognized.

Narcissus remains transfixed by his image in the pool, neither eating nor drinking, 'perque oculos perit ipse suos', consumed by his own eyes. His eclipse is rather like the fate that once threatened habitual masturbators, that they would exhaust the bodily substance that was needed to build them up to robust manhood. The Narcissus story has such a clear and present relevance to youthful self-obsession that the story has been regularly retold in all kinds of moralizing literature since the Old French metrical romance *Narcisse* was written in the third quarter of the twelfth century. Guillaume de Lorris retold the story in the *Roman de la Rose*; Boccaccio referred to it repeatedly in his writings on love; Christine de Pizan retold it at the end of the fourteenth century, Alamanni, Jean Rus, Ronsard and Gregorio Silvestre Rodriquez de Mesa in the mid-sixteenth. Though paintings of Narcissus gazing at himself are relatively few, the theme continued to inspire hundreds of writers, some of whom were clearer than others about the connection between Narcissus' behaviour and his youth. John Clapham called his Latin verse allegory of 1591 *Narcissus, sive, Amoris iuvenilis descriptio*.

As long as the boy is a boy, behaviours that would dishonour the head of a family are acceptable and even becoming; boyhood is after all the time of 'sowing wild oats'. A boy may play the role of passive partner in sex with both men and women; the ritual of transition will relegate such play to the past, as the man will husband his seed for the serious purposes of reproductive sex. No such self-denial is to be expected from a boy. Boy sex is irresponsible, spontaneous and principally self-pleasuring. Though the sexual drive of young males has now been recognized, it is expected to be expressed in masturbation rather than in non-reproductive sex with others, which has been to a large extent criminalized. Age limits for consent to sexual activity may be gradually coming down but at the same time it is more likely than ever before in our history that intimacy between individuals of disparate ages will be stigmatized as perverted. If vu nerability to paedophilic assault peaks between the ages of ten and twelve, tinkering with definitions of what can be legally consented to

Left and above Benvenuto Cellini's marble Narcissus was designed to be reflected in a pool in the Boboli Gardens in Florence. Originally Cellini had been asked to carve a Hercules from the marble he had been given but when he found that it had two holes through it, he decided upon the sinuous languid figure of a Narcissus instead. In the elegant wall-painting discovered on the wall of a house in Pompeii the unknown artist has supplied both pool and reflection.

Opposite In two films, *Kids* (1995) and *Another Day in Paradise* (1998), and various photo essays, Larry Clark, born in 1942, claims to present the world from the point of view of the young. In *Oklahoma City*, 1975, from his 1992 series *Teenage Lust*, the boy's excitement at the sight of himself with his pants down may be a deliberate recollection of Narcissus.

Top and above In his portrait of Master John Heathcote
(*c*. 1770–74) Gainsborough emphasizes the boy's frailty, so that
he seems almost more fragile than the flowers he holds. When
Reynolds painted fourteen-year-old Alexander Hamilton in 1782
boys were to be seen, according to an impressed German visitor,
'with their bosoms open, and their hair cut on their forehead
while behind it flows naturally in ringlets'. Boys could continue
dressing in this informal style until they were eighteen or twenty.

at age sixteen, say, can have nothing to do with child protection. As far as we can tell, about 11% of boys will have sexual experiences with males; fewer than 2% of boys then go on to become exclusively homosexual in their preference. Latin cultures foster heterosexuality by encouraging even small boys to be in love with small girls, teaching them the arts of courtship and, eventually, how to pleasure females without running the risk of impregnating them, by making love to them as if they had no vaginas, as if indeed they were male. Boyhood is a playground and the game is polymorphous perversity.

Among the variety of rituals that terminate boyhood, many involve hair, usually the cutting or shaving of hair. A boy's hair can grow as luxuriantly as any girl's. Keeping it long, full and flowing has been a privilege accorded to boys in many societies where grown men were expected to keep their hair cropped or their heads shaved. At the ceremony which will signal the Masai *moran*'s irrevocable entry into manhood his mother will shave off his elaborately braided tresses, leaving him as bald as a billiard-ball, and she will comfort him as he weeps for the loss of his beauty. Shearing of a boy's hair often coincided with the coming in of his beard. In Ancient Rome the day a boy's face was first shaved was held to be the day of his entry into manhood, and as such was held sacred. The first shavings from the cheeks of the Emperor Nero, together with the long curls cut from his head, were placed in a gold box ornamented with pearls and dedicated to Jupiter Capitolinus, and the day was rubricated as the first of the festival of the Juvenalia.

Male anthropologists, who evidently share the phallic anxiety of their adult male subjects, have been more interested in the social construction of manhood than the condition of boyhood and have little to say about it. They were fascinated and, one suspects, appalled to find that among several groups in the New Guinea Highlands, the Sambia, Etoro, Onabasulu, Kaluli and Gururumba, for example, boys were expected to fellate men in order to ingest their semen so that they might grow tall and strong. No attempt was made to find out how the boys felt about the practice, whether they enjoyed doing it or whether it was an ordeal for them, or even at what stage they could cease being takers and become givers of the nourishing semen. Female anthropologists, having principally concerned themselves with studying the largely undescribed lives of women, have had even less to say about the condition of boyhood.

The psychologists have been more interested. Freud described the earliest phase of a male child's life, when he fails to distinguish between himself and his mother, as 'primary narcissism'. As he grows, the male child must separate himself from his mother and assume an identity and a social role that are unlike hers, in that they are predicated on independence and courage, while still yearning for the security of the engulfing maternal presence. 'While it is true that the boy's first love object is heterosexual, he must perform a great deed to

Below This portrait of two-year-old Francis George Hare was commissioned from Sir Joshua Reynolds in 1788 by the child's aunt. His imperious gesture is the only clue to his sex. Reynolds liked the picture so well that he, or his assistants, painted at least three replicas of it.

make this so: he must first separate his identity from hers. Thus the whole process of becoming masculine is at risk in the little boy from the day of birth on; his still-to-be-created masculinity is endangered by the profound, primeval oneness with the mother, a blissful experience that serves, buried but active in the core of one's identity, as a focus which, throughout life, can attract one to regress back to that primitive oneness. That is the threat latent in masculinity.'

A version of this argument that underlies the sex role theory of the 1960s and '70s goes like this: 'Males start as FFs (unconscious and conscious feminine identity) totally identified with the mother, then progress to the FM stage [unconscious-feminine-conscious masculine] acquiring superficial masculine traits but maintaining their deep feminine identity, and complete their maturation as MMs, developing inner masculine identification to match the surface behavior they earlier acquired.'

Many mothers, conscious of the boyishness of their sons from birth and their different attitudes from their sisters' to such basic matters as food, waste elimination and play, would want to reverse the story, making the femininity of their boys superficial and temporary, and their masculinity deep, virtually instinctual. Others might want to argue that both femininity and masculinity are superficial, cultural or even arbitrarily imposed, and that both boy and girl are more androgynous than the finished product of civilization, man and woman. It is man and woman who are the subject of gender studies; the boy is all but elided in the various descriptions of manhood in the making which tend to present him as an incomplete man, and entertain no suspicion that the finished man might be an incomplete version of the boy. The old adage that the child is father of the man might be truer than we think.

When and how a boy-child becomes aware of the necessity of separating himself from his mother would appear to be dependent on external factors, such as when those around him identify him as a boy and what they take a boy to be. Confronted with a boy who was timorous or easily moved to tears, our great-grandfathers concluded that his mother's milk was not yet out of him and called him a 'milk-sop'. Even now a soccer player who tackles another without due ferocity is said to have 'gone milky'. It is from his mother's caresses that the boy learns to express affection and how to give and take pleasure. By the time he is a man he will have learned how to subordinate that search for mutual pleasure to the exercise of dominance. Boyhood is the blessed time when he still remembers how to give and take pleasure without troubling himself about power.

Opposite Sir Thomas Lawrence, *Lydia, Lady Acland, with her Two Sons, Thomas and Arthur*, 1818. Though Lawrence was obliged to paint boy and girl children in the undifferentiated dress that they actually wore, and often in the control of the mothers who dressed them, he took care to show his boys as boisterous. standing in their mothers' laps or climbing over and around them, even shouting.

As boyhood is but a preparatory phase in the emergence of a man, the archetypal boy cannot survive. He is typically struck down on the eve of manhood, whether he is Adonis gored by a boar, Orpheus dismembered by the Maenads, Hyacinthus brained by a discus deflected from its true path by a lovesick god, Antinous swallowed up by the Nile either accidentally or on purpose, or Sebastian stuck full of arrows. Over the centuries more boys than men have died, felled by war and childhood diseases. Those diseases are now conquered, in the rich world at least, but, even if AIDS were not a javelin aimed at their throats, boys will still be annihilated because civilization has little use for them. The corporate world requires one-dimensional men not polymorphous boys. Brian Jones, James Dean, Jimi Hendrix, Jim Morrison, Marc Bolan, Jean-Michel Basquiat, Freddie Mercury, Kurt Cobain are our new immortals. Like Apollo and Dionysos they can never outgrow their dazzling boyhood.

Above James Dean was well aware of his appeal to both sexes and flirted outrageously with the camera, while affecting to be unconscious of it. Though he made only three films in a career that lasted little more than a year, he posed for thousands of photographs, some of a distinctly compromising nature, before writing himself off in a car wreck at the age of twenty-four.

Opposite Kurt Cobain was the talent and the beauty behind the successful Alternative Rock band Nirvana. His suicide by a single shotgun blast to the head in 1994 at the age of twenty-seven made of him a cult figure.

chapter 2

The Boy is Beautiful

The brightest figure on Olympus is the boy-god Apollo. As the personification of brilliance, 'the far-shooter with the unshorn hair … the Lord of Song, his head adorned with locks that bloomed in freedom', he is also the personification of youth. Apollo is good at the things that young men are better at than their elders, pure mathematics, abstract thought, archery, composition of poetry and playing the fiddle. He is almost always shown naked as a jay-bird because 'Apollo knoweth how to make naked to them who inquire of him the decrees of Fate or because he appeareth to all alike, for King Phoebus is the sun and his pure brilliancy is seen from afar'.

Zeus begot both Apollo and his twin Artemis on Leto, daughter of the Titans Coeus and Phoebe. Hera, infuriated with jealousy, sent the dragon Python to hound Leto to a place where the sun never shone. At Ortygia she went into labour. Artemis issued from her womb first and, immediately taking control, helped her mortal mother across the straits to Delos and assisted her through the nine days of labour that elapsed before she brought forth the other twin, Apollo. He was only four days old when he demonstrated the strong attachment of all boy-gods to his mother, calling for a bow and arrow so that he could revenge her. He tracked Python to Parnassus but only succeeded in wounding it, The dragon found sanctuary at Delphos but Apollo entered the sacred shrine and killed it. In trouble with his father for this sacrilege, he sought out Pan from whom he learned the art of prophecy, returned to Delphos and took the priestess into his service. One of his duties was to guard the cattle of the gods in Pieria; the cows were stolen by his younger half-brother, Hermes, who fashioned the first lyre from a tortoiseshell. His use of cowgut for the strings betrayed him as the cattle thief and Apollo arraigned him before the gods on Olympus. Hermes pleaded guilty, returned the rest of the cows and sang the praises of Apollo, accompanying himself on the lyre. Apollo was so

Though this performer at an up-market club in Pattaya is usually identified as a 'katoey', the photograph shows not a 'lady boy', that is, a male-to-female transvestite, but a boy who has painted one side of his face like a man and the other like a woman. The suggestion, that the boy underneath may be neither, is worth consideration.

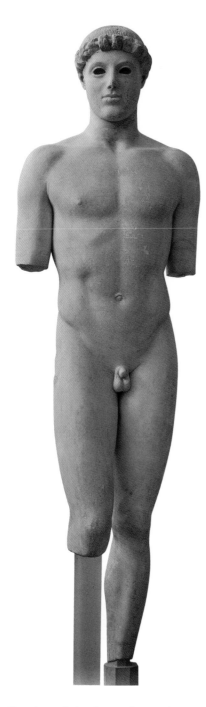

charmed with the instrument that he accepted it in exchange for the cows and from then on was seldom seen without it.

So thoroughly is Apollo associated with physical perfection that every idealized representation of a young male nude is likely to be given his name. The first known Greek statues are the kouroi, erect, striding nude figures that were placed in cemeteries as long ago as 700 BCE. The earliest of these are monumentally stylized to give an impression of stillness and permanence rather than movement. Over the centuries the clenched fists held rigidly against the stiff thighs relaxed and the outlines of the body began to soften, so that they became less monumental and more human. Different styles of representation of ideal male youth existed side by side; what they had in common was that they were all likely to be identified as Apollos, as in the case of the kouros in the British Museum that used to be known as 'Strangford Apollo'.

A hymn of 600 BCE describes Apollo as 'like unto a man, lusty and powerful in his first bloom, his hair spread over his broad shoulders'; this type can still be seen in the Etruscan Apollo of Veio of *c.* 500 BCE (see p. 43). Gradually the type became more refined until Praxiteles produced the very much more delicate and younger-looking figure of the Apollo Sauroktonos, now known to us from a number of Roman copies (see p. 41). By far the most famous effigy of Apollo is the figure that is known as the Belvedere Apollo (see p. 40). A Roman copy in marble of a lost Hellenistic bronze, it was dug

Kouroi were designed to stand as guardians over the remains of the honoured dead. The earliest example shown (opposite), a stone kouros from Melos *c.* 550–540 BCE, is typical of the older form. The bigger than life-size bronze kouros (right), also of the sixth century BCE, and found in a sewer in 1959, is dubbed an Apollo but is more likely to represent an attendant or devotee, whose hands would have held a vessel or tray for offerings. The contours of the third figure (above), dating from the beginning of the fifth century BCE, are beginning to relax from the rigid columnar form.

up somewhere near Rome *c.* 1490 and presented to Cardinal Giuliano della Rovere who put it in his garden. When della Rovere was elected pope in 1503 he took it with him to the Vatican where it was installed in the Cortile of the Belvedere. Every artist who came to Rome went to see it, study it and draw it from every angle. Thousands of plaster casts were made and dispersed throughout Europe.

When the Belvedere Apollo was found, it was missing all of its left hand and part of its right. In 1532 the sculptor Giovanni Angelo Montorsoli was commissioned to restore the statue, which he did by removing the original right arm and supplying a rather feeble one of his own, complete with a hand that is gesturing limp-wristedly at nothingness. He also supplied a left hand which is grasping a bow; on the plinth at the statue's feet he planted a marble laurel tree. He did not apply the fig-leaf that covers the god's genitals, which was added at a later stage. Montorsoli thought that Apollo's pose represented the moment when he drew his bow to kill Python. In fact we do not know and cannot tell which event in the Apollo myth the Greek sculptor originally sought to represent.

What we see is a tall boy, naked but for a mantle thrown over his outstretched left arm and a pair of strappy sandals, striding forward on his right foot, while looking back along his extended left arm. His body is slender and graceful, with delicate articulations and smooth musculature, suggesting power without effort. Luxurious curls cluster at the nape of his neck and are tied in a lover's knot on the crown of his head, as in other depictions of Apollo familiar to us from the excavations of Graeco-Roman ruins, such as those at Aphrodisias in Anatolia. The art critic Kenneth Clark was at a loss to explain how 'the eye could overlook weak structure and slack surfaces which, to the aesthetic of pure sensibility, annul its other qualities'. He continued: 'In no other famous work of art, perhaps, are ideal and function more distressingly divorced, and in so far as we believe that they must be inseparable if art is to take on the quality of new life, the figure of the Vatican is dead.'

A work of art that is being copied in every conceivable medium and so endlessly reproducing itself, could be accounted dead only by an 'aesthetic of pure sensibility'. Successful or unsuccessful, the figure was recognized as an embodiment of young male beauty, and not simply because the other types that are liked better by Clark were not available to the critics. The Belvedere Apollo is certainly an odd structure: the contrapposto of

body turning right and head turning left is daring and unsettling, and the outstretched left arm rocks the balance of the whole, especially as the left heel is lifted and the weight should be thrown further to the right. Another oddly unsettling note is the heaviness of the cloak thrown back as if simply to reveal the boyish body; we do not here have a warrior scarfing his arm against his enemy's blows. The face that looks along the outstretched arm is expressionless, the lips slightly smiling as if in recollection of the kouroi of old. Kenneth Clark does not explain why he wanted the figure to be stronger and less decorative. In any case, his was a received opinion. In 1920 Guy Dickins had rejected the Belvedere Apollo on the grounds of its 'ultra-refinement of surface in every direction' and 'its affected stage pose and gesture', calling it 'little short of abominable'. He was followed in 1929 by A. W. Lawrence who deplored its 'feeble prettiness' and 'undeserved reputation', stating firmly that 'comparison with many statues of greater merit makes the encomiums of older critics appear ridiculous'. Dickins and Lawrence might have paused to consider the obvious fact that hundreds of artists, as distinct from 'critics' and scholars, had responded to the beauty of the Belvedere Apollo. Turner, for example, drew it repeatedly; it would be a daring 'critic' indeed who would suggest that even as a student Turner didn't know what he was looking at. What the critics of the 1920s didn't like about the statue was, simply, that it was not sufficiently masculine, and this moral defect they translated into an aesthetic quality, calling it 'vulgarity', or its opposite, 'ultra-refinement'.

Earlier artists had fewer anxieties about masculinity and were happy to give homage to the Belvedere Apollo in their work. Michelangelo took from it the suggestion of an immature man's slouch; as the weight is taken off the left leg, the torso curves forward to the right. This he developed in a drawing of a nude youth now in the Louvre. Though the figure is knotty with sinews and bone shapes that would never disturb the calm of the Belvedere Apollo or any other Hellenistic sculpture, the tilt of the pelvis and the counter-tilt of the slightly dropped shoulder refer back to it, and at the same time remind us of the would-be toy-boys strutting their stuff around the bar on the Piccola Marina. This real-life version of the classical contrapposto Michelangelo would repeat in his David (see p. 178). Raphael, Vasari, Sansovino and Dürer all admired the Belvedere Apollo and paid it the sincere compliment of imitation and adaptation. Every atelier and every connoisseur possessed a cast of the statue. Goethe asked a friend to come and look at his 'cast of the Apollo … even by candlelight' and see if he could agree that it was beautiful.

Opposite In the nineteenth century the Belvedere Apollo was derided as 'disgusting' and either 'vulgar' or 'over-refined'. Earlier observers, from the time of its discovery in Rome in the 1490s, had thought its boyish beauty unsurpassed. Every young artist who made the journey to Rome visited the Vatican to draw it from every angle.

Below The Greek original of the Roman figure of Apollo Sauroktonos, the lizard-killer, is thought to have been carved by Praxiteles late in the fourth century BCE. Monumentality has been abandoned for grace, expressed in the softly rounded contours of a body that has relaxed so far that it has become unstable and must use the tree trunk as a prop.

Johann Joachim Winckelmann, considered the founder of the neo-classical movement and arbiter of revolutionary aesthetic taste, wrote: 'It is the highest ideal of art among all the works of antiquity. Enter, o reader, with your spirit into this kingdom of beauty incarnate, and there seek to create for yourself the images of divine nature.' Winckelmann's judgment that the male nude is the epitome of the aesthetic is nowadays assumed to be one 'in which desire is clearly instrumental', the implication being that straight people would not share his homosexual's preference, when they clearly did. The key to the attraction of the Belvedere Apollo to both straight and gay men and women is that it is not the depiction of a man, but of a boy. Its skittishness is a boy's skittishness and the cold arrogance of its look bespeaks the amorality of the kind of young hooligan who could skin Marsyas alive.

The oldest Apollos are by no means always so naked. The Apollo of Veio, thought to be carved by the master Etruscan sculptor, Vulca, strides forward forcefully, the flat monumental contours of his powerful body enhanced by the rippling folds of a thin chiton. His stride is the same as the stride of the Greek kouroi, and the ancestor of the step being taken rather more languidly by the Apollo of the Belvedere. His braided and plaited hair hangs thickly on his neck and back, and his lips are curved in a smile that seems to anticipate pleasure. A related type, the Apollo kitharoidos, has his hair elaborately dressed in a later fashion and wears a flowing pleated gown, with only his height, his broad shoulders and the contours of his groin as evidence of his maleness. In the Middle Ages the problem of Apollo's troubling appeal was dealt with by the simple expedient of depicting him clothed; after the discovery of the Belvedere Apollo his nudity became once more an essential aspect of his emblematic significance. As his entire body must be seen to be without flaw, he is almost always shown, even when he is involved in such dangerous activities as break-ing the horses of the sun to his rein, wearing nothing but a laurel wreath and sandals, accessories that tend to emphasize the starkness of his undress. Part of the shock effect of the few pictures that show naked females with clothed men is that the combination of nude male plus clothed female is so common in European art as to be ubiquitous. Now that Andrea Sacchi's picture of Apollo placing his own laurels on the head of Marcantonio Pasqualini has been restored, and a clumsy drape removed from the god's loins, we can see that his rosy genitals are the focus of the composition, all its diagonal lines intersecting at just this point. The naked figure, derived from and justified by the example of the Belvedere Apollo, entirely upstages the musician, who is bizarrely clad in

Opposite In Andrea Sacchi's hyperbolic *Marcantonio Pasqualini Crowned by Apollo* (1641) the castrato's upright harpsichord is decorated with the figures of Daphne and a bound satyr. Marsyas can be seen behind; beside him a shepherd's bagpipes.

Below The head of the terracotta Apollo of Veio, with its elaborately braided curls and lazy smile, contrasts with the massiveness of the torso and the tortuous detail of the muscles of its striding legs.

The Boy is Beautiful **43**

Below As a painter Jusepe de Ribera was more interested in the contours of suffering humanity than in divine pagan beauties, but in the mid-1630s he painted several versions of Apollo and Marsyas, all of which show the god's nude body amid billowing drapery hovering weightlessly over the struggling earthbound satyr, who is usually more human than mythical.

a billowing starched surplice over which a shaggy leopardskin has been knotted, with bright red stockings and brown shoes tied with red laces. Pasqualini was himself a castrato; what he felt about the contrast between himself and the god can only be imagined. The composition is balanced by the swarthy figure of Marsyas waiting tied to a tree for Apollo to strip his skin off.

The Marsyas episode is repulsive and can be repulsively painted. Showing the young god in the act of flaying an older man certainly dramatizes his bodily intactness along with his effortless implacable power. Marsyas, always a mature man, bearded, his body muscular and dark-skinned, is reduced to helplessness before the divine power of the shining boy. Though Marsyas is supposed to have been a satyr, most versions do not show him with goatish extremities. Marsyas's crime was to offend the gods by claiming to have invented the flute and then challenging Apollo to a musical contest which he lost, whereupon the boy musician bound him to a tree and skinned him alive. The boy who punishes the man shows his power as the Belvedere Apollo does, by remaining

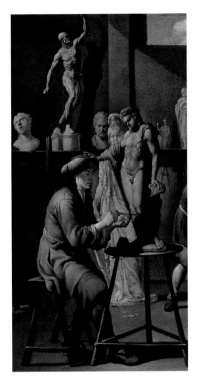

completely impassive, while Marsyas bawls like a child. Most painters do as Ribera does and use the subject simply as the occasion for a contrast between two physical types, the white and tranquil boy and the red and frenzied man, with little evidence of the grisly process of dividing a man from his skin.

Only great artists can create convincing ikons of invincible power-without-force, and not all their efforts succeed in establishing a balance between delicacy and strength. Critics of different generations will interpret the same visual clues differently, in response to the concepts of gender appropriateness prevailing at the time. The figure of Apollo that dominates the foreground in Rubens's *Council of the Gods*, with its extended left arm holding a bow, leading right leg, and turned head is clearly derived from the Belvedere Apollo as restored by Montorsoli. Rubens turns the mass of the sculpted figure into flickering light and movement, exaggerating the stride and twisting the glimmering body with the red mantle billowing and swirling around it, so that to a modern sensibility the god might seem to be mincing. Rubens's contemporaries, who expected a gentleman to be a graceful dancer and able to make a good leg on any of the many occasions that required it, would not have seen it this way. In the Circle of Michael Sweerts's painting of the interior of a sculptor's studio, the figure in the foreground is putting the finishing touches to an Apollo of a distinctly feminine type. He stands in a version of the Belvedere

Above left The unknown painter of *Interior of a Sculptor's Studio*, which can be dated by the costume and other details to about 1655, makes his own ironic comment on the story of Apollo and Marsyas. The Apollo whose knee the young sculptor is finishing is amply covered in flesh; the figure with arm raised behind him is a flayed man, modelled in wax on a wire armature so the boys could study muscle structure.

Above right In *Council of the Gods, c.* 1623, with characteristic verve and dazzle Rubens translates the sculpted Belvedere Apollo into colour and light. The figure is more Netherlandish than Greek in physical type, but the attitude is identical, even to the hands added by Montorsoli, and the draping of the cloak.

pose with left leg relaxed and his mantle thrown over his extended right arm, leaving his smooth, plump body open to view. The contrast to be seen in the iconography of Apollo and Marsyas is here implied and exaggerated by the contrast with the virile figure of a sinewy *homme écorché* to be seen on a shelf behind the Apollo, a figure as rough as the Apollo is smooth. Modern taste does not appreciate plumpness, partly because we see far too much of it; to the boy-watchers of the seventeenth century, who saw too many undernourished boys scratching a living in the streets, plumpness was a positive attribute.

In 1769 when Sir Joshua Reynolds undertook a full-length portrait of Frederick Howard, fifth Earl of Carlisle, he took the pose from the Belvedere Apollo, of which a full-size plaster cast had recently been acquired for the Royal Academy. Reynolds was a fan. 'He is supposed to have just discharged his arrow at the Python; and by the head retreating just a little towards the right shoulder, he appears attentive to its effect. What I would remark, is the difference of this attention from that of the Discobolus, who is engaged in the same purpose.… The graceful, negligent, though animated air of the one, and the vulgar eagerness of the other, furnish a signal instance of the judgment of the ancient sculptors in their nice discrimination of character.' Carlisle was twenty-one years old, a smooth-cheeked pouting boy, with a fine leg in rose-coloured silk stockings; Reynolds shows him in the robes of the Order of the Thistle with which he had been endowed in Turin when he was on the Grand Tour. The portrait might seem to modern eyes outrageously effeminizing, but to his contemporaries it suggested youth, power and poetry, to which the young earl had pretensions that were at one point acknowledged by his cousin, Lord Byron. Where Apollo wears his vine leaf dangles the foot-long gold tassel of the cord securing the youth's velvet cloak, between slender thighs riotously garlanded with bunches of ribbon. Reynolds modified the Hellenistic pose; the extended left arm is shorter, the hand held lower, while the right hand rests upon the pommel of a sword.

Reynolds used variations on the Belvedere pose at least twice more, for the full-length portraits of Augustus Keppel (*c.* 1752) and the Tahitian Omai (*c.* 1774) sold at Sotheby's in 2001 for more than £10 million. There are those who think that the fact that Keppel's head is turned to his left as he looks along his outstretched left arm and lifts his left heel, as the Apollo does, is mere coincidence. 'That it turned out rather like the famous antique statue of the Apollo Belvedere was probably almost accidental, though not of course entirely so. The pose itself was already in circulation, one of the many "stock" poses used

Opposite In 1768 Frederick Howard, fifth Earl of Carlisle, was elected a Knight of the Order of the Thistle. The following year, the twenty-one-year-old sat to Sir Joshua Reynolds for this full-length portrait in the robes of the Order. He would later become addicted to gambling but then abandon the vices of his youth and enter politics, with great success.

by the drapery painter van Aken: Ramsay's *Chief of MacLeod at Dunvegan Castle* and Hudson's *Gentleman* (said to be Charles Douglass), sold Christies on 21 November 1975 (88) are two striking examples.' What such evidence goes to show is that the pose of the Apollo was thoroughly embedded in the

pictorial language of the aggrandizing portrait, and that the effeteness that so revolted later critics had not yet been diagnosed. Reynolds, who never studied from the nude and had no grounding in anatomy, was as likely as many a lesser painter to resort to a plaster cast for a coherent pose. Though the twenty-seven-year-old Keppel is decently dressed and holds his arm rather lower than the Belvedere Apollo, he has legs as slender and as long as the Apollo's, and his confident striding without looking where he is going conveys the same subtle sense of power without force that distinguishes the classic original. It was not until 1867 that the critic F. G. Stephens pounced on the reminiscence of the Belvedere Apollo and denounced it as 'attitudinizing', 'theatrical' and 'most unworthy of the man'. Contemporary judgment was very different; the Keppel portrait made Reynolds's reputation.

The case of the Omai portrait is less clear because Reynolds has turned the head away from the outstretched arm and the hand that emerges from a superfluous fall of cloth as the Belvedere's hand would have done. Though the twenty-something-year-old subject is swaddled in classical draperies, their very voluminousness, as well as the nakedness of the emerging hands and feet, suggests the

Taddeo Zuccari's drawing of a *Seated Youth Surprised by Two Soldiers* may be one of many illustrations of an episode from Tasso's *Gerusalemme Liberata* in which Rinaldo, having gone AWOL from the crusades, is tracked down to Armida's enchanted bower by two of his fellow paladins. The episode dramatizes the conflict between boyish susceptibility and sexual appetite, which are condemned as effeminate, and manly continence and discipline.

dark slender body beneath. His averted gaze together with a slight flush beneath his eyes suggests the kind of vulnerability usually associated with female subjects. Reynolds liked this picture so well that he kept it by him until his death, when it was bought by none other than Frederick, fifth Earl of Carlisle. A century later the sculptor Charles Lawes was reputed to be so physically perfect as a young man at Eton College and Cambridge University that his father got an artist to model his son's figure in silver, in the attitude of the Belvedere Apollo.

What later generations have interpreted as effeminacy in the Apollo figure began as no more than evidence of its youthfulness. Intolerance of the boygod's 'softness' (a word that also means 'amorousness' in the early modern period) may stem from intolerance of boyhood itself and a desire to translate the boy instantaneously from child to man, so avoiding the troubling phase of misrule and extravagance out of which Apollonian brilliance may be said to rise. Before the British developed their system of thrashing and bullying male children into men at boarding schools, the charms of extended boyhood were apparent to all, even to females. Ladies have left little in the way of evidence of their susceptibility to the androgynous appeal of boys, but grown men were sufficiently jealous of it to speak for them. In 'Her Man described by her own Dictamen', Ben Jonson speaks in the persona of a woman explaining what she looks for in a lover:

> Young I'll have him too, and fair,
> Yet a man, with crispèd hair
> Cast in a thousand snares and rings
> For Love's fingers and his wings...
> Eyebrows bent like Cupid's bow,
> Front, an ample field of snow,
> Even nose, and cheek withal
> Smooth as is the billiard-ball,
> Chin as woolly as the peach,
> And his lip should kissing teach,
> Till he cherished too much beard
> And make Love or me afeared.

In her poem 'In Imitation of Horace' printed in 1684 Aphra Behn apostrophizes a boy who has beautified himself in order to attract the eyes of women.

> What mean those amorous curls of jet?
>   For what heart-ravished maid
> Dost thou thy hair in order set,
>   Thy wanton tresses braid,
> And thy vast store of beauties open lay,
> That the deluded fancy leads astray?

Behn writes often of male beauty in terms that would seem to us excessively feminizing but, at this juncture in the development of taste, beauty in a boy is identical with the beauty of a girl. Both should have radiant and unblemished skin, brilliant eyes, entwining tendrils of hair and a slender, graceful form. The boy has the advantage in that his clothing outlines and reveals his form; girls, being encased in busks and stiffened skirts, their hair coiffed rather than allowed to flow over their shoulders, offered fewer opportunities for voyeuristic pleasure than boys.

Behn's allusion is to Ode 5 of Book 1 of Horace which is addressed to a girl, Pyrrha. Behn addresses the self-beautifier as 'fond, charming youth', an expression that was less sex specific in the 1680s than it is now, so that this poem can possibly be read as describing an amorous interaction between women. Lady Mary Wortley Montagu adapts the same ode to reflect slightly more bitterly on the havoc wrought by a male flirt:

> For whom are now your airs put on,
> And what new beauty's doomed to be undone?
> That careless elegance of dress,
> This essence that perfumes the wind,
> Your very motion does confess
> Some secret conquest is designed.
> Alas! The poor unhappy maid,
> To what a train of ills betrayed!

When Lady Mary was forty-eight she fell hard for a twenty-four-year-old Italian, who was carving out a brilliant career by allowing powerful men and women to fall in love with him while committing himself to none of them. While he was following his fortunes to Berlin and winning the heart of Crown Prince Frederick, Lady Mary travelled to Venice expecting him to join her there; they eventually met up in Turin, with the outcome that would have been expected by anyone but the lovesick Lady Mary. Algarotti was, of course, extremely handsome in a fair-skinned, dark-eyed, heavy-lidded sort of way and knew how to make the best of himself.

Until relatively recently boys were expected to be interested in prettifying themselves. Indeed, in societies where well-to-do women were to be seen only in their own houses, it was the boys who supplied all the glamour to be seen in the streets. They were all too aware that from the screened windows of their apartments the rigorously segregated daughters of the middle class were gazing down upon them. In the Venetian crowd scenes painted by Carpaccio, Mansueti and Gentile Bellini at the beginning of the sixteenth century can be seen knots and couples of posing boys. The broadness of their shoulders is emphasized by padding, the tininess of their nipped-in waists by all kinds of stitched panels and slashings in contrasting colours, the length of their legs by a variety of longitudinal stripings and patternings. The skirts of their doublets are not only cropped to reveal the contours of the buttocks, but split and folded back. All the boys make the most of their hair which has been bleached, put up in curlers and then brushed out to froth over their shoulders and round their faces. Hats come in all shapes and sizes, but the most popular are pill-boxes and beanies, all sporting a feather or several.

Whether the self-beautification of the sixteenth-century boy was limited to his hair is not so clear. In the paintings of Pisanello we can see that neither men nor women used cosmetics, but both shaved their foreheads and necks to produce a clean hair-line. While the women's hair is braided and bound, the men's is curled and clipped, and, one suspects, bleached. The truth seems to be that boys are as vain as girls and spend as much time pondering their reflection in the mirror but, although we are told every year that the market for male cosmetics is growing and will at last take off, boys still do very little to render themselves attractive. Elvis Presley took a risk of being denounced as effeminate in using kohl and eye-shadow long before rock musicians began to sport make-up. When bands did begin to appear with painted faces it was in the hope of provoking a homophobic response in order to deny it. Interestingly girls responded as passionately and obsessively to the heavily made-up features of Boy George as they did to any of the fresh-faced, clean-cut pop idols. In the *Erotes,* the author pseudo-Lucian says of the heterosexual disputant, Charicles, that he 'shows some evidence of the skilful use of cosmetics, because, I imagine, he wished to attract the women'. One of the most

Frank Sinatra, who became the idol of bobby-soxers in the mid-1940s, was the first teen heart-throb. Though he was well into his twenties when he became a solo artist, it was his skinny boyish appearance and his wide blue eyes as well as the sentimental ditties he sang that made teenage girls swoon.

frequently touted advantages of loving boys was that in contrast to women they had unpainted faces; we can only wonder if Charicles as a grown man was using cosmetics to counterfeit the appearance of youth.

In allegories of youth, boys are often shown with mirrors, a fitting attribute for them but not for the men they will become. Yet Native American Osage braves all carry mirrors in which they are expected to adjust their elaborate coiffures. In many cultures young males are required to beautify themselves in order to catch the eyes of females both old and young, like so many cock birds in their mating plumage, and they will parade themselves thus bedizened, even dancing to show their grace as well as their strength and endurance, or jumping to great heights. Instances of this kind of behaviour are so numerous that we might wonder whether preventing boys from beautifying themselves and displaying that beauty is not both counter-instinctive and counter-productive.

Above Boy George, born George O'Dowd in 1961, became a household name in the 1980s with his band Culture Club. Though he affected an extremely camp manner, wore heavy make-up and made no secret of his sexual orientation, he had a huge following among teenage girls.

Opposite Though exclusively heterosexual, Elvis Presley began using eye-liner, mascara and eye-shadow when he was still at school, to dramatize his eyes and project his version of a smouldering look. He was intensely aware of the value of sexual display and of musical performance as a part of that display.

Though the boys of the nomadic Wodaabe of the Sahel are beautiful to start with, tall, lithe and fine-featured, they have an exacting and elaborate beauty culture which requires them to darken their eyes and lips and highlight their noses, cheekbones and chins, in order to don intricately hand-embroidered tabards and charm women by dancing and rolling their eyes. Dinka men, most of whom are over six feet tall, call themselves 'the men of men'; at fifteen years old a Dinka boy will begin wearing, in addition to his ivory and silver bangles and necklace, a tight beaded corset, which accentuates the narrowness of his waist compared to his shoulders as well as the tightness of his buttocks (see p. 57). Such male display is not in the least incompatible with male exploit, but seems rather a part of it. Young men expert in all kinds of martial arts are expected to dress the part. The best stick-fighters among the Surma of south-western Ethiopia wear, besides their silver earrings and bracelets, and

Opposite The Surma are a tiny community of herdsmen in south-west Ethiopia, numbering no more than 30,000. In this photograph of 1991 Kolaholi, a famed body painter, decorates a renowned stick fighter with finger painting in chalk and ochre. Both wear necklaces, bracelets and earrings.

Right For the 'yaake' or charm competition at the festival of Geerewol, when the young Wodaabe men of Niger will display themselves to attract a wife, they shave their foreheads, powder their skin with ochre, outline their eyes with kohl and sharpen their noses by painting a line from brow to chin.

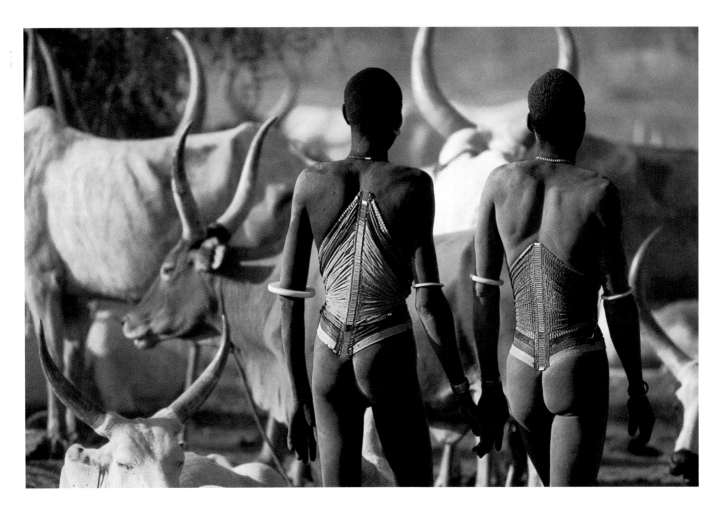

hair shaved and clipped into narrow bands, intricate finger-painted body designs in white, from neck to knee. The more fearsome the New Guinea head-hunter the more likely he is to wear a toque of vivid parrot feathers, recycling the brilliant plumage donned by a male bird to attract the female.

All such beautification implies that the boys want and expect to be looked at by women. Where women till the earth, carry heavy loads, especially water, and even erect the houses, a man who cannot attract one of these useful creatures is in trouble, for a man alone cannot survive. The women know that they are free to follow the 'nice direction of a maiden's eyes', singling out the most graceful dancer, the highest leaper, the most creatively adorned of all the boys, who may turn out to be as well the bravest hunter or the strongest wrestler. The same combination of beautification and prowess survives in post-industrial society in the figure of David Beckham who, defying the braying of less secure men, speaks in a soft high-pitched voice, wears diamonds in his ears, a skirt when he feels like it, topiarizes his hair, poses for thousands of modelling photographs, and is also rather good at playing soccer. Apollo lives.

Above Now that the Dinka people have been driven off the savannahs of southern Sudan by decades of persecution and civil war, their tall slender menfolk are seldom to be seen following their herds of cattle as in this photograph of 1984. At puberty a Dinka boy would no longer be required to milk the cows, would be painfully initiated in a ceremony involving deep cuts to his head, and assume a beaded corset, as a sign that he had become a warrior guardian of the cattle.

Opposite At the yam festival for which this young man is preparing, adolescent boys as well as girls will have their bodies oiled and dusted with golden pollen. His headdress is made of cockatoo feathers, and the tiny dots he is applying to the dark stripes of his face paint are powdered coral mixed with water.

chapter 3

Love is a Boy

In 1787 Canova made a preparatory plaster cast for a frankly erotic sculpture of Cupid reviving Psyche after she has swooned from inhaling poison perfume. The project languished until 1793 when the sculptor received a private commission which resulted in the group now in the Louvre, in which Psyche's reduced drapery reveals her legs and thighs and she has lost her butterfly wings. In 1796 Prince Yusupov commissioned a third version, now in the Hermitage, in which Cupid has acquired a fig-leaf as well as more massive wings. In all three versions Cupid's hand cups Psyche's breast.

Cupid, with his bow and fiery arrows, is always male and always immature. He is male because he is the aggressor: in no myth does Cupid play a passive sexual role. He is a boy because a boy is more sexually active than a man, has more erections, produces more sperm and ejaculates more often. If society provides no legitimate outlet for boys' sexuality it will be expressed in ways that are chaotic and destructive. Therefore Cupid is both blindfolded and in charge of a lethal weapon. His arrows infect individuals with infatuation and sexual obsession, bringing havoc and anguish, disrupting friendships, households and the state. Nowadays we like to pretend that small boys, such as Cupid is usually shown to be, have no awareness of sex. This fond hope is part of the myth of childhood innocence that grew up in the nineteenth century and managed to exist side by side with the belief that children would be wicked unless they were regularly thrashed. This was only possible because parenting was bifurcated: mothers trusted, fathers thrashed. Mothers enacted mercy, fathers justice. The nineteenth century replaced the common awareness of original sin with a conception of childhood as both innocent in itself and unaware of the sexuality of others. The results of this delusion were in some ways tragic, as adults abused children who could find no redress because even to speak of such things exposed them as bad, while innocent children could be abused with impunity because they really did not know what was happening. The nineteenth century largely lost sight of Cupid's boyhood; though he still turned up wherever there were hearts or flowers he was presented as an unsexed baby. The dreadful boy of antiquity had been obliterated.

Cupid is the Roman version of the Greek Eros whom some among the Ancients held to be the oldest of the gods since none of the others would have come into being without him; he is supposed to have hatched out of the world-egg laid in the womb of Darkness after the Wind had made love with

Below left The original of the type of Eros stringing his bow is thought to have been sculpted by the Greek sculptor Lysippus in the fourth century BCE. The legs and feet, right arm, bow and wings of this Roman copy have been restored, by analogy with other examples surviving in different fragments.

Below right Parmigianino, who created *Cupid Carving a Bow* in about 1533, was himself a child prodigy and said to have been as beautiful as an angel. The wood that Cupid is working on is Hercules's club; the figure is another emblem of love conquering all, even the strongest. Rubens liked this picture so much that he copied it.

Night, so that he could set the universe in motion. This is one way of illustrating the philosophical notion that love, also known as desire, prompts all movement, vulgarly rendered as 'it's love that makes the world go round'. The early Greeks represented Eros as a winged figure rather like a djinn, who existed to torment human beings and disrupt the social order. Later versions accept that his mother was Aphrodite but cannot agree as to whether his father was her half-brother Hermes, Ares the god of war or her father Zeus. This very confusion reflects the way that Eros represents all that is ungovernable in human sexuality, including jealousy, rage, violence and incest. Though Eros is a tyrant and all the Olympian deities are afraid of him, in all his incarnations he is a boy, sometimes a very small boy. For Praxiteles Cupid is a refined and beautiful boy of twelve or so; a fourth-century Lysippan type shows him rather younger, twisting himself a bow out of Hercules's club, in an emblem of the unmanning of the male hero in the grip of lust. In about 1533

Right The Eros of Praxiteles,
which has come down to us via
Roman copies, is a graceful boy
rather than a mischievous child,
and appears more the object of love
than the instigator of love in others.
He looks and gestures downwards,
as if from an altar to a suppliant.

'for the knight Baiardo, a gentleman of Parma and intimate friend of his', Parmigianino painted a different view of 'Cupid who is making a bow with his own hand', which shows him whittling it rather than stringing it. Vasari continues: '… and at his feet he depicted two putti, both seated, one of whom is catching the other by his arm and laughingly urging him to touch Cupid with his finger, and the putto who does not want to do this is weeping, expressing his fear of burning himself at the fire of Love.' It is an interesting indication of the changed assumptions of the twenty-first century that the putto who is weeping is often assumed to be a girl.

Renaissance notions of the character of the boy Love were greatly influenced by Ερος Δραπετις, 'Runaway Love', by the Greek poet, Moschus, writing about 150 BCE, in which Venus sets up a hue-and-cry after her delinquent son and gives a detailed description of him.

> He is a notable lad; he shall be known among twenty: complexion not white but rather like to fire; eyes keen and beamy; of an ill disposition but fair spoken, for he means not what he says — 'tis voice of honey, heart of gall; a wily brat makes cruel play.

Moschus' rather clumsy poem had no sooner surfaced in Italy than it was translated into elegant Latin hexameters by Politian, and then into Italian terza rima first by Geronimo Benivieni and then by scores of others. The early church, under the influence of St Augustine, had adapted the Ciceronian view that Eros, under his Latin name of Cupid, was 'a wild boy, who showed no respect for age or station but flew about on golden wings, shooting barbed arrows at random or wantonly setting hearts on fire with his dreadful torches'. The success of Moschus' poem stemmed as much from the support it gave to the prevalent notion of lawless love as from its intrinsic merit. The iconography of Eros/Cupid/Amor, as moralized in allegorical paintings like Gherardo di Giovanni del Fora's *Combat of Love and Chastity*, painted at the same time that Moschus' poem was being disseminated in Greek, Latin and Italian, reflects a pre-existing Christian tradition. Love, a naked winged boy with a floating mane of red-gold hair, has fired into the shield of Chastity at point-blank range an arrow which has snapped in two. Chastity is represented as a fully-clad female figure, brandishing the chain with which she will bind the youth when his last arrow is broken.

In 1532 the Florentine banker Bartolomeo Bettini asked Michelangelo to design a fresco of Venus and Cupid. Michelangelo produced the design but

Above *The Combat of Love and Chastity* painted by Gherardo di Giovanni del Fora some time in the last quarter of the fifteenth century is thought to be one of a series of panels illustrating Petrarch's *Triumph of Chastity*. Love irrupts into the picture space like a skater, but Chastity holds her ground, as his arrows break against her shield, and she brandishes the chain with which she will bind him once disarmed.

ultimately Bettini had to ask Pontormo to carry out the painting and several of his younger contemporaries made their own copies. The nude and rather massive body of Venus with her right leg bent behind her occupies the whole of the foreground; she appears to be rolling away from her son, Cupid, who has flung his left leg over her right hip in an odd version of the leg-over pose that signifies coitus in the art of classical antiquity. He has thrust his left arm under her chin and is pulling her face round, apparently so that he can kiss her on the lips, as with her right hand, as if inadvertently, she plucks a single arrow from his loaded quiver. 'The little Cupid has already attacked Venus; approaching from behind, he has climbed up her body and embraces her.'

To modern sensibility such an image of an apparently lustful child is intensely disturbing. Indeed, in 1819 one of the pictures based upon the cartoon was listed among the 'quadri osceni' in the Royal Bourbon Collection. To Correggio's educated contemporaries the notion of infantile sex play carried no threat; Eros here stands for non-reproductive sex which Venus Urania, as a nature goddess and daughter of Heaven and Earth, must

Below Michelangelo's monumental design for a fresco of Venus and Cupid, featuring one of the most dynamic female forms to appear in Western art, staggered all those who saw it. It was never executed and has come down to us through copies by other artists, such as this one thought to have been made by Pontormo. The child's aggressiveness towards his mother would be disturbing enough even without the tiny figure lying as if dead in the cupboard-like pedestal to the left of the picture.

control in the interests of fertility. Nowadays we do not think of uncontrolled and indiscriminate sexual desire as childish, but Correggio's contemporaries certainly did. As Cartari explained in *De i Dei degli Antichi*, 'Love is depicted as a child because while it is directed solely towards lust, it is no other than a mad desire, and because the thinking of people in love is weak and imperfect, like that of children.'

According to Ovid, Venus was infected with passion for Adonis, a mere mortal, when Cupid kissed her and one of the arrows in his quiver accidentally grazed her bosom. The landscape in the background of the paintings after Michelangelo's cartoon certainly appears to be the mountains, woods and rocky places set with thorns where Venus will hunt with Adonis and he will be killed. A version of the subject by Bronzino's nephew Alessandro Allori, though it still refers to Michelangelo's design, in that Venus is again attacked from behind, shows her seizing Cupid's right wrist in her right hand to restrain him, while in her left hand she holds aloft his bow. The allegory has been consciously disinfected. Cupid is older; his mother does not attempt to ignore him but gazes as deeply into his eyes as he into hers; white doves bill in the foreground. We are now confronted with an icon of tranquil monogamy,

Venus genetrix triumphans. With this useful moralization Allori was onto a winner: besides the version in the Musée Fabre, there is another in the Uffizi, another in the Kress Collection, another at Hampton Court, and another in the Galleria Colonna in Rome, and the subject was twice engraved.

As the go-between and facilitator of adulterous love, Cupid is seldom defeated. In Correggio's *Danaë* he has cast aside his bow and arrows, and sprung on to the bed, his legs spread in a mirror image of Danaë's receptive position, ready to snatch away the sheet so she can be penetrated by Zeus in the form of a shower of gold. Cupid alone is aware of the imminent arrival of the god; Danaë seems lost in some complacent dream of her own. A pair of amorini, one winged and the other not, play with one of Cupid's arrows.

Above Nineteenth-century critics esteemed Correggio as everything that was delicate and pure, but he is the only artist ever to have depicted the anus and scrotum of an airborne angel, who can be seen among his decorations for Parma Cathedral along with another nude angel sitting astride a cloud in the same pose as the Cupid who assists the impregnation of Danaë in Correggio's painting of 1531 or so.

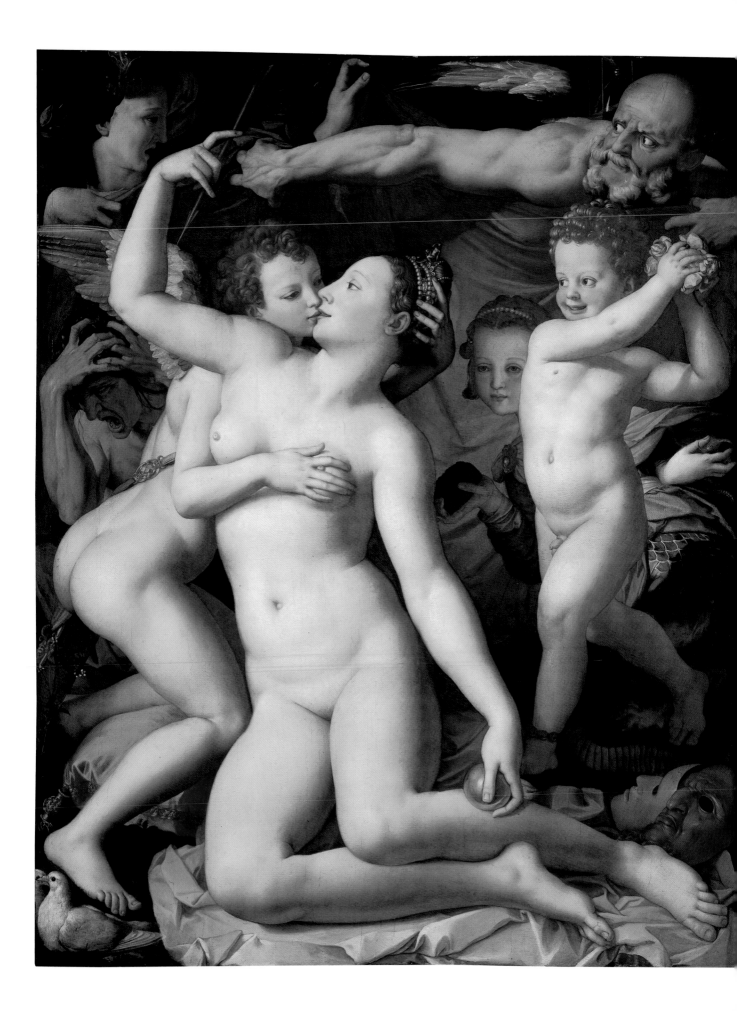

The winged one, who represents sacred love, is inscribing on a tablet held by wingless earthly love, signifying the character that divine love inscribes on worthless clay. The image may be one of adulterous passion, but the interpretation is purely neo-platonic, so that the cognoscenti get to have their cake and eat it too.

Correggio's Cupid may be an obedient servant of divine will, but the dominant image was still that of Cupid as a demonic force. In the painting by Bronzino now known as *Venus, Cupid, Folly and Time* Cupid is once more advancing on his mother from behind in unambiguously erotic fashion. His right hand passes under her right breast to squeeze her left nipple between his spread fingers, while his left hand, as in the Michelangelo cartoon, holds her head so that he can reach her parted lips with his own. Her gaze appears unfocused but he is looking intently at the lips he is about to kiss. Cupid's buttocks are conspicuously presented, to the point where his posture seems anatomically impossible. Despite its overt erotic content the picture is another moral allegory. The doves of harmonious monogamy appear in imminent danger of being crushed by Cupid's foot, while a veritable horde of sinister personifications throngs in the background, forces that will be unleashed if the lips of mother and son should meet. Once more we are in the realm of the pseudo-Moschus. Though a more refined age might simply rejoice in this complex image as a neo-platonic mystery celebrating the power of perfect beauty to subdue lust or some such, the picture is one of a beardless youth intent on seducing a woman who is old enough to be his mother and appears to have given him no encouragement. She does not return his embrace but turns away from him, one hand lifting one of his arrows and the other clutching the golden apple awarded her by Paris.

Bronzino's picture is a highly sophisticated puzzle which will keep scholars occupied for some years yet, but at a superficial level it raises the questions of just when male children begin to feel sexual desire and whether they are moved to translate desire into performance of some kind. Bronzino's amorous boy appears to be a teenager; in a drawing made at more or less the same time by Bartholomäus Spranger, the boy who has climbed onto Venus and straddles her thigh is even younger than Michelangelo's toddler. He appears moreover to have deliberately wounded his mother with his arrow, and it is contemplation of the wound that brings their mouths within kissing distance.

Lorenzo Lotto's *Venus and Cupid* is obviously an allegory of marriage but what it plainly shows is a smiling toddler standing legs apart, holding his penis

Above Bartholomäus Spranger's drawing is another that deals with the infection of Venus with love through a wound from one of Cupid's arrows. In 1581 Spranger, a Fleming by birth, became chief painter to the court of the Holy Roman Emperor Rudolf II in Prague. His extravagantly sexy conceits were fed by the works he saw in the Emperor's Kunstkammer, then the largest collection of art works in Europe.

Opposite Scholars will probably never agree about what is going on in Bronzino's *Allegory with Venus and Cupid* (*c.* 1540–50). A teenaged boy appears to be making unequivocal advances to an older woman who, apparently in a state of suspended animation, allows him to kiss her open mouth. The picture could conceivably refer to the unrequited love of boys for older women and to the ills that would follow if such untimely love were to be returned.

in his right hand and aiming a stream of urine at the belly of a naked woman reclining in front of him in yet another version of the Michelangelo pose. The child's body is more accurately observed than the woman's. The myrtle wreath he wears at a roguish angle and his lazy, even tipsy smile both indicate a knowingness that would nowadays be considered most undesirable in a child of his age. We know the toddler is Cupid because he wears grey pigeon wings and has slung his bow over his left shoulder. Venus, wearing crossed bracelets on her wrists, is holding up a ribbon upon which a myrtle wreath is suspended and from that an incense burner, all indicative of the ceremony of marriage. The child's action recalls the popular superstition that a wife is more likely to conceive if her husband urinates through his wedding ring.

Above In his *Venus and Cupid* of *c.* 1540, Lorenzo Lotto shows Cupid as a toddler urinating accurately through a myrtle wreath onto his mother's petal-strewn pelvis, in an allegory of fruitful wedlock. The child's stance and expression indicate that he knows what he is doing (as a god should) and is a willing participant in this adult scenario.

The magic depends on the parallellism between ejaculation within the vagina and peeing through a ring. Properly speaking the attendant of marriages should be the torchbearer Hymen rather than Cupid the archer. Lotto's allegory appears to relate less to monogamy and marital chastity than to the importance of physical desire to marital fertility, so that Cupid, young and all as he is, is playing his usual role in fomenting lust.

Caravaggio's *Love Triumphant* is seldom seen as anything but visual indulgence of homosexual paedophilia. Cupid's pose has even been interpreted as climbing off his adult lover after anal penetration, his relaxed smile being taken as a sign of Caravaggio's sharing the common delusion of paedophiles that children invite and enjoy their attentions. Other elements of the picture are not so easily read and suggest that the superficial reading may be the wrong one. It is Caravaggio's method to subvert the humbug of patrician aestheticism by choosing for his Baptists and Davids unrefined types whose bodies appear real rather than ideal. The child's body is here presented more awkwardly than seductively. The total exposure of his nakedness is also the exposure of his unreadiness; he holds two arrows not in his quiver but in his hand, their barbed tips invisible somewhere beyond the picture's edge. The only bow visible is the bow of the viol that lies with a theorbo and a sheet of music on the floor, next to an abandoned cuirass and a crown of laurel. The instruments are two, the armour is one; a couple may have been playing and singing in consort and retired to make love, hence Cupid's victory. This pictorial topos may not have been new in 1601 when Marchese Rodolfo Giustiniani commissioned the picture from Caravaggio. A version of it painted in the 1580s is credited to the Ferrarese Ippolito Scarsella, called Lo Scarsellino; four more are credited to Caravaggio's younger contemporary, Orazio Riminaldi.

Though the cognoscenti would have been aware of the import of Caravaggio's allegory, the audacity of the representation and its lack of refinement did provoke a reaction, led by the Marchese Giustiniani's brother, Cardinal Benedetto Giustiniani, who commissioned a

Below Caravaggio's *Love Triumphant* (c. 1599) is another illustration of the difference between early seventeenth-century attitudes towards childhood and those current now. There is nothing innocent about this boy, but the assumption that he has been involved in some kind of paedophilic exchange is purely twenty-first century. He is acting, as Correggio's Cupid does (see p. 65), as the facilitator of adult intercourse.

corrective from Caravaggio's erstwhile follower and principal antagonist Giovanni Baglione, showing earthly love in the person of Cupid overcome by heavenly love personified as the Archangel Michael. Baglione's plump Cupid, naked except for a diminutive breech clout, lies helpless on his back in a mess of broken arrows, as the Archangel Michael, resplendent in full armour and parti-coloured feathers, bestrides him wielding an arrow of light.

Neither Caravaggio nor Baglione thought of the boy Cupid as worthy; where Caravaggio represents him as audacious, irrepressible and virtually invulnerable, the other shows him like Saul on the road to Damascus, about to be thunderously enlightened and blinded at the same time. In a contemporary treatment of a related subject Bartolomeo Manfredi shows Cupid subjected to a boy's more usual punishment, a merciless flogging at the hands of his father Mars. The same plump boy as in Baglione's painting writhes in the same position in the picture space but he is blindfolded and twisted over to reveal more of his buttocks, as Mars goes at him hammer and tongs with flailing knotted cords and Venus, newly alighted from her dove-drawn chariot, tries in vain to appease him.

Greek and Roman love poetry is written by men about consummated love with both boys and women. In feudal Europe the boy-lover began to write for himself. The troubadours of eleventh-century Provence were teenagers, recruited from the ranks of the squires who attended on the war lords in the field and at table. The woman they idealized was their lord's seldom visible wife, whom they did not expect to bed, because she was the incarnation of virtue, but for whom they burned with implacable desire. In an Avignon church in 1327, twenty-three-year-old Francesco Petrarca caught sight of a married woman and fell in hopeless love. Though he had active sexual relationships, he remained true to his unenjoyed Laura, and celebrated her in sonnets all his life long, though she died a few years after he first saw her. Petrarch's *Canzoniere* established the literary conventions of courtly love that ruled European poetry for half a millennium. All European love poetry is rooted in the overmastering passion of frustrated boys. The twenty-year-old squire in Chaucer's Canterbury Tales is an embodiment of the type, inspired to deeds of daring in the hope of standing in his lady's grace, singing and fluting all day long, a writer of songs, a dancer, and such a hot lover that at night he slept 'no more than doth the nightingale'.

To understand how traits that we would associate with masculinity are mixed with others that we would characterize as feminine in the figure of the

Above In Giovanni Baglione's *The Triumph of Sacred Love over Profane Love, c.* 1602, the weapon which armoured Sacred Love aims at the eyes of naked Profane Love aka Cupid, who is without his blindfold and has had all his arrows broken, is a sword of light. The pointed ears of the male figure on the left indicate that he is a satyr, an incarnation of animal lust.

Opposite The violence of Bartolomeo Manfredi's image of Cupid being flogged by his father is accentuated by the composition in which the action spirals against strong transverse elements that push and pull. In Manfredi's Rome, boys could lose their lives at the hands of masters who were legally entitled to flog them. Cupid's nakedness is an important element in the depiction of his helpless vulnerability.

boy-lover it is important to grasp that intense amorousness in the early modern scheme of things is considered an attribute of women rather than men. Early modern sexology held that boys share the female's propensity to ungovernable desire, amorous obsession and emotional incontinence. Polymorphous play sex was considered part of the birthright that boys would grow out of as life became earnest, when they were saddled with reponsibility and authority, and their lusts harnessed in the service of the body politic. Shakespeare's Rosalind, played by a boy actor and playing the boy Ganymede, describes it as the job of a 'moonish youth' to

> grieve, be effeminate, changeable, longing and liking, proud, fantastical, apish, shallow, inconstant, full of tears, full of smiles, for every passion something and for no passion truly anything…

Over the centuries, as boys were expressing their longings in endless songs and poems, women, being under the control of husbands and deprived of the advantages of education, remained silent. In our own time, women have had more power and less shame. Even so Elizabeth Sargent took a risk in her frank description of 'A Young Lover':

> Five times a day is what he really likes
> If he misses a day he becomes morose
> If he misses two days he turns mean and bites
> He is apt to bite, also, when held close;
> He bites the left breast and then the right,
> He bites the neck and face   God knows
> He bites! any place the fancy strikes
> him; he has even been known to bite toes.
> After he has bitten, he turns up the whites
> Of his eyes   and   grows
> A high tower of flesh   spike
> Of living steel, into which the semen flows
> Like tap water — Nature's loveliest sight
> (as least to me) as I take happy hold
> Of my young lover, my fifteen-year-old.

The boy's speciality is play and mutual pleasuring rather than domination, impregnation or, save the mark, relationships. He is incontinent but his juvenile rate of sperm production is such that it matters not. A boy is made for

Opposite In a preparatory two-figure study for a morally improving print called *Love Seduces Innocence, Pleasure Draws her On, Repentance Follows*, Prud'hon renders Love as the same size and same age as Innocence, and allows the boy to caress the girl just as if they were any young citizens stepping out together.

love only until his skin hardens and his beard comes. Then, to adapt Eminem, his dick gets shorter and his balls get bigger. He is no longer fit for dalliance or inclined to it.

In traditional Hindu communities a husband's unmarried younger brother, living alongside him in the extended household, is expected to be in love with his brother's wife. A common street jibe in India is 'brother-in-law', a more or less genial insult with about the same force as 'wanker'. The situation brought about by the impact of the loveliness of the young bride on over-active adolescent gonads may be remedied by indulgence in the riper charms of an aunt. 'Aunties' traditionally initiate young men sexually and reward them with money and presents. Such relationships are only possible because the boy's sexual readiness does not rely on the efficacy of the stimulus that he is being offered, but is pre-existing and almost impersonal. The money and the presents are an added bonus which the auntie is only too ready to provide. Usually the boy admitted to the favours of a mature woman gets a bad press from his jealous elders who call him 'gigolo' and 'toyboy'. It took considerable daring for Hugo von Hofmannsthal to suggest to Richard Strauss that they might make a hero of Count Octavian Rofrano, the Rosenkavalier. Octavian was seventeen when he became the lover of the Marschallin, Princess von Werdenberg, and when the opera opens they are actually waking up in bed together. The boy (sung by a contralto) wants nothing more than to stay with the Marschallin and continue being her boy-lover. So inexhaustible is his amorousness that when day comes he draws the curtains against the light, crying 'What is the day for? … It should be dark!' It is the Marschallin who decides that he should extricate himself from her clutches and embark on his adult life as the husband of a young wife, though to lose him catapults her headfirst into her own old age.

Colette's novel, *Chéri*, tells of the love of Frédéric Peloux for Léa de Lonval who is twenty-four years older than he; as in *Der Rosenkavalier*, the affair must end because Chéri is to be married. Six years before it was the boy who initiated the affair by turning his head and kissing Léa on the mouth when she bent to give him an aunt-like peck on the cheek. There is a good deal that is maternal in Léa's love for her *nourisson méchant,* and a good deal of the infantile in Chéri, who lets Léa teach him about pleasure and indulge his costliest whims. When Chéri leaves Paris on his honeymoon, Léa is so unprepared for her own reaction that at first she thinks she must be ill. Chéri is bored by his young wife, who correctly interprets his lack of interest in her as a

consequence of his perverted attachment to an old woman. When the lovers meet again, it is only to part forever as, in their very re-enactment of the bliss they both missed so unbearably, both realize that Léa is now too old. Colette had had an affair with a younger man before she wrote *Chéri*, and she was to have a longer relationship with a much younger man afterwards. In *La Fin de Chéri*, we see that Léa has survived menopause and become a bluff and hearty but entirely sexless being; it is Chéri who cannot adjust to the ravages of time and kills himself.

Schoolboy lovers are by no means rare in literature. By his own account Gustave Flaubert was six months shy of his fifteenth birthday when he went on holiday with his family to Trouville and fell in love. In a memoir written when he was sixteen, he recalled the way he stalked a woman he saw on the beach:

> I gazed at her from afar underneath the water, I envied the soft, peaceful waves lapping against her sides and covering with foam that heaving breast, I could see the outline of her limbs beneath the wet clothes enwrapping her, I could see her heart beating, her breast swelling, I mechanically contemplated her foot placing itself on the sand, and my gaze remained fixed to the trace of her steps and I could almost have wept at the sight of the waves washing them slowly away.

> And then when she came back and passed by me, and I heard the water dripping from her clothes and the swish of her walk, my heart beat violently, I lowered my eyes, blood rushed to my head — I was suffocating — I could feel that woman's half-naked body passing by me with the odour of the waves. Even deaf and blind, I could have guessed at her presence, for there was within me something intimate and tender which was submerged in ecstasy and graceful imaginings, whenever she passed by like that.

He felt something mystical, strange '*comme un sens nouveau*'.

> I was immersed in infinite tender feelings, I was rocked by hazy vague images, I had grown and at the same time become more proud.... I was in love.... Oh! a man's first heartbeats, his first throbbings of love, how sweet and strange they are! ... It was at first a singular state of surprise and admiration; — a quite mystical sensation in some degree, all idea of pleasure excluded. It was only later that I felt that frenzied and sombre ardour of the flesh and soul, an ardour that devours both of them.

Above Egon Schiele's uncompromising exploration of eroticism resulted in his imprisonment for obscenity in 1912, when he was twenty-two. In *Schiele's Wife with her Little Nephew*, Edith Harms, whom he married in June 1915, embraces her nephew in maternal fashion, but the boy's clutching arm and his fingers in her hair suggest his desire for something more than mere compassion.

Opposite In Benjamin West's *Venus Consoling Cupid Stung by a Bee*, exhibited at the Royal Academy in 1802, divine power is vested entirely in the sumptuous figure of the goddess with her swags of red-gold hair. Her son is just a little boy in need of mothering. West's subject is drawn from the Anacreonta and Theocritus.

It would be difficult to argue that at the age of fourteen years and six months Gustave Flaubert was not ready for sex with a woman. Indeed, if he had consummated his love with an understanding and skilful partner at this stage, his adult sex life might have been less chaotic. He went on to visit brothels with his cronies, choose the least attractive prostitute and have public intercourse with her without bothering to remove the cigar from his mouth, and at the same time involve himself in long and mutually frustrating relationships with women he feared and disliked more than he desired them, most of them older than he and married. Investigations of Flaubert's personality find nothing abnormal in his feeling a keen sexual passion at the age of fourteen and a half, but commiserate with 'the torment of his unrequited passion', and even accuse Elise Schlesinger of 'turning her back on him', as if she should have granted him her favours.

The eponymous hero of Bernhard Schlink's novel *Der Vorleser* was fifteen when he met the love of his life, Hanna Schmitz, who was twice his age. He had vomited on the sidewalk in front of her house; Hanna cleaned him up and walked him home. Three months later he went back to thank her, saw her putting on her stockings and ran away. A week later he came back, had an accident fetching coal for her and had to get out of his soiled clothing and take a bath.

> From behind she wrapped me in the towel from head to foot and
> rubbed me dry. Then she let the towel fall to the floor. I didn't dare
> move. She came so close to me that I could feel her breasts against
> my back and her stomach against my behind. She was naked too.
> She put her arms around me, one hand on my chest and the
> other on my erection.

Michael is afraid that he might not be equal to the situation but Hanna reassures him. It would be hard to argue that he was too young for love, when he describes his feelings like this:

> The next night I fell in love with her. I could barely sleep, I was
> yearning for her, I dreamed of her, thought I could feel her till I
> realized that I was clutching the pillow or the blanket. My mouth hurt
> from kissing. I kept getting erections, but I didn't want to masturbate.
> I never wanted to masturbate again. I wanted to be with her.

If there is an element of child abuse in Hanna's seduction of the boy, it is that no love he ever experienced afterwards could match either the comfort or the intensity of this relationship, in which the boy was never in control but so quick to regain his erection that it didn't matter. There was much about Hanna's behaviour that was maternal, but relationships with older men can be every bit as maternal. In this case the power balance was adjusted because the boy was educated and the woman was not. Years after their ways diverge he marries a girlfriend who is pregnant by him but the marriage fails.

In Milan Kundera's *Ignorance* Josef is given his high-school diary and is amazed to find himself as a 'virgin boy' recounting how he did 'everything possible to see his girlfriend suffer'. Josef is repelled by the mixture of 'sentimentality and sadism' that characterizes 'this little snot'… '[T]he diary finishes with the closing days of the school year (he has one more to go) just when an older woman (this one he remembers very well) introduced him to physical love and moved his life on to other tracks…' In this case the love of an older woman transforms Josef so that he is capable of faithful and happy love in a union with his Danish wife that ends only with her death.

Conventional wisdom holds that all these relationships were dysfunctional, and would point to Chéri's suicide and the failure of Michael's marriage as evidence of the damage the boy-lovers had suffered. It will not do to say simply that these were the great love affairs of their lives and nothing else measured up. What happens to a boy is apparently not life itself but only a curtain-raiser to the main event. This view is the more bizarre when we consider that the proper study of mankind, to judge from the yearly output of novels, is 'myself when young'. Whatever sexual rights the boy may have had in the past, he seems now to have lost them altogether. All over the world boys are seducing their betters, but campaigners against twenty-first-century sex tourism see the traffic as one-way. Their activities are inspired by horror and compassion for children who are forced by economic necessity to have sex that they are not ready for with older people they could not possibly desire. (This assumption itself should cast some doubt on the campaigners' own motives.) When she was studying the 'bad', sexualized mother, the great Melanie Klein asked herself in a note, 'Who is seducing whom?'

chapter 4

The Castration of Cupid

In the fifth century BCE a new emphasis began to be laid on Cupid's youth and childishness, so that he dwindled from a devil to an imp, and was allowed to frolic unchecked on the fringes of adult activity much as small boys do in life. Infant clones of Eros called Erotes, all born of Aphrodite, appeared in attendance at all kinds of human events, betrothals, marriages, births and deaths. Mournful Erotes are often shown in Roman funerary art, leaning on down-turned torches. A fragment attributed to Sappho in the Orations of Himerius describes the Erotes, their wings and tresses adorned with gold, waving their torches before the progress of Aphrodite in the chariot of the Graces. They may be fine-feathered, rose-crowned, soft-haired and gentle or raucous and cruel, as they are to women who treat their lovers with scorn. These millions, even billions of Erotes, who like Eros carry bows and arrows to pierce the hearts of their victims with love, are always babies or toddlers, ancestors of the Roman cupidines amores, who have come down to us as cupids, amoretti, cherubs, putti and even kewpee dolls.

In his *Metamorphoses*, more commonly known as *The Golden Ass*, written in the second century CE, Apuleius gives the fullest version of the story of the transformation of Cupid by his love for Psyche. When Venus wishes to punish Psyche, whose mortal beauty is drawing men away from the worship of the goddess, she can think of no worse torment than unrequited love. 'She quickly sent for her son, that winged and headstrong boy who, with his bad character and his disdain for law and order, goes running about at night through other folks' houses armed with flames and arrows, ruining everyone's marriages, and commits the most shameful acts with impunity and accomplishes absolutely no good.' The plan misfires; Cupid himself falls in love. When the oracle of Apollo tells Psyche's father to expose her on a mountain-top where her husband-to-be, a winged

The Guatemalan photographer Luis Gonzáles Palma, born in 1957, trained as an architect and studied art history in Europe, before returning to Guatemala, where civil war has been raging for thirty years. Using props and models he creates haunting images of the multiple ironies of post-colonial culture, such as *Corazon I (Winged Man with Heart)* of 1989.

monster who has power over everything and everyone, will find her, Cupid spirits her away to a sumptuous palace. He comes to her there by night, warning her that if she should ever see him she will lose him forever. Her sisters, jealous of the magnificence in which she lives, persuade Psyche that her invisible husband must be a monster and that he will eat her as soon as she has borne his child. Psyche decides to kill Cupid while he is sleeping beside her. She lights a lamp so that she can see to stab him but, overwhelmed by his radiant beauty, she accidentally pricks herself with one of his arrows and falls in love. The lamp sputters and a drop of hot oil falls onto Cupid's shoulder. He wakes and immediately soars upward. Distraught, Psyche beseeches the goddesses for protection but they leave her to the wrath of Venus who, after having the pregnant girl flogged, sets her a series of superhuman tasks, which Cupid covertly helps her to perform. Finally she is sent to the underworld to bring Venus a vial of beauty cream from Proserpina. When Psyche inhales the lethal contents of the vial and falls unconscious to the ground, she is once more rescued by Cupid, who pleads with Jupiter to allow her to drink nectar and so become immortal. Amidst great rejoicing in the company of all the gods, Cupid and Psyche are married and live happily ever after.

Apuleius's account of the transformation of the god of unbridled sexual passion into a husband was not his own invention. Funerary art of an earlier period also shows figures that can be identified as Psyche or the soul being borne to heaven by the god of love. Erich Neumann has argued that the fact that images of Cupid and Psyche can be found in art before they emerge as characters in literature shows that the story contains elements that are as old as the matriarchal culture that existed in the Mediterranean before the Graeco-Roman ascendancy. For the Early Christians the story immediately suggested parallels with biblical stories and with the Redemption itself. Apuleius's text survived in manuscript but it was known only to a handful of scholars before a Latin translation was published in Rome in 1469. By the 1490s editions were appearing every year. In 1517, when a vernacular translation by Boiardo was printed in Venice, Raphael accepted a commission from the Sienese banker Agostino Chigi to design a series of decorations for the entrance loggia of his villa in Trastevere (now the Farnesina), illustrating the story as told by Apuleius and other sources. Raphael died before he could finish the cycle but his designs were realized by Giulio Romano and Giovanni da Udine. Giulio later went to work for the Gonzaga family in Mantua where in 1528 he created a 'Sala di Psiche' in the Palazzo del Te. From then on the story of Cupid and Psyche has furnished innumerable subjects for artists in all kinds of media.

In Apuleius's version, when Cupid tells Psyche that she is pregnant, he says, 'Your womb, still a child's, bears another child for us…' and Venus, taking Cupid to task for disobeying her instructions, says angrily, 'At your age, a mere boy, you couple with her in your unrestrained immature love-making' and threatens to punish him by shaving off his hair, so both Cupid and Psyche are young, even adolescent. Artists as different as Gérard, Picot, Canova, Hugh Douglas Hamilton, Romney, Bouguereau, Burne-Jones and Rodin have been happy to show them as such. Raphael, however, chose to depict his Cupid throughout the cycle as a half-grown boy and Psyche as a full-grown woman. One of Raphael's most influential designs for the cycle, surviving in a copy from his workshop, shows Jupiter kissing Cupid as he consents to his marriage with Psyche. The naked child is so small that, though Jupiter is seated, he has to stoop to kiss him. Rubens was so impressed by this conceit that he reproduced it in his tribute picture *Mercury Bearing Psyche to Olympus*. Cupid's relationship with Psyche in some ways mirrors his relationship with

All the gesturing arms in Pompeo Batoni's *Marriage of Cupid and Psyche* (1756) converge on the diminutive figure of Cupid who restrains his enormously tall Psyche with an imperious left hand, while concentrating on slipping the ring on her finger with his right, under the watchful eye of a muscular Hymen. The maternal posture of Venus, who has taken temporary charge of Cupid's bow, adds to the feeling that somewhere a small god is in trouble.

his mother and scholars have confused them often enough. In Schiavone's *Marriage of Cupid and Psyche* the naked Cupid is half a head shorter than his fully clothed bride. In Pompeo Batoni's *Marriage of Cupid and Psyche* (1756) Psyche is more than common tall, as tall as Venus who is witnessing the marriage and holding the bridegroom's bow. Hymen, who supports the bride's hand, and Zephyr who puffs away in the upper right hand corner are both shorter than Psyche but much taller than her child-bridegroom. The ostensible intent of representing Cupid as a child may be to delete the sexual element in his marriage with Psyche, and to celebrate it as a figure of the union of the soul with divine love.

In the eighteenth century artists who chose to depict both Cupid and Psyche as teenage lovers manage to desexualize the subject by feminizing Cupid. His genitals are represented out of scale, his penis shrinking until it is smaller than some clitorises. All signs of musculature disappear from his nakedness and his face becomes more and more girlish. Towards the end of his life Jean-Baptiste Greuze was working on an ambitious composition called *Psyche Crowning Love*, which was never finished. Cupid kneels, naked except for a scarf, before a seated and fully clothed Psyche who holds a 'white crown of purity' over him. Cupid's boneless body is a replica of what can be inferred of Psyche's, in all except her exposed breast. Behind Psyche stands a figure of Modesty who reveals her own naked body by lifting what there is of her diaphanous drapery to veil Psyche, all the while resting her cheek on her hand and gazing blankly out of the canvas. None of the figures makes eye contact

with any other. The whole flat composition breathes tired melancholy, despite the two Erotes, one of whom lays rose garlands on the nuptial bed while the other adds incense to a brazier. On the altar behind the not very joyous couple can be seen a pair of white turtle doves, emblem of life-long monogamy and marital chastity. An empty basin and ewer, with a damp napkin testifying to ritual purification already carried out, stand on the left of the picture foreground, balancing Cupid's abandoned quiver on the right.

Greuze was right on the money. Sexless Cupid proved very popular. In 1795 Angelika

Left In *Psyche Receiving Cupid's First Kiss* exhibited at the Salon of 1798 Gérard continues the tradition of draped woman with nude male. In accordance with the canons of public art sex gives way to gender, as Cupid conceals his manhood but behaves in a manly and protective fashion. Both figures, posed by professional models, seem frozen.

Kauffmann felt able to paint the Plymouth children, who were brother and sister, as Cupid and Psyche. To a modern sensibility the enactment of innocence seems something of a posture. Once again we are confronted with the familiar combination of clothed female figure and naked boy, whose genitalia are coquettishly scarfed in floating drapery. Cupid's maleness having been elided, he is nevertheless required to display masculine protectiveness towards his sister, as Cupid did towards Psyche when he rescued her from the underworld. Kauffmann's image is conscientiously one of gender without sex. In Gérard's *Psyche Receiving Cupid's First Kiss* exhibited at the Salon of 1798, Psyche's lower limbs are decently veiled and Cupid is, as usual, quite naked, yet perfect propriety is maintained because he does not touch her with hand

Above Angelika Kauffmann painted several pictures of Cupid and Psyche; her portrait of two children of the Earl of Plymouth, five-year-old Lord John Windsor and his elder sister Mary as Cupid and Psyche, was probably commissioned by one of their relatives. The children's hands are 'fasted' as if for a betrothal. As we have come to expect, the girl is draped, the boy nude except for a wisp of cloak.

Below In keeping with neo-classical republicanism, Jacques-Louis David presents the Cupid who slips out of Psyche's bed as a cheeky sunburnt son of the people. In other respects *Cupid and Psyche* (1817) represents a departure from the austerity and high moral purpose that distinguish David's best work, being frankly decorative and erotic. The interlacing of arms and legs is particularly daring.

or lip and even their limbs are in no way entwined. In defiance of perspective and probability Cupid has managed to raise his leg and insert his knee in a non-existent space behind Psyche, so that his foot is standing on nothing, and all to conceal his genitals. He does not even make eye contact with Psyche because he is supposed to be invisible. When David painted his *Cupid and Psyche* in 1817 and placed in the foreground a sun-tanned, hard-bodied Cupid who grins knowingly at the viewer as if he were a street boy slipping out of the bed of a sated princess, he was reacting against years of representation of love as effete and sexless. The limit had been reached by Prud'hon in his treatment of such improving subjects as *Innocence Preferring Love to Wealth* (1804), in which Love, winged and naked except for a diaphanous scarf knotted rather suggestively over his genitals, is a kind of hermaphrodite, slender, boneless and broader in the hip than the shoulder. When François-Edouard Picot came to exhibit a *Cupid and Psyche* in 1819, he not only made

sure that Cupid's body was not in contact with Psyche's, as he reaches for his bow and quiver as if grabbing a briefcase before going to work, and reduced his genitals to infantile dimensions, but also backlit him, leaving Psyche's ripe nudity as the focus of the composition.

In the nineteenth century sexual passion was gradually transformed from a diversion of the élite of the *ancien régime* to the foundation of the bourgeois family. Husband having been transformed into lover, the lover also had to be transformed. Physical desire had to wait upon sentimental commitment and the modest shrinking of a virtually sexless partner. It has been suggested that the feminization of the boy-figure in the revolutionary period is a consequence of the growing importance of homosociality in building the modern state; at least as important is that, with the rise and rise in every major

Above For his *Cupid and Psyche* painted in Rome in 1817, François-Edouard Picot chooses a moment early in Apuleius's story, before Psyche has glimpsed her husband's celestial beauty and fallen in love with him. By leaving Cupid unlit, while Psyche's nude torso is bathed in light, he makes the female nude the focus of interest.

European city, of public academies with their yearly expositions and awards, not to mention the proliferation of reproductions in various media, the imagery of painting and sculpture had to be suitable for female members of the public to see. It was no longer sufficient that male genitalia should be reduced in size; they now had to disappear from view altogether. Love was officially de-sexualized.

Given a new boys' own culture of manly pursuits that prized knockabout boisterousness and derided sensitivity, no boy could model the god of sentimental love. No boy could be seen like Antoine-Denis Chaudet's Cupid, offering a rose to a butterfly. A daring painter like Annie Swynnerton might show a boyish boy Cupid trying rather ineptly to kiss a girl his own age, but the mainstream took a different path. The boy-god turned into a girl, as more in keeping with an innocent, faery incarnation. Though a hint of male anatomy may be meant to lurk behind a wing-tip artfully positioned over his groin, the *Cupidon* painted by Adolphe-William Bouguereau in 1875 must have been modelled by a girl. She is apparently but not quite leaning against a tree, her left foot propped on her right, and her arms wreathed so that each hand rests on top of the opposite shoulder while her very feminine cheek has come to rest coquettishly on her left hand. This is possibly the most disturbing image of all for she projects, rather than the audacity proper to Cupid, consciousness of exposure and vulnerability. For *Venus Chiding Cupid and Removing his Wings*, *Cupid Considering* and *Cupid Reposing*, Julia Margaret Cameron used as the model for Cupid a rather miserable small girl, tentatively identified as one Daisy Taylor.

As the redeemer of Psyche, Cupid was purged of his diabolic character and became to all intents and purposes a figure of Chaste Love. In other contexts Eros is identified with sexual passion only, and is to be seen opposed by or co-operating with other kinds of love. His counterpart is Anteros, which may

Above left The French neo-classical sculptor Antoine-Denis Chaudet created *Cupid Trapping a Butterfly* (1802) in which a winged child tenderly offers a butterfly a rose, as a figure of Love seducing the soul with pleasure. Reliefs carved by the artist on the plinth show Love subjugating the soul and trying to destroy it, until it finally breaks free with the help of bees, in all a complete inversion of Apuleius's fable of the soul redeemed by love.

Above right It is but a short step from innocent androgynous child to coy little girl. Before Bouguereau began to paint little girls nude, as in *Child at Bath* and *Temptation*, the subject was never depicted. It is possible that the model for his *Cupidon* of 1875 was male, but a boy would hardly have been expected to take such a coy nipple-concealing pose.

Opposite In foregrounding the female figure, which is sedulously cleansed of pubic features, and upstaging an awkwardly boyish Cupid, whose genitals are screened by a prong of purple feather, Annie Swynnerton's *Cupid and Psyche* of 1891 reflects nineteenth-century aesthetics, which saw the beautiful as both feminine in gender and devoid of sexual associations.

Above The topos of Venus scolding Cupid is an old
one, but before Julia Margaret Cameron posed her female
models for *Venus Chiding Cupid and Removing his Wings*
the goddess had never been shown actually removing her
son's wings. Whereas the classic Cupid is knowing and
mischievous, the little girl as posed by Cameron with
her legs crossed appears defensive and unaware.

mean love of virtue, or love of learning and hence ambition, or loyal but un-requited love. As Amor Virtutis the winged youth is shown crowned with laurel and carrying laurel wreaths. Sometimes Eros and Anteros are shown as little boys fighting. In early Greek vase-painting Eros is often shown with two of his brothers, Pothos, the god of obsession, and Himeros, the god of sexual desire. To these may be added Hermaphroditos, a figure of intercourse itself, Hedylogos, the god of wooing, and Hymen, the god of marriage. As the god of sexual passion Cupid is sometimes opposed to Hymen and sometimes allied with him as a necessary partner in the nuptial enterprise, in which case he may assume Hymen's attributes, abandoning his bow and arrows for a chaplet of flowers and a torch. Where love is represented as rational and virtuous, he is shown as old enough to have reached the age of reason, while most often irrational love is still personified as a naughty toddler, and often blindfolded.

Below Guido Reni's *Triumph of Sacred Love over Profane Love*, 1622–3, is yet another commentary on the topos of the Triumph of Cupid. Behind Sacred Love, represented as a beautiful youth who is tranquilly burning Cupid's arrows, can be seen the music and instruments that prefigure the harmonious consort of Cupid's triumph. The image of the struggling toddler, blindfolded and bound to a tree, is disquieting, to say the least.

The sexless and boneless figure of Guido Reni's *L'Anima Beata*, also called *Amor Divino*, was greatly admired in the eighteenth century when Guido's fame was at its peak. In 1797, as part of the spoils of war, Napoleon took the picture with him to Paris, where it remained until the Congress of Vienna ordered its return in 1815. It is thought to be one of the last works carried out by the master, but as it has been several times restored its exact place in Guido's canon cannot be established.

The only preparatory oil sketch left by Guido Reni shows a winged youth standing on a globe, his naked body entirely revealed despite a fluttering drape, with his arms raised in the pose of Amor Divino from Ripa's iconography (which otherwise shows the blessed soul as a veiled and fully clothed female). The figure is virtually hermaphroditic, with minute genitals and a pronounced curve of fleshy hip. In the finished picture, Guido has pulled a fold of the drapery over the genitals and elongated the figure more than somewhat, though it is still relatively boneless and clothed in pearly opalescence shed on it from an overhead burst of effulgence. This Love is entirely angelic and bodiless. Not for nothing was Guido the favourite Italian artist of a sentimental and prudish generation.

Eros is sometimes opposed not by Anteros but by Thanatos, the god of death. Thanatos is either brother or father of another winged boy, Hypnos, who brings sleep by merely placing his hand on the heads of the weary or by administering a sleeping draught from a horn he carries. He lives either in a cavern on the Isle of Lemnos or in the far-off land of the Cimmerians. An Etruscan head in the British Museum shows him as a calm-faced, beautiful boy, with large wings growing from his temples. In art Hypnos is often shown with Thanatos carrying the bodies of fallen soldiers from the battlefield. Morpheus, the god of dreams, who is also often depicted as a boy with huge wings that beat without noise, is variously described as the son or the brother of Hypnos.

Thanatos, Hypnos and Morpheus are less closely related to Eros than they are to the numberless tribe of genii. The term 'genius' in classical antiquity is understood to mean 'the tutelary god or attendant spirit allotted to every person at birth, to govern his fortunes and determine his character and finally to conduct him out of the world'. In a later development this bodiless abstraction bred out of identity is endowed with proclivities for good or evil, leading to the notion that we all have two genii, one good and one evil, who prompt us to act well or ill. Places too have each a *genius loci*, an in-dwelling spirit. All the combinations of abstractions called genius are properly represented as winged boys. The spiritual realm being even more crowded with winged boys than the streets were with flightless boys, it was inevitable that their spheres of activity should overlap so that genii tended to morph into one another and into abstract qualities. One of the best-known examples of a genius is the impressively virile boy soaring diagonally across one face of the base that is all that remains of the column erected in 161 CE in honour of Emperor

Antoninus Pius by his successors Marcus Aurelius and Lucius Verus, now in the Vatican Museum. The wings of this boy, who is carrying the emperor and his wife to heaven on his back, occupy the full width of the space, dwarfing the imperial eagles that attend him. In keeping with the tendency to treat genii as personifications he is sometimes identified as Aion, or Eternity. Genii are agents and not abstract qualities, which are always (barring deliberate departures from the canon) personified grammatically and pictorially as feminine.

After the Sack of Rome by the Visigoths in 410 CE the iconography of paganism was eclipsed. The austere early Church not only cut down the number of gods to one but depeopled heaven of its hordes of winged boys, replacing them by the angels of biblical tradition who are spirits like human souls but without bodies. According to some the angels are what became of the other gods when Judaism adopted monotheism. It is now recognized that Hebrew iconography is an outgrowth of both Ancient Egyptian and Ancient Assyrian art, which peopled heaven with winged creatures that were usually chimaeras or female and often both. The descriptions of cherubim and seraphim in the Scriptures reveal them to be creatures that are not so much superhuman as inhuman. According to Isaiah vi: 2, the six-winged seraphim formed a double choir around the throne of God, unceasingly and deafeningly singing the Trisagion, 'Holy, holy, holy. Lord God of Hosts. Heaven and earth are filled with thy glory. Hosanna in the highest.' The name 'cherubim' for the angels of the Old Testament was a borrowing from an Assyrian word that simply meant 'those nearby'; the cherubim who guarded the gates of Eden with a flaming sword were simply recruited from the throng that stood about the throne of God. In some accounts they are covered with eyes and each has four sets of wings and four faces. The fourth-century doctor of the church, Augustine of Hippo, envisioned a constant traffic between angels and men, as signified in the name 'angel' itself, from the Greek 'angelos', meaning messenger, but he gives us no indication of what shape these bodiless creatures might take if they needed to assume physical form.

In the fifth century angels began to appear in church decorations and manuscript illuminations, as the court of heaven was gradually peopled with plenipotentiaries in parallel with the court of the Byzantine emperors. The result is three hierarchies, the first comprising the seraphim, cherubim and thrones, the second the dominations, virtues and powers, and the third the principalities, archangels and angels. Only the last two ranks, the archangels and their subordinate angels, are often seen in art as supernaturally beautiful

Opposite As the patron of travellers the Archangel Raphael, known to us only from the apocryphal book of Tobias, is a popular subject in votive painting. Pollaiuolo shows the angel incognito, as he escorts Tobias to the house of Sarah, whom he hopes to marry, though seven preceding bridegrooms have been killed by the demon Asmodeus on their wedding night. The little dog features in the scriptural account. Gradually Raphael the escorting archangel morphs into the (sometimes female) Guardian Angel of later iconography.

Above left In the groundbreaking design of his *St Michael*, Raphael creates a powerful impression of downward movement by the driving vertical elements of the wing, through the axis of the twisting body and the down-dropping spear. St Michael, dressed not in contemporary armour but the warrior dress of classical antiquity, is a figure of power and authority rather than prettiness.

Above right In painting *St Michael* on silk, sometime before 1636, probably for a processional banner, Guido Reni attempted to portray ideal beauty, rather than divinely sanctioned power and authority. Reni's design was engraved, and at least a dozen copies were made of what was an enormously influential image.

boys. Of the seven archangels, we are familiar with only three, Michael, Gabriel and Raphael. As the leader of the army of good angels and enactor of divine justice, Michael becomes an important patron of the church militant; Gabriel is the angel chosen to announce the Incarnation; and Raphael is known to us from the book of Tobit. The Byzantine tradition required them to be dressed alike in sumptuous ecclesiastical robes which obliterated any sign of feet or legs which, being airborne, the angels did not need, though in this period they were seldom shown as actually flying. The half-lengths in the Cambridge Polyptych attributed to Simone Martini and painted *c.* 1320 are lineal descendants of this orthodox tradition. The Archangel Raphael who accompanies the young Tobit in the representations of the favourite story from the Apocrypha by Verrocchio, Pollaiuolo and Botticini, though he does not wear the cope and dalmatic familiar from mediaeval representations, is still elaborately gowned, cloaked and shod. If the disturbing connotations of the presence of a handsome young man in a virgin's bedroom are to be suppressed, the Archangel Gabriel needs to remain decently covered by priestly vestments. Michael is too grand a functionary of heaven to be divested of his shining armour, but it gradually dwindles from the full shiny metal suit seen in Botticini's picture to a version of classical Roman armour that fits his angelic torso like a coat of paint, while the brevity of his flying kilt of slit leather leaves his thighs and legs exposed. In this guise Michael's iconography can be seen to be identical with that of Sacred Love, as it was expressed by Baglione (see p. 71).

In the European art of the late Middle Ages angels of the rank and file follow the example of their superiors, appearing to men in over-long

Below Francesco Botticini, *The Three Archangels and Tobias*. According to Catholic tradition only three archangels are mentioned in the Bible: Michael, depicted by Botticini in 1467–71 in full armour, Raphael identified by the presence of Tobias, and Gabriel, the angel of the Annunciation, who seems to have carried off the lily that is usually to be seen in the Virgin's boudoir. As bodiless beings angels can have no sex; their sexlessness is usually rendered as boyhood.

garments that swirl and billow around their bodilessness. Whether they are clutching the instruments of the passion, or awarding palms and crowns to saints and martyrs, or serenading the newborn Christ on lutes, viols, portative organs and trumpets, their sleeves are apparently glued to their wrists. Nakedness was reserved for humans like Adam and Eve and the throngs of the blessed and damned souls. When Giotto filled the sky of the Entombment in the Scrovegni Chapel in Padua with mourning angels, he allowed their fully clad nether limbs to disappear in the mist and their wide sleeves completely to conceal their outflung arms. The stern-faced angels of Piero della Francesca are covered from neck to knee to ankle. The first sign of a change on the way is the slit in the tunic of one of the five wingless angel musicians in Piero's Nativity. The slit extends almost to the hip but it is held closed, as if for the time being, by a single button. In about 1460 when Giovanni Bellini painted a dead Christ supported by two angels, the angels were small boys wearing sleeveless classical tunics slit to the thigh. When he treated the subject again some years later the number of angels was increased to four and the tunics were not only shortened but slit, to reveal teasing segments of hip and buttock. One boy's tunic is even slipping off his shoulders. These angels are so boyish, so engagingly human that we are almost surprised to notice their wings, which are anything but conspicuous. Their bare-bottomed brothers play lute and flute for the Enthroned Madonna in the Church of the Frari in Venice. Bellini was aware of the classical tradition; Erotes frolic across the floors of his secular allegories. Indeed, it is doubtful if the Erotes had ever quite gone away. The mosaic floor of the basilica built by Bishop Theodore at Aquileia in the fourth century is peopled with Erotes gaily fishing. In the 1430s when Donatello and Luca della Robbia competed to decorate the Cantoria of the Duomo in Florence with singing boys, they modelled their friezes on classical reliefs.

For all we know Bellini's innovation was not well received. As the nature of angels was a matter of Catholic doctrine, confusing them with Erotes was likely to lead to trouble. Bellini's other dead Christs are supported by less controversial figures of decently clad older angels. Vasari records Luca della Robbia as having made two nude angels for the cornice over the sacristy door of the Duomo in Florence. The precedent did not become a fashion. Though naked cherubs had begun to proliferate in religious painting of the High Renaissance, the bodies of the grown angels remained shrouded, so that only head, hands and feet could be be seen.

It was probably Michelangelo who first decided to represent the bodiless-ness of angels as ideal body. In the ceiling of the Sistine Chapel (1508–12) the beings who transport God the Father towards Adam's beautiful inert body are of various ages, all masculine and stark naked. They are also, oddly, wingless, as are the hordes of partially draped angels who carry the instruments of the passion in the *Last Judgment*. Where Michelangelo went other artists were usually bound to follow but wingless angels did not catch on. In Giovanni Girolamo Savoldo's *Tobias and the Angel* (c. 1534), for example, Raphael sports a vast pair of seagull's wings and is moreover festooned from head to foot in such voluminous drapery that we might suspect an implicit criticism of Michelangelo's practice. If he had lived longer Raphael would probably have been the one to remove the clothing of winged angels while letting them keep their wings. His study for the *Lapidation of Saint Stephen* shows grown angels who are to all intents naked but do have wings. When Giulio Romano executed Raphael's design for the Church of Saint Stephen in Genoa, he altered the angels but left them as scantily clad as they were in the bozzetto – and retained their wings. The fresco of *Pope Urban I between Justice and Charity* in the Sala di Costantino in the Vatican shows him attended by two stalwart angels who sport robust wings and little in the way of clothing. The elaborately clad angels of the older tradition were usually equipped with brilliant wings in jewel colours encrusted with lapidary detail; these new-style angels had actual birds' wings painted from life. Thus equipped they took to the air. Titian's Gabriels, though certainly more human and animated than any before them, keep their suffocating draperies.

It took minor painters to release the pent-up eroticism in the figure of the angel that swoops into the Virgin's boudoir. In the mid-1550s Titian's follower Lo Schiavone was commissioned to paint an Annunciation for the wooden doors of a church organ. He took the opportunity to show an airborne Gabriel who has yet to touch down and whose diaphanous draperies foam about his shapely loins rather than his calves. From then on sexy angels began to show up not only in Annunciations but in treatments of all kinds of subjects. Lot and his daughters provided an excuse to portray a full-length boy nude leading the way; St Cecilia could be accompanied on the viol da gamba by a naked winged boy; the Holy Family could be serenaded by a ravishing youth; Hagar could be solaced in the wilderness by a boy wearing

In a fresco of 1727 in Palazzo Dolfin, Udine, Giambattista Tiepolo illustrates Genesis xviii, when Sarah overhears the angels telling her husband that she will bear a son and and laughs 'within herself, saying, "After I am waxed old shall I have pleasure, my Lord being old also?"' Tiepolo creates an ironic parallel with the Annunciation by having her visited in person by a single gorgeous angel who displays a shapely leg and thigh through the slit in his skirt.

Below Because angels are messengers between the divine and the human, with souls like ours, Caravaggio can show the pigeon-winged angel in *Rest on the Flight into Egypt* (1596–7) performing human music as written in the book that St Joseph holds. The music has been identified as the cantus of a motet by Noel Baulduin, first published in 1519, a setting of 'Quam pulchra es et quam decora', from the Latin version of the Song of Songs.

nothing but a floating scarf; St Jerome could be rapt in a vision of semi-naked male loveliness. A reaction set in almost immediately; angels not only resumed their clothes but fundamentally altered their character, as a new emphasis was placed on angels as guardians of human souls. At first, as in the image designed for Cardinal Odoardo Farnese by Annibale Carracci (1603), sexless guardian angels were shown towering over generic figures of the human soul, but the souls gradually turned into children and the angels

Above For *The Deliverance of St Peter*, 1624, Hendrick ter Brugghen adapted the techniques he had learned in Rome from the Caravaggisti to produce a homely image of a confused old man being infused with new life by a much younger one (who just happens to be an angel). The image, which brings the two figures into almost mouth-to-mouth contact, is stunning in its tenderness and immediacy.

Above In Lanfranco's *Hagar in the Wilderness*, which
illustrates an episode from Genesis xxi, the angel, being lit
by the same light source as the woman, seems less heavenly
than human. Though according to scripture Hagar had left
her baby beneath a shrub a bow-shot away, Ishmael's ghostly
child-face can be seen squeezed between her and the angel,
an afterthought perhaps, intended to mitigate the
suggestiveness of the image.

Opposite *The Vision of St Jerome*, painted in 1602
for Cardinal Aldobrandini by Domenico Zampieri, called
Domenichino, is remarkable for the nakedness of the angel
who has flown in to inspire a naked St Jerome in his biblical
studies. In later works all Domenichino's personages,
including angels, tend to be decently clad.

Naked boys sporting wings are to be found on all kinds of public monuments. This bronze *Genius of Liberty* by A.-A. Dumont hovers over Paris on the summit of the column in the Place de la Bastille, as Gilbert's Eros does over Piccadilly Circus in London.

became so maternal that they began to grow breasts. The images of angels on cards, trinkets and figurines that are now big business are all revoltingly kitsch and mostly ultra-feminine.

As the Age of Revolution approached, the reign of the angels came to an end. Religion having been driven out of art by a combination of anti-clerical republicanism and enthusiasm for classical antiquity, in the place of angels came genii of all kinds, of liberty, of fame, of individuals, of countries, of parties, of movements. The pioneer was Anton Raphael Mengs, whose fetching genii floated across ceilings all over Europe, often crowned with laurel and carrying wreaths of laurel, but otherwise indistinguishable from his genial angels. For his *morceau de réception* to the Académie, the French sculptor Jean-Antoine Houdon chose to offer a life-size representation of Morpheus as a winged youth asleep; he began the project in 1770 and was finally successful in 1777. When Franz Anton Zauner was asked to design a memorial to Ignaz von Born he returned to the Eros of Praxiteles as the model for his Genio Bornii of 1785. In 1783 Canova chose to show, rather than an angel, a mourning Genius on the tomb of Pope Clement XIII. In the years that followed it looked as if a throng of airborne females called Victory, Wisdom, Truth, Public Instruction, Rights of Man and so forth might jostle the winged boys out of the sky but they hung on, if only as naked winged secretaries, also known as Genii of Fame, recording the achievements of the age. In 1795 Jean-Baptiste Regnault exhibited *Liberty or Death*, in which the seated figures of female Liberty and skeletal Death are indicated by the outstretched arms of the winged Genius of France, in a deliberate recollection of the Genius on the base of the Column of Antoninus Pius. By the mid-nineteenth century the winged boys had clawed their way back to the forefront of public art. When the Parisian authorities sought a design for a figure to place atop the huge column that was erected in the Place de la Bastille in 1845, they looked no further than A.-A. Dumont's *Genius of Liberty*.

chapter 5

The Passive Love Object

The poet Rochester's 'Platonick lady' could be speaking for all boy-lovers:

> I love a youth who'll give me leave
> His body in my arms to wreathe,
> To press him gently and to kiss…

A love object is the wooed, not the wooer. Whether male or female it is by definition passive, its function not to do love but to allow love. The easiest way to reduce the boy to passivity is to immobilize him utterly in sleep. As he sleeps amorous eyes may feast upon his beauty; when those eyes belong to a woman she is for once powerful and dominant, free to feed her own desire as slowly and deeply as she wishes, building her own excitement and deliciously delaying any consummation, as mother-like she takes pains not to wake the sleeping beauty. Byron, who knew more of peremptory female passion than most of his contemporaries, develops a wonderful account of women's love of the passive boy in his comic epic *Don Juan* which he began in 1818 and did not live to finish. Juan's adventures begin when he is seduced at the age of sixteen by his mother's friend Donna Julia. When the affair is discovered by Julia's husband, Julia is sent to a nunnery and Juan to sea. He is eventually shipwrecked and cast up naked on a Greek island, where 'like a young flower snapped from the stalk, Drooping and dewy on the beach he lay', 'As fair a thing as e'er was formed of clay'. As consciousness comes and goes he becomes aware of 'a lovely female face of seventeen' 'bending close o'er his'. It belongs to Haidée, who raises Juan up, pillowing 'his death-like forehead' on her 'transparent cheek, all pure and warm'. She and her maid carry him into a cave, where they tend him and make him a bed of Haidée's furs and their spare

Bartholomäus Spranger has angled his *Hermaphroditus and the Nymph Salmacis* of *c.* 1585 so that we look along the eyeline of the nymph as she spies on the boy who is bathing as innocently as any Susannah. The serpentine lines of the desiring female body that lurks behind an upheld mantle dramatize the predatoriness of an intent female voyeur.

Below In *The Finding of Don Juan by Haidée* of 1878 Ford Madox Brown is careful to follow the detail of Byron's poem, showing how Juan's 'stretched hand drooped dripping on the oar' as he lay 'like a young flower snapped from the stalk' but he is also careful to keep Haidée at a seemly distance from the unconscious naked boy, as Byron does not.

petticoats. They leave him fast asleep and he is still sleeping when Haidée returns next morning and once more drinks 'his scarce-drawn breath'. Altogether Juan sleeps for thirty-seven stanzas during which Haidée, without the least encouragement, manages to fall in love with him. It is only a matter of time before they make love, whereafter Juan sinks once more to sleep.

Haidée's deep pleasure in watching her boy-lover asleep has something in it of mother-love. There is an old Polish expression of the mother to her child, 'I love you when you're asleep', that is, when the child is not being restless or demanding and the mother can sit in quiet contemplation of how lovely it is. In the days when adolescent boys were woken at dawn and packed off to labour beside their fathers in the fields or the mines, their mothers would sit by their beds for a few minutes gazing at their childish sleeping faces, savouring their sweetness and agonizing over the privation that was making them old before their time, delaying as long as possible the unpleasant moment when they had to be shaken awake and pushed out of the house.

The female sleeping beauty of the fairy tale is always shown lying fully clothed upon her bed like a funerary sculpture on a bier. In Western painting reclining female nudes abound but their limbs are always demurely arranged, their thighs decorously together, with a hand sometimes draped over a hairless, lipless pubic mound. Even reclining Venuses are conscientiously unsexed, which is why Manet's *Olympia* caused such a fuss when it was first exhibited. Reclining male nudes are often to be seen fast asleep, legs akimbo, arms flung up in total abandonment. One explanation for the recurrence of the sleeping boy motif is that posing a model lying down permitted the artist unlimited contemplation, without the necessity of allowing the model regularly to relax and change position. If he actually went to sleep, so much the better.

The story of the sleeping male nude begins with the larger than life-size Hellenistic marble sculpture known as the Barberini Faun, now in the Staatliche Antikensammlung in Munich. Hard facts about the sculpture are hard to come by. Its subject has been identified as both a satyr and an athlete, its heavy slumber interpreted as the result of drunkenness, or relaxation after physical effort or sex. When the statue was unearthed close by Castel Sant'Angelo in 1627, it was thought that it had lain there since being thrown

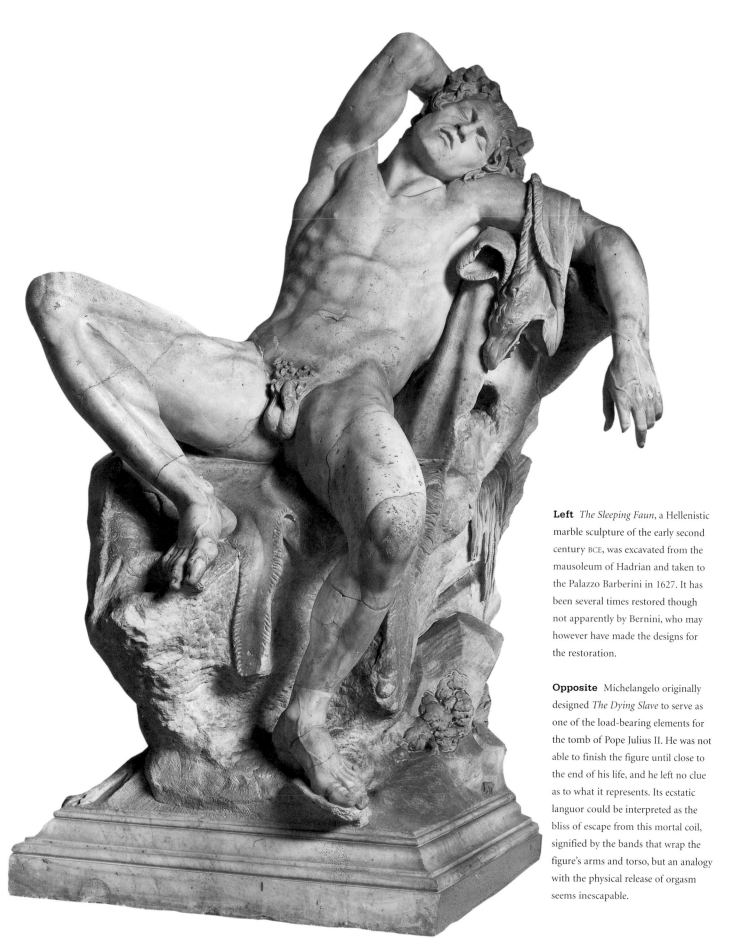

Left *The Sleeping Faun*, a Hellenistic marble sculpture of the early second century BCE, was excavated from the mausoleum of Hadrian and taken to the Palazzo Barberini in 1627. It has been several times restored though not apparently by Bernini, who may however have made the designs for the restoration.

Opposite Michelangelo originally designed *The Dying Slave* to serve as one of the load-bearing elements for the tomb of Pope Julius II. He was not able to finish the figure until close to the end of his life, and he left no clue as to what it represents. Its ecstatic languor could be interpreted as the bliss of escape from this mortal coil, signified by the bands that wrap the figure's arms and torso, but an analogy with the physical release of orgasm seems inescapable.

down by the Goths in the sixth century, but later versions hold that it had been hidden in the mausoleum of Hadrian, which gives support to the notion that it is a masterpiece of homoeroticism. It is thought to date from *c.* 200 BCE and to have been carved somewhere in the Eastern Mediterranean, perhaps in Antioch, or to be a good copy of some such work; a decision on this point is rendered more difficult because the statue has been several times restored, some say by Bernini, others not (Bernini was the sculptor patronized by Cardinal Barberini, first owner of the recovered statue, which was eventually bought from the Barberini family by Ludwig II of Bavaria).

The figure has few of the attributes of a satyr or faun, no pointy ears, no goat feet, no bony animal penis, only the panther-skin of a Dionysiac devotee to suggest the identification. Michelangelo adapted the Faun's raised elbow and forearm cradling his curly head for the figure of his own that is usually given the title of 'The Dying Slave'. Both are stunning ikons of young male passivity, with bodies left open and unguarded to the view. Both are replete with erotic suggestion but whether the appeal is homoerotic or not depends on the prejudices of the beholder. In 1844 Eugène-Louis Lequesne's copy of the Faun was positioned in the foyer of the Comédie Française for the world and his wife to see; the subject was not then considered to be erotic let alone homoerotic. Despite this rather egregious blindness it seems safe to say that the figure of the sleeping boy always carries some sort of charge, even when the boy is the young Christ as painted by Guido Cagnacci in 1630–40. Cagnacci has emblematized the fragile beauty of the unconscious boy by the parallel of the bowl of roses on the table beside him (see p. 110). Like the Faun's and the Slave's, Christ's arm is lifted above his head and his fingers are sunk in his curly hair. The pose seems unavoidable; Ludovico Carracci's sleeping boy has his knees bent and his legs parted and an arm cradling his head in a similar way to the Faun's (see p. 111), but no one has interpreted his abandonment to sleep as the consequence of drunkenness or sex or as the indulgence of the artist's lust.

Eros himself is often to be seen asleep. One of the most popular classical depictions shows him as a sleeping toddler. The type has him, legs apart, lying on his back with his upper body twisted so that his right arm hangs by his left side, as if he has fallen asleep in the midst of playing, as a small child will. Later versions show Cupid in the same pose pillowed on the skin of the

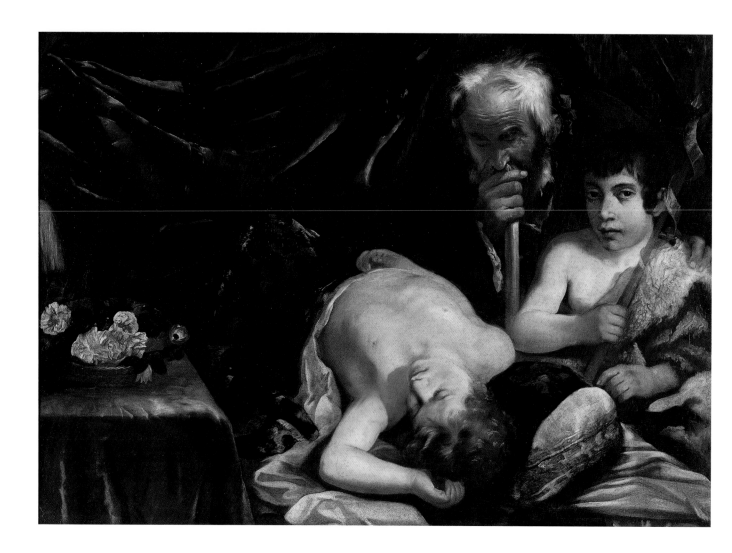

Nemean lion, reminding us that this sleeping infant is a god of such power that, as love unmans the strongest of men, he overcame Hercules himself. In other versions, used as conventional ornaments for the tombs of children, the sleeping infant clasps a bunch of poppies. A sleeping Cupid carved on the Hellenistic model by the young Michelangelo was sold to Cardinal Raffaello Riario di San Giorgio as a work of genuine antiquity; it was later acquired by Isabella d'Este. A version of the subject used on lids of boxes and the like in the fourth century shows Eros in the same pose as the Barberini Faun. When Alessandro Algardi carved the subject in touchstone, he too altered the pose to something resembling that of the Barberini Faun. Caravaggio's nuggetty little *Sleeping Cupid* of 1608 lies in a more covered and defensive fashion with his legs together, as if Caravaggio were denying his possible complicity in embraces of any kind, a suggestion borne out by the broken bow and scattered arrows. The *Sleeping Cupid on the Island of Cyprus* at Kedleston Hall is a

Above Compared to the plethora of images of Christ as an infant and as a man alive, dying, dead or resurrected, there are very few depictions of Christ as a boy. *Sleeping Christ with John the Baptist* by Guido Cagnacci can only be identified as such because the boy by the bedside carries the Baptist's banner and wears a camel skin. All Christ has to identify Him is a dazzlingly white boy's torso.

Opposite Though almost certainly drawn from life, the foreshortened body of Ludovico Carracci's *Nude Boy Sleeping* once again makes use of the upflung pillowing arm, and the parted knees of the Barberini Faun. There being no wisp of drapery trailed across the boy's genitals, his nakedness retains its innocence, even though he is smiling in his sleep.

frankly delicious image of the tumbled limbs of a flushed and cuddlesome child. At much the same time Caravaggio's Roman colleague Giovanni Battista Caracciolo arranged the naked limbs of an auburn-haired ephebe on artistically rumpled red velvet in a version of the Roman pose, with his left arm crossed to his right side and his bow lying by his fingers, demonstrating nothing more than the radiant beauty of his youth. Though Caracciolo shows the boy's genitals, they are unrealistically tiny, yet someone in the mid-seventeenth century still felt it necessary to obscure them with a painted drape, which was not removed until the end of the twentieth century. It should not be forgotten that Psyche falls in love with Cupid when she sees him asleep.

The archetype of all sleeping boys beloved of women is Endymion. Ovid, Lucian and Apollodorus of Rhodes agree that he was a shepherd boy and fast asleep on Mount Latmos when Selene, the moon goddess, fell in love with him. Some (Cicero) say that she lay down beside him and gently kissed his closed eyes, others that she caressed him in his sleep so that he awoke amazed and appalled to find himself in the radiant embrace of a goddess. So that Selene could gaze at him and caress him to her heart's content the young earthling was given the gift of immortality plus eternal youth – on condition that he remained eternally asleep. Some versions of the story hold that Selene

bore Endymion fifty daughters before casting him into eternal sleep which she did, perhaps, according to Graves, 'because she preferred kissing him to being the object of his too fertile passion'. The astonishing ubiquity of Endymion in European culture is probably to be explained by the fact that artists in all media found the beautiful boy sunk in eternal sleep a useful emblem of ideal beauty which may be caressed and admired but never owned or enjoyed and therefore can never cloy. The subject of Selene feasting her eyes on the sleeping boy is to be found on many Roman sarcophagi. The first vernacular poem on the subject is probably Benedetto Cariteo's 'Endimione a la Luna', published in 1506, at the same time as Pinturicchio and his workshop were carrying out frescoes of Diana and Endymion in the Piccolomini Library, and Cima da Conegliano was painting his *Endymion Asleep*, now in the Galleria Nazionale in Parma. Baldassare Peruzzi, Titian, Carpaccio, Parmigianino, Giulio Romano, il Garofalo, Jacopo Zucchi and Tintoretto all painted their own versions of the subject.

The story of the sexless passion of a virgin goddess was especially suitable for the entertainment of a virgin queen. When the boys of the Chapel Royal played John Lyly's *Endimion, the Man in the Moone* before Elizabeth I at Greenwich 'on New year's day at night' in 1591 some suspected that Endymion represented the queen's beloved but unenjoyed Earl of Leicester. Michael Drayton, a tradesman's son who was brought up as a page in the household of Sir Henry Goodere, wrote his *Endimion and Phœbe* in 1595 in celebration of the marriage of Lucy Harington to the Earl of Bedford.

Above Henry Fuseli saw himself as conducting a one-man campaign against effete art; in *Selene and Endymion*, he endowed the sleeping Endymion with the symbolic anatomy of a superhuman hero, who begins to respond to the imperious advances of the arriving woman-moon even in his sleep.

Below Canova's *Sleeping Endymion* (1819–22)
is sometimes said to be inspired by the painting by
the younger artist, Girodet. The ultimate source for
both must be the Barberini Faun. Canova may also
have known the figure of Ilissus from the Elgin Marbles.
Endymion's smile is to be explained as a response
to the moon caressing his face, but the sculpture has
never been placed where moonlight could reach it.

For this boy's love the water-nymphs have wept,
Stealing oft times to kiss him whilst he slept:
And tasting once the nectar of his breath,
Surfeit with sweet, and languish unto death…

The myth was particularly useful for prefiguring the love of a lady of the highest degree for a commoner. Certainly, when Gombauld wrote his *Endimion* in 1624, it was understood to be a response to the love that he believed that the Queen, Marie de Médicis, bore for him. Sonnets and all kinds of allusions proliferated; Gaspar de Aguilar and Marcelo Díaz Calcerrada narrated the story at length in Spanish verse; Monteverdi and Lully and dozens of lesser composers wrote operas, ballets and other musical entertainments on the theme. The singers in Johann Sebastian Bach's cantata 'Was mir behagt, ist nur die muntre Jagd' are Endimion and Phoebe. Both Gaetano and Auguste Vestris created ballets about Endymion. Annibale Carracci, Domenichino, lo Scarsellino, Van Dyck, Poussin, Rubens, Guercino, Francesco Albani, Pietro da Cortona, Luca Giordano, Boucher, Van Loo and Mengs are among the hundreds who painted the combination of sleeping boy, usually naked, and gazing goddess. In 1776 Gavin Hamilton restored a Hellenistic marble Endymion, asleep in a rather more decorous version of the Barberini pose, and wearing a shepherd's straw bonnet. When the Palazzo Milzetti in Faenza was restored in splendid style after the earthquake of 1781, Pier Francesco Cavalli decorated the 'gabinetto d'amore', that is, the duchess's boudoir, with a series of murals featuring a large Eros, holding aloft a flaming torch, a sleeping Endymion, and a Diana swooping down from the sky to kiss him. Keats is thought by some to have been influenced in his typology of Endymion by the jasperware plaques copied for Wedgwood in about 1789 from a Roman relief of a very boyish Endymion with his curly head sunk on his breast in sleep, while his dog bays at the moon and tries to wake him with his paw. After the acclaim which greeted the twenty-four-year-old Girodet's *Sleep of Endymion* at the Salon of 1793, there was hardly an artist who did not

attempt the subject. In 1819 the sixth Duke of Devonshire commissioned a sculpture from Canova, paid him some money on account and left the choice of subject up to him. The subject Canova chose for this, his last work, was Endymion. Though the figure, with the right arm supporting the head and the right knee drawn up, has clear affinities with the Barberini Faun as well as the figure of Ilissus from the west pediment of the Parthenon, its grace and pliability are those of youth suspended in the fleeting moment of boyhood, its loveliness abandoned to the gaze of the invisible moon goddess and a wakeful little dog. When George Frederick Watts's life was drawing to a close, he too bethought himself of Endymion, a subject he had painted thirty years before.

Aphrodite was not above imitating Selene in making love to a sleeping boy. As Anchises slept in his herdsman's hut on Mount Ida, she visited him clad as a Phrygian princess and eventually bore his son Aeneas. Phineas Fletcher's description, first printed in 1628, presents Anchises as a niggard in love.

> A dainty boy there woned whose harmless years
> Now in their freshest budding gently swelled;
> His nymph-like face ne'er felt the nimble shears;

Above Anne-Louis Girodet was twenty-four in 1791 when he painted *The Sleep of Endymion*. When it was exhibited in Paris two years later no one objected that Selene had been reduced to an off-stage moon or that in her place a bouncing boy Zephyr was contemplating Endymion's loveliness. Girodet exhibited the picture repeatedly and was known to sign his letters 'Endymion'.

Youth's downy blossom through his cheek appears:

His lovely limbs (but love he quite discarded)

Were made for play (but he no play regarded)

And fit love to reward and with love be rewarded.

Like Ovid's Narcissus, 'This dainty play fellow for naked love' 'thousand boys (ah fool!) and thousand maidens denied'.

A sleeping boy is necessarily passive; the woman gazing at him, whether she be Venus, Selene, Psyche or the average gallery visitor, who is middle-aged and female, probing his effigy with a penetrating eye, is the aggressor. Generally speaking, women who make advances to reluctant boys are not looked upon favourably. The biblical story of Joseph and Potiphar's wife has dozens of analogues, and seems to well up from a deep-seated fear of the sexual power of the mother. In Genesis xxxix we read how in Egypt young Joseph prospered as a slave in the house of Potiphar until his master's wife cast desirous eyes upon him.

And it came to pass, as she spake to Joseph day by day, that he

hearkened not unto her, to lie by her, or to be with her.

And it came to pass about this time, that Joseph went into

the house to do his business; and there was none of the men of

the house there within.

And she caught him by his garment, saying, Lie with me: and he left his

garment in her hand, and fled, and got him out.

And it came to pass, when she saw that he had left his garment in her

hand, and was fled forth,

That she called unto the men of her house, and spake unto them,

saying, See, he hath brought in an Hebrew unto us to mock us; he came

in unto me to lie with me, and I cried with a loud voice:

And it came to pass, when he heard that I lifted up my voice and cried,

that he left his garment with me, and fled, and got him out.

And she laid up his garment by her, until his lord came home.

She repeated her story to her husband who believed it and Joseph was thrown into prison. The biblical story, which is thought to have originated in Canaan, has many analogues in pagan literature. In the mythology of ancient Boeotia, Phrixus was a handsome young man who had the misfortune to attract the lustful eyes of his aunt Biadice. When he repelled her advances she publicly accused him of attempted rape. The men of Boeotia believed both her and the false oracle that had already decreed that he should be sacrificed to Zeus on Mount Laphystium. The sacred flint was poised to slit Phrixus' throat when he was rescued by Hercules. An old Corinthian legend tells how an older woman's scorned passion placed young Bellerophon in mortal danger. Bellerophon, fleeing punishment for killing two men, one of whom was his brother, had taken shelter in the house of King Proetus of Tiryns, when the queen fell in love with him on sight. When he rejected her advances she accused him to her husband of having attempted to ravish her. Proetus believed her but, though he wanted to kill Bellerophon in his rage, he dared not anger the Furies, so sent him to his father-in-law, Iobates, King of Lycia, carrying a sealed letter in which were instructions to put him to death. Instead Iobates asked Bellerophon to destroy the Chimaera which, with the help of the flying horse Pegasus, he eventually did. When the Aeginian hero, Peleus, was very young he was married to Polymela; he was obliged to flee Iolcos after accidentally killing a man while hunting the Calydonian boar. Cretheis, wife of Acastus, his host, tried to seduce him. When he refused her she told Polymela that Peleus meant to desert her and marry her daughter instead. Polymela believed her and hanged herself, but Cretheis did not consider herself fully avenged until, in floods of tears, she told her husband that Peleus had attempted her virtue. Tenes was set adrift on the sea in a chest, after his stepmother Phylonome, who was in love with him, had called false witnesses to support her claim that he attempted to rape her. The most harrowing tale of the catastrophic fallout from an older woman's lust for a boy must be that of Hippolytus, object of the criminal passion of his stepmother, Phaedra. Hippolytus, son of Antiope, was like his mother a devotee of Artemis to whom he built a new temple, incurring the wrath of Venus who saw to it that, when he attended the Eleusinian Mysteries, Phaedra would see him and fall desperately in love with him. When he returned to Troezen Phaedra followed and built a temple of Peeping Aphrodite there so that she could watch him unobserved as he worked out, stark naked. When he went to Athens for the games she followed him. Phaedra's old nurse, shocked at how unslaked passion had worn her darling to skin and bone, besought her to write a letter to Hippolytus, confessing her love and begging for his. Ovid included his own version of the letter in the Heroides, in which Phaedra explains how she fell in love.

It was then most of all (though you had pleased me before)
that piercing love lodged in my deepest bones. Shining white
was your raiment, bound round with flowers your locks, the
blush of modesty had tinged your sun-browned cheeks and
what others call a countenance hard and stern, in Phaedra's
eyes, was strong instead of hard.

Hippolytus's reaction was immediate and furious. He burned the letter and
came to Phaedra's chamber to rebuke her. Phaedra's response was to rip her
clothes, throw open the doors and scream 'Rape!' Then she hanged herself
from the door-beam, leaving a note accusing Hippolytus of terrible crimes.
His father, Theseus, banished him from Athens and prayed to his own father
Poseidon to send a sea monster to kill the boy on his way back to Troezen.
The monster appeared and pursued Hippolytus's chariot, terrifying the
horses. A loop of the rein caught on a crooked olive tree, the chariot veered
and was smashed on wayside rocks. Hippolytus's beautiful body was flung

Above Francesco Albani's erotic treatments of
the Salmacis and Hermaphroditus episode from the
Metamorphoses had such success in the 1620s that his
patrons vied to commission versions in different formats
for their private enjoyment. Curtains were hung before
the pictures for fear that children, servants and women
might be corrupted by the sight of them.

first against the tree, then against the rocks and then dragged along behind the bolting horses. One version of the story has it that Artemis then revenged herself for Aphrodite's cruelty to her devotee by causing the death of Aphrodite's beloved Adonis.

A different fate befell the nameless boy who caught the eye of the nymph Salmacis, who there and then begged him to become her husband.

> … the boy blushed rosy red; for he knew not what love was.
> But still the blush became him well. Such colour have apples
> hanging in sunny orchard or painted ivory … when the nymph
> begged and prayed for at least a sister's kiss and was in act to throw
> her arms round his snowy neck, he cried: 'Have done, or I must flee
> and leave this spot — and you.'

Salmacis pretends to go, but hides and watches him.

> Then quickly, charmed with the coolness of the soothing stream,
> he threw aside the thin garments from his slender form. Then did he
> truly attract her, and the nymph's love kindled as she gazed at the naked
> form… Scarce can she endure delay, scarce bear her joy postponed,
> so eager to hold him in her arms, so madly incontinent.

Stripping off, she dives in beside him.

> … she holds him fast though he strives against her, steals reluctant
> kisses, fondles him, touches his unwilling breast, clings to him on this
> side and on that. At length, as he tries his best to escape, she wraps him
> around with her embrace, as a serpent … or as the ivy oft-times
> embraces great trunks of trees, or as the sea-polyp holds its enemy
> beneath the sea, its tentacles embracing him on every side.

She prays that they may never be separated and the gods, hearing her prayer, weld the two of them into a single being, Hermaphroditus.

Eos, or Aurora as she is known in Latin, was less unfortunate. Aphrodite, having found her once in bed with Ares, cursed her with an unquenchable lust for young mortals. Eos was driving her chariot over the Western Ocean when she caught sight of Orion, described as the handsomest man alive and fell in love with him. Orion had gone there seeking a cure for his blindness, which Eos persuaded her brother Helios to perform. She then fell in love with the young shepherd Cephalus and carried him off in

Below Tithonus was the first of the mortal boys ravished by the goddess Aurora. She succeeded in having him granted eternal life, but forgot to ask for eternal youth to go along with it. When he became unable to function as a lover she went about other conquests, making sure that he was looked after at home, until she grew so tired of his senile babble that she changed him into a grasshopper. Rodin's sculpture group of *Aurora and Tithonus* presents an aggressive female figure and an inert male, but whether he is a boy being ravished or an old man being abandoned is not clear.

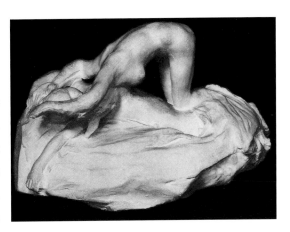

Above Male fantasies of submission to masterful females result in a proliferation of images of wounded boys being tended by amorous nurses, images which women might well find equally interesting. Pietro Ricchi's *Tancredi Succoured by Erminia* is one of many in which the young crusader's languid body fills the foreground.

Opposite The sexiness of Rubens's drawing of *Venus Lamenting over the Dead Adonis* has not escaped feminist art historians. The impact of the image is as much a matter of the fluid rhythm of the drawing as of the event depicted. Much as we may appreciate the unusual energy in Venus's twisting figure, it is less clearly visualized than the yielding body of the boy, which remains the focus of the composition.

her chariot, then Cleitus, a grandson of Melampus, then Ganymede who was taken away from her by Zeus in the form of an eagle, and lastly Tithonus. The most painter-friendly of these episodes is the one involving Cephalus, which provides yet another opportunity for the woman-watching-boy-asleep motif, and was treated by Rubens, Boucher and Francesco Furini, to name but three. Annibale Carracci used the theme for the decorations of the gallery of the Palazzo Farnese. In 1790 or so Thomas Hope commissioned a Cephalus and Aurora group from John Flaxman to serve as the centrepiece of the Star Room in his house in London, where it was endlessly reflected by mirrors on either side.

The best known example of a reluctant male love object in English literature is Shakespeare's Adonis. His extreme reluctance is Shakespeare's invention; it is not to be found in the classical sources. In the many paintings of Venus and Adonis together, Adonis is portrayed as Venus's sexual partner, and any included emblems, usually poured out ewers, snoring cupids and such, are those of slaked passion. The usual Adonis simply wants to hunt as well as make

The only part of *Venus Mourning Adonis*, a preparatory oil sketch for a picture of *c.* 1614 (now in a private collection in New York) that Rubens drew from life, is the figure of the dead man, which he reproduced from a study of two recumbent figures made in Rome some years earlier.

love to Venus; Shakespeare's boy has no interest in Venus whatsoever. The poem begins with a frustrated goddess pursuing the boy and pleading with him:

'Thrice fairer than myself,' thus she began,
    'The field's chief flower, sweet above compare;
    Stain to all nymphs, more lovely than a man.
    More white and red than doves and roses are…
        Here come and sit where never serpent hisses,
        And being set, I'll smother thee with kisses.'

Before he can reply she seizes his hand and manages 'courageously to pluck him from his horse'.

Over one arm the lusty courser's rein,
    Under her other was the tender boy,
    Who blushed and pouted in a dull disdain,

With leaden appetite, unapt to toy:
>She red and hot as coals of glowing fire,
>He red for shame, but frosty in desire.

The description of Venus's struggle is both comic and erotic; Adonis lies in her arms like 'a bird tangled in a net', looking up 'like a die-dapper peering through a wave'. She does not accept that his coldness is merely the effect of his youth.

>The tender spring upon thy tempting lip
>Shows thee unripe; yet mayst thou well be tasted.

The young huntsman himself becomes the prey in this upside down rape story. Overcome with feeling, she faints and he, to revive her, kisses her. She presses her advantage and kisses back.

>He now obeys and now no more resisteth,
>While she takes all she can, not all she listeth.

She pulls him on top of her, but 'he will not manage her, although he mount her'.

Venus and Adonis was a best-seller, going through at least eleven editions before 1620, and it was regularly reprinted thereafter. Later, Augustan taste was revolted by what seemed a strange mixture of genres within the poem, the tragic with the comic , the 'wanton' with the 'witty'. As Shakespeare's plays grew in importance, *Venus and Adonis* languished as the very notion of a woman eager for sex with a boy who pleaded his age as an excuse for avoiding it became increasingly repugnant. By the nineteenth century the British bourgeoisie had become obsessed by the threat posed by sexually aggressive women, whether intrigantes or prostitutes, to their sons' future prospects, which could so easily be blighted by venereal disease or by a forced marriage with a female of easy virtue who had contrived to 'get herself' pregnant.

Frederic Lord Leighton was taking a calculated risk when in 1858 he exhibited at the Royal Academy in London *The Fisherman and the Syren: from a ballad by Goethe* showing a boy being dragged off a rock into the sea by a blond syren whose erect nipple is almost piercing his diaphragm. Her long fish tail is wound around his right leg much as Salmacis wound herself around Hermaphroditus long ago in a stream in Ida. Leighton was rather stretching a point to justify his picture of an apparent seduction as an illustration

of Goethe's ballad, 'Der Fischer', of which the last two lines were quoted in the exhibit:

> Half drew she him, half sunk he in,
> And never more was seen…

Goethe's short ballad certainly relates how the waters of a turbulent stream parted and a dripping woman set about tempting a fisherman on the bank to descend with her under the water, but she does this not by displaying her charms but by arguing that, like the sun and moon that refresh themselves underwater, he will be much better off in mind and body at the bottom of the stream. No mention is made of her snow-white skin or golden hair or of the youth and beauty of the fisherman, or of her pressing her body against his, but, by passing the buck to Goethe, Leighton escaped censure.

Edward Burne-Jones was not so lucky. When his *Phyllis and Demophoön* was shown at the Old Watercolour Society in 1870 the passivity of the male figure, together with the physical similarity between it and the female figure and the smallness of its exposed genitals, provoked the ire of the critics. In Burne-Jones's fantasy, based on an episode from Ovid, Phyllis, transformed into an almond tree after her suicide because Demophoön does not return to her as promised, arises from the flowering tree in her own persona and locks her arms about her fleeing lover, into whose eyes she is staring from a distance of two or three inches. Though Shakespeare could exploit the erotic and ironic possibilities of a courtship in which the sex roles were reversed, Burne-Jones found that he could not. When the President of the OWS approached him to suggest alterations to render the picture less objectionable, Burne-Jones 'withdrew not only the picture from the walls but himself from the society'. It was by then official: women who initiated sexual contact, who pursued boys who were unwilling, who attempted to persuade, cajole and seduce their juniors were unnatural, even unbelievable. Men were in charge in sex, as in everything else. Any woman who actively desired sex, instead of simply submitting to it, was a bad lot and unfit to be seen about her unnatural business in public. The age-old collaboration between mature women and boys in search of sexual enlightenment was at an end, officially at least.

Above When Burne-Jones exhibited *Phyllis and Demophoön* in 1870, the picture was reviled. Demophoön's limbs were considered too gracile, and his unnecessarily visible genitals undersized. Moreover, in attempting to escape from a predatory Phyllis he was behaving in an unmanly fashion. Public art could not be seen to encourage either male submissiveness or female sexual desire.

Opposite The drooping neck and arms of Lord Leighton's fisherman suggest that he is already drowned. Though the source, Goethe's poem 'Der Fischer', is German, the fisherman's exotic features, bright red cap and matching knickers suggest that he is a native of hotter, more languid climes. The Nordic blonde mermaid shooting up from the depths impales him on her breast as if it were the nose-cone of a torpedo.

chapter 6

Play Boys

Playing is a boy's prerogative. The world over, if you see a child with a toy, whipping a top, flying a kite, bowling a hoop, floating a piece of wood with a paper sail, or whacking at a makeshift ball with a stick, it will be a boy. In portraiture any child holding a toy, regardless of whether it is dressed in petticoats or breeches, will be a boy. Though women are now insisting on the right to play sports and to become athletes, girls' participation in sport is still tiny compared to the number of boy-hours devoted to it. There are good historic reasons for this. When and where men's work is mostly physical labour, boys cannot be expected to do it before they get their strength, and so they are allowed to pass their days in play, which builds up that strength. Boys can roam free while girls are kept at home, to look after their little brothers and sisters or fetch water or wash dishes and clothes in the sink or in the river. Boys who have to help the family will do it by fishing as I have seen hundreds of boys doing along the rivers of the Nordeste of Brazil (and not a single girl) and by herding, and even then a boy will play, with other boys, with animals or by himself.

The divine prototype of the playing boy is Dionysos, the dancing god. At first he was represented as a bearded man. The earliest surviving image of the god of ritual dance, song and play-acting as a youth is a bronze in the Louvre, which is dated about 455 BCE. From then on Dionysos is usually depicted as a youthful long-haired figure clad in nothing but a leopard-skin mantle. Dionysos is a paradoxical figure, both divine and human, savage and gentle, aggressive and submissive, feminine and masculine. As the god of the priapic Phallophoria festival, he is the beardless male for whom sex is inexhaustible play. Since the teasing figure of the sexually active boy was elided in our culture, scholars have had much ado to account for the apparent contradictions in the character of Dionysos, wondering if he might be hermaphrodite or the god of pederasty, which would hardly

A bronze head of the first century CE, now in the Getty Museum, can be identified as a Dionysos or Bacchus by the garland of ivy that encircles it. The impression of rapture conveyed by the parted lips is intensified by the silvering of the eye-whites; within the hemispherical incisions are to be seen screws for mounting corneas carved out of semi-precious stone.

explain the shrieking hordes of slavering Maenads who followed him everywhere, or his being represented by a bull in Thrace and Crete, or his association with snakes 'with darting heads' and panthers 'breathing fire'. In the usual version of his life, his mother, Semele, fearing that the wrath of Hera would strike him as the fruit of another of Zeus's infidelities, had him brought up as a girl, a mythological reflection perhaps of the period of time that all male children spent among the women, when children were not distinguished by sex. As a boy-god Dionysos may be considered still under the influence of his mother, and his connection with orgiastic women to represent his connection to her and to the immanent state of pregnancy when the female body houses the male child. This uterine attachment is expressed in the myth by the way that, when Dionysos was finally raised to be one of the twelve Olympian gods, he used his power to descend to Tartarus where he bribed Persephone to release his dead mortal mother and he brought her to live on Olympus. At the annual Lenaea, the Athenian Festival of Wild Women, Dionysos was represented by a yearling bull which was cut into nine pieces, of which one was burnt as a sacrifice to his mother and the rest eaten raw by his devotees. In earlier versions of the same rite, the creature that was torn in pieces and eaten raw, under one of the god's many names, was a human child, needless to say, a boy.

In Euripides's play, *The Bacchae*, Dionysos comes to Thebes in the person of a young priest of his own cult. Pentheus describes him as an 'effeminate stranger',

> from Lydia, one of those charlatan magicians,
> with long yellow curls smelling of perfumes,
> with flushed cheeks and the spells of Aphrodite
> in his eyes. His days and nights he spends
> with women and girls, dangling before them the joys
> of initiation in his mysteries.

Insultingly Pentheus announces his intention to cut off the stranger's 'girlish curls' and is quietly told that the stranger's hair is holy. Pentheus grabs the thyrsus out of the stranger's hands, chains him up and throws him into a stable. The smiling boy-god offers no resistance, but wordlessly causes an earthquake that reduces the palace of Thebes to rubble. Unabashed, Pentheus sets out disguised as a woman to spy upon the Maenads among whom is his mother who, possessed by the god, tears him limb from limb in her frenzy.

Above The earliest known representation of a beardless Dionysos is a bronze statuette of the fifth century BCE now in the Louvre.

Scholars bewildered by Dionysos's combination of effeminate langour and implacable violence might look about them and see how male adolescents incarnate both principles. Soccer is a game, but young men have been killed in the frenzy that it can generate. The same recklessness that prompts them to experiment with states of euphoria and trance as the Maenads did, impels them also to acts of mindless aggression and violence, to commit offences against life and property in a spirit of mere gamesomeness, for the hell of it. In the 1980s Bill Buford travelled about England with soccer supporters, to learn the truth about hooliganism. The following scene took place not in Ancient Greece or in the Ngongoro but in Bury St Edmund's, a small market town in England.

…. the music was now brutally loud. The room was hot and filled with smoke and smelled of dope. The air had grown heavy and damp. Sixty or seventy lads were in the middle of the room, clasped together, bouncing up and down, rubbing their hands over each other's heads and chanting in unison:

> *Wogs out! White power!*
> *Wogs out! White power!*
> *Wogs out! White power!*

They had taken off their shirts and were stripped to the waist, their braces dangling over their sides, knocking against their legs; sixty or seventy pale, narrow chests, covered in perspiration, pressed tightly together. They were bouncing so vigorously that they all fell over, tumbling on top of each other … they all clambered up over each other and, with difficulty, resumed their dancing. They fell over again, wet and hot. I don't know if it was the drink or the drugs or the delirium of the dancing or that chorus, over and over again, but there was a menacing feeling in the air – sexual and dangerous.… Some of the lads appeared to be in a trance.

I looked at the women, sitting in the dark, smoking cigarette after cigarette, none of them dancing.

The occasion was a disco run by the National Front, a white supremacist organization that found a fertile recruiting ground among soccer supporters, but what Buford witnessed had less to do with politics than with the condition of boyhood itself. As it turned out, the youngsters were being

Above Dionysos with Kantharos, an alabaster figure from Eleusis, accentuates the effeminacy of Dionysos whose legs are draped as if the figure were female, as would also be suggested by the plump curve of the exposed hip, while at the same time its male genitalia are rather coquettishly revealed. The identity suggested by the wine jug is established by the suggestion of the thyrsus in the pine-cone under the figure's left hand.

effortlessly manipulated by older men who were following their own political agenda. The boys Buford travelled with did not only dance and play; they also inflicted terrible injuries on other people and on themselves, re-enacting the Dionysian sparagmos.

A similar phenomenon had been recorded eighty years earlier by none other than Lord Baden-Powell, founder of the Boy Scout movement, who sounds rather like Pentheus when he writes, 'Thousands of boys and young men, pale, narrow-chested, hunched-up, miserable specimens, smoking endless cigarettes, numbers of them betting, all of them learning to be hysterical as they groan or cheer in panic unison with their neighbours – the worst sound being the hysterical scream of laughter that greets any little trip or fall of a player…. Get the lads away from this. Teach them to be manly.' Lord Baden-Powell may not have been aware of the etymology of his own word 'panic'. It takes us back in an un-broken line to Lord Dionysos and his goat-footed hordes.

Graphic artists have been less puzzled than stimulated by the combination of languor and sudden frenzied violence in the figure of Dionysos and his Roman counterpart Bacchus. The Hellenistic Greeks saw him as finer-limbed than Apollo, his neck drooping under its weight of grapes and vine-leaves, and his lips parted with some unnameable excitement. Michelangelo took the cue for his Bacchus of 1497 from Roman copies of Hellenistic figures and produced an androgyne who smiles in true Bacchante fashion, his limbs sagging so that the whole figure appears almost to reel. Caravaggio's *Bacchus* plays the same game of combining boyish characteristics, such as the muscularity of the foreshortened left arm, with the extreme femininity of the disproportionately tiny rosy-fingered right hand that holds the cup, but he

Above If it were not for his riotous crown of grapes and vine-leaves, the grave Bacchus painted by Caravaggio *c.* 1597 would be more readily identified as an apathetic Ganymede than as the god of intoxication. He shows no trace of the Dionysiac smile and his dark eyes are mournfully abstracted rather than entranced. What he does share with the classic Bacchus is the hint of hermaphroditism in the contrast of his muscular shoulder and chest with the girlishness of his face and fingers.

adds an extra layer of meaning. The pose is languid, the expression less languorous than bored, as the dark eyes of the model rest on the viewer with conspicuous absence of desire. This impassivity is mocked by the ebullience of the vine-leaves of his headdress, as if the god had less vitality than a vegetable or than the fruit in front of him, evidence as it is of fertility and reproduction. The model bears a strong resemblance to the Spanish castrato Pedro Montoya, who sat for Caravaggio as *The Lute-player*. A workshop copy of *The Lute-player* was bought in Rome by the third Duke of Beaufort in 1726 as 'Girl with a Guitar', the guitar being no more a guitar than the subject was a girl. The same type and possibly the same individual, with the same cleft chin and round face, dominated by large brown eyes set under heavy brows, can be seen tuning his lute in Caravaggio's picture of four musicians. As a castrato Montoya was condemned to eternal boyhood: his beard would never come in, he would never father a child, and he would always be the equivalent of an upper servant in another man's household.

Below Caravaggio's *The Musicians* (1595–6) casts an ironic reflection on the depictions of carolling putti that featured on the cantorie of Renaissance churches. These church musicians are all professionals; at least one of them has been castrated so that puberty will not rob the church of his services. The claustrophobia of the composition reflects the cloistered circumstances in which such church servants were obliged to live.

Western art and literature abound with musicians, all of them boys. Though flute girls were an indispensable part of the entertainment at the symposia of ancient Athens, few images of them have survived. Athene was quite capable of contriving a double-flute from the bones of a stag but when she made music with it the gods laughed at her. Perplexed by their reaction, she looked at her reflection in a stream as she played and realized that the effort of blowing into the flute reddened her face and distended her cheeks, so she threw her flute away. The Muses of Helicon certainly made music but they did not start an iconographic fashion, whereas boyhood and music-making are so closely connected that one of the ages of man can be signified by the figure of a musician (see p. 18). Hermes was still a child when he fashioned a lyre out of a tortoise-shell and cow-gut and gave it to Apollo, who was thereafter never without it. Hermes then fashioned reeds into a shepherd's pipe, so inventing the musical scale. Reed pipes were later re-invented by the goat-footed god Pan after his beloved Syrinx turned herself into a reed; Pan's attendant satyrs and fauns are all musicians. Pan also taught Hermes's Daphnis to play the pipes, and every Arcadian shepherd boy followed his example. In equipping shepherd boys with instruments Pan seems to have done no more than shepherd boys will do for themselves. All over the world boys following herds will play and sing to themselves or with their work-mates, playing bag-pipes, flutes, ocarinas or makeshift instruments made of anything they can find.

Orpheus was presented with a lyre by Apollo and taught to play it by the Muses. He played so beautifully that he could charm wild animals and make trees and rocks dance. When he accompanied the Argonauts to Colchis he saved them more than once by the power of his music. The story of Orpheus's marriage with Eurydice, his loss of her and his unsuccessful trip to the underworld to find her, which represents a later tradition, lent itself to all kinds of allegorical interpretations and became a central theme in moralizing literature. After wandering around Thrace singing of his lost love, Orpheus met his death in true Dionysian fashion by being torn to pieces by wild women. The Muses collected the fragments of his body and buried them, but his still-singing head and his lyre floated down the Hebrus and out to sea to be washed

Above The pan pipe appears to be a global instrument and its player is usually a boy. This Erigbaagtsa lad, whose face is beautified with judicious application of the juice of the seeds of the annatto tree, and valanced by strings of toucan feathers threaded through slits in his ears, was photographed in Mato Grosso, Brazil, in 1964.

Opposite The notion that heaven is peopled with choirs of angels derives from the theologians' description of the seraphs continually intoning the praises of the Almighty. Since the earliest times the angel singers have been accompanied by angels playing manmade instruments. Two of the ravishing angel musicians included by Melozzo da Forlì in his fresco of the Ascension with Christ in Glory, commissioned for the choir of the church of the Apostles in Rome in 1478 or so, can now be seen as detached fragments in the Vatican Art Gallery.

up on the island of Lesbos, where they were dedicated to Apollo. Because Orpheus is a figure of the creative artist, the story has inspired artists in every medium that human ingenuity has ever invented. Politian's poem, *La Fabula di Orfeo*, served as a libretto for two musical dramas that were performed during the poet's brief lifetime. Mantegna, Signorelli, Baldassare Peruzzi and Primaticcio frescoed noble residences with the subject, while in easel painting any depiction of a boy with an instrument is likely to be identified as an Orpheus. In 1538, during negotiations to secure the hand of Eleanor of Toledo for Cosimo de' Medici, Bronzino painted a nude portrait of his brilliant young patron as Orpheus confronting Cerberus at the entrance to Hades. The first opera ever written is usually taken to be Monteverdi's *Orfeo* of 1607. Hundreds of composers followed the precedent, producing cantatas and oratorios without number, down to Franz Liszt's symphonic poem of 1854 and Kurt Weill's *Der Neue Orpheus* in 1925. Jean Cocteau, for whom Orpheus was a figure of the homosexual as much as of the artist, depicted the subject in graphics, sculpture, jewelry and ceramics, in a tragedy of 1925, and in two screenplays and a ballet. Perhaps the most successful Brazilian film ever was Marcel Camus's *Orfeu Negro* (1958) based on a music-drama by Vinicius de Moraes. Ted Hughes wrote a radio play called *Orpheus.* The theme, which gathered momentum through the nineteenth and twentieth centuries, is still irresistible in the twenty-first. In a recent production by the New York-based Adobe Theater Company, Orpheus is a baby-faced rock star who writes and performs songs with a band called In Your Thrace.

In Virgil's eighth eclogue Orpheus is linked with Arion, who hardly rates a mention unless he is in Orpheus's company. Originally from Lesbos and the most renowned minstrel living in Corinth during the reign of King Periander (625–585 BCE), Arion was returning to Corinth loaded with money and gifts from a successful tour of Magna Grecia, when the ship's crew decided to kill him and keep his treasure. They offered him the choice of committing suicide or jumping overboard. Arion accepted the second option but asked if he might perform on deck one last time. As he sang, accompanying himself on the lyre, dolphins were drawn to the ship, and when he leapt overboard a dolphin took him and his lyre on its back and bore him safely to shore. There is nothing to suggest that Arion was particularly young, but a persistent iconographic tradition linking the dolphin with the boy can be traced as far back as the fourth century BCE. Arion's arrival on the dolphin being the founding myth of Tarentum, two-drachma coins minted there in the archaic period feature a

Opposite Agnolo Bronzino devised his flattering portrait of Cosimo de' Medici as Orpheus, to be a wedding present for Eleanor of Toledo, whom Cosimo married in 1539. Eleanor so appreciated the implied compliment – and the implied casting of herself as Eurydice – that she chose Bronzino to decorate her private chapel and to paint portraits of all her children.

naked youth astride a dolphin. The motif of a putto holding a dolphin, as in the bronze in the Palazzo Vecchio in Florence usually attributed to Verrocchio, is a commonplace of Renaissance decorative art. Like many such motifs the boy on a dolphin may have had its origins in observations of real life, for attachments between boys and dolphins happen just often enough to remain remarkable and memorable.

At other times Orpheus may be in consort with Amphion who was given a golden lyre by Hermes. Like Orpheus, Amphion was half-divine, he and his twin brother Zethus being sons of Zeus by Antiope, a mortal woman who was so afraid of what her husband's vengeance might do to the boys that she abandoned them to be found and brought up by a shepherd. When Antiope did not return to her husband, his brother Lycus abducted her and gave her as a slave to his wife Dirce who treated her cruelly. Antiope managed to get a message to her sons who came with their fellow herdsmen to Thebes and overran the city, restoring their mother to her dignity just as Dionysos did. Queen Dirce they punished with true Dionysian cruelty, tying her hair to the horns of a wild bull so that she was dashed in pieces. Amphion helped his brother build the walls of Thebes by playing such enchanting music on his golden lyre that the stones danced to their places.

Dionysos himself neither sings nor plays; he dances. In the evolution of the human race dance has been an essential aspect of male display in every society. It was not until the nineteenth century that European men stopped dancing for the appreciative eyes of women and confined themselves to leading the ladies out on to the floor. Elsewhere men were still dancing, hoping to attract the female in the same way that the bower bird attracts his hen. In some Masai groups young men seeking to attract a wife still perform a ceremonial dance in which they leap stiff-legged into the air. Before the massacres of the late twentieth century the noble Tutsi warriors were famous for their dancing (see p. 139). The spectacular whirling dance of the Sufi dervishes is performed only by men. In flamenco dancing the *zapateado*, in which the male dancer drums complicated patterns with the stacked heels of his boots, while clutching his abbreviated jacket under his breast bone, well clear of trousers cut so narrowly as to leave nothing to the imagination, is male display at its most gratuitous. Before his descent into reclusive strangeness, Michael Jackson performed startlingly original dances that needed every ounce of sinew that his lean young body had to offer, raw, syncopated and angular, bred out of the improvised break dancing that boys (not girls) were doing on the street.

At the entertainments mounted at the courts of Renaissance Italy all the dancers were male and masked. Female parts were danced by slender boys. When Catherine de Médicis imported the Italian fashion to the French court she also set up daily classes so that her courtiers could learn the moves. In 1653 Louis XIV, who had been taught since the age of seven by Pierre Beauchamp, danced the Sun God in *Le Ballet de la Nuit*. In 1658 the exiled George Villiers, second duke of Buckingham, danced the part of Fire in Benserade's *Masque Royale de la Nuit*. At the same time professional dancers like Louis Pécourt were rising within the royal establishment. In 1661 Louis XIV set up an Académie de Danse at the Louvre. In 1681 Beauchamp danced the female role in Lully's *Triomphe de l'Amour*. At the fête of the duchesse de Maine, Jean Balon (1676–1739) danced in Corneille's *Horace*, the forerunner of the new vigorous 'ballets d'action'. Though women stars were beginning to appear, men like Jean Blondy and Louis Dupré, who was solo dancer at the Paris Opera for thirty-six years, dominate. Dupré taught Gaetano and Angiolo Vestris and Jean Georges Noverre. When Gaetano Vestris and his son Auguste came to London in 1781, parliament went into temporary recess to allow members to attend their performances at Covent Garden. Female roles were still being danced by boys in many places in Europe right up until the end of the eighteenth century.

All the contradictory Dionysian aspects of the dancing boy meet in the fragile, brilliant figure of Vaclav Nijinsky. He was born into a Polish dancing family and began training with the Imperial Ballet in St Petersburg at the age of seven. By the time he had completed his training and joined the ballet as a danseur noble in 1907, he was already being called 'the Vestris of the North'. Strong as steel and light as a feather, he could lift himself so high that he seemed to hang in the air before landing noiselessly. His lean, flat torso and graceful arms contrasted teasingly with his muscled thighs and very evident masculinity. Nijinsky knew how to exploit his boyish allure by stressing his own energy and masculine endowment and at the same time indulging in narcissistic prettinesses of costume and attitude. St Petersburg society feted him and he basked in their adulation. He was enjoying the attentions of a Russian princeling when the impresario Diaghilev decided to take him in hand, to educate him and develop his creativity, and appointed him principal dancer of the new company he had formed to dance in Paris in the off-season, the Ballets Russes. In 1909 Diaghilev took the new 'god of the dance' to Paris to dance with Anna Pavlova. In 1911, again in Paris, Nijinsky caused a sensation

when for the first time he danced Le Spectre de la Rose. With his narrow torso emerging naked as if from the petals of the rose, his lips reddened and his eyes darkened under his cap of rose petals, he seemed polymorphous sexuality incarnate. Back in St Petersburg he rebelled against the traditional costume he was expected to wear to dance Albrecht in *Giselle*, and came on stage in the revealing costume he had worn in Paris, knowing that he would be dismissed and could concentrate full-time on the Ballets Russes. Diaghilev had had the idea of a ballet based on Mallarmé's poem, *L'Après-midi d'un Faune*, which Nijinsky would choreograph for himself. As a satyr aroused by seeing nymphs bathing to the point where he appears to masturbate with a discarded scarf, Nijinsky had the perfect opportunity for boyish exhibitionism and he used it to the full. Rodin was so impressed that he sculpted him as the Faun.

In 1913 Nijinsky travelled to South America with the Ballets Russes and, away from Diaghilev for once, succumbed to the advances of a young

Above When they ruled over the subject Hutu in Rwanda, the culture of the aristocratic Tutsi people involved a good deal of ceremonial dancing. In this picture, taken in Uganda in 1971, young Tutsi refugees relive past glory by performing their traditional victory dance. In the 1990s the Tutsi people were virtually wiped out.

Opposite In 1912 Diaghilev devised a ballet based on Mallarmé's poem *L'Après-Midi d'un Faune* for his protégé Vaclav Nijinsky. Léon Bakst, artistic director of the Ballets Russes, designed for the Faun an unconventional costume that was no more than a sleeveless body-stocking, so that both the strength and the delicacy of Nijinsky's boyish body could be displayed to the full in movements that were, inevitably, denounced as obscene.

Hungarian noblewoman who had been following him for eighteen months. They were married in Buenos Aires. Ballet historians tend to be waspish about Countess Romola de Pulszky, who did what male lovers could not do and very soon became pregnant by her boy-husband, who suffered along with her and missed a performance in Rio. Diaghilev sacked him. In 1914 Nijinsky had what is usually described as a nervous breakdown. He was then interned in Hungary. Diaghilev got him out of detention for an American tour in 1916, but he was already showing signs of the mental illness that would eventually become so severe that he would be in and out of Swiss clinics for the rest of his life. He danced for the last time in 1919. In 1920 he became a father for the second time. Nijinsky would not have been the dancer he was if he had been capable of acquiring manly discretion. He was, as it were, a faun trapped in the corporate world, at the mercy of wiser heads than his own, who treated him as a property and effectively prevented his transition to autonomy. He was certainly committed to his wife and his two daughters, and they cared for him. They managed to keep him alive until 1950, not an easy matter in the case of someone who is described variously as suffering from dementia praecox or schizophrenia, or both.

Nijinsky's mantle is commonly supposed to have fallen on the strong shoulders of Rudolf Nureyev. Certainly Nureyev worked tirelessly to achieve the same combination of power and passion, but he was much less androgynous in his stage presence. Though Nureyev was exclusively homosexual

Above Grace Lau, founder of Exposures, the National Association of Women Photographers, is one female artist who subjects young men to an assessing female gaze and poses them in ways that are replete with sexual suggestion.
Opposite Though Rudolf Nureyev made no secret of his exclusively homosexual sex orientation, he was best known to adoring women of all ages as the devoted boy-partner of Margot Fonteyn, who was old enough to be his mother.

Above In his enthusiasm to return to nature, the American painter and art teacher Thomas Eakins took his male students swimming, which they did naked, as did most men of the period. The composition for *Swimming*, of *c.* 1889, is based on figures in photographs Eakins took at the time. In the painting he takes care to keep their backs to the viewer and avoid any suggestion of contact between one another.

in his sexual preferences, he did not have the option of dancing as a boy. He could not appear self-pleasuring on stage but had to act his various princes, corsairs and what have you as adorers of the succession of females who got to ride on his shoulders. In art as in life sexually active boyhood had disappeared. Young males had to commit themselves to sexual orthodoxy rather than spontaneity, and devote themselves either to sex with men or sex with women, and no mucking about, which is what boys do. In 1984 Nureyev was found to be HIV positive; before his untimely death he made the transition to seniority, becoming at last his own master as a director of performances.

Like dancers, male athletes are boys as long as they continue to perform. Whether they compete for a club or a country they are under the control of others, of trainers, managers, owners and the various boards of control.

Soccer players are bought and sold like slaves in the marketplace, and shifted about like merchandise. Only a very few athletes ever manage the transition from performer to controller. More athletes will break down than will grow up within their sport and come out on top. To be identified with bodily prowess is to be feminized, regardless of the obvious activities of testosterone, because the athlete is regarded as body rather than mind, strength rather than power, junior rather than senior. Sport has been called with justification 'a system of failure'. In every competitive sport there are always more losers than winners, and every winner knows that his defeat at the hands of a younger man is already on its way. 'You're only as good as your last game.' The figure of the athlete is therefore suffused with pathos. Even as the diadoumenos ties the victor's garland round his brows his moment is passing.

No such reflections disturb the ebullience of the boy at play. His spontaneous activity may seem to have little in common with the concerted effort of the athlete in training or the tireless self-discipline of the dancer, but both

Below The nakedness of the boys pictured by Henry Scott Tuke in *August Blue* (1893–4) is largely to be intuited. The brilliance of the light bleaches out the contours of flesh. None of the boys makes eye contact with any other or with the viewer, who might as well be looking at the scene through a spy-glass on the pier, as if the boys were some kind of wildlife.

have their origin in play and continue to bear the stamp of not-quite-serious-ness. The exuberance of the boy that rode his dolphin on the coinage of ancient Tarentum has no equivalent in modern times. Michelangelo's *Bathers* are not bathers at all, and the painters of later 'bathers' are offering homage to Michelangelo rather than revisiting the self-pleasuring world of boyhood. Females, when bathing, are never in the water; in Antonio Carracci's *Landscape with Bathers* the sole female is bone-dry and fully dressed. The *grandes baigneuses* of Renoir, Gauguin, Monet and Cézanne lie about the landscape like beached whales. The bathers exhibited by Frederick Walker in 1867 are almost as dry, being all on the bank except for two or three in the distance and Seurat's *Bathers at Asnières* demonstrate a similar ratio of wet to dry. Thomas Eakins wanted to paint not 'Bathers' but 'Swimming'. As a preparative he had invited the male students from his art class to go skinny-dipping with him at the local swimming hole so that he could photograph them. The painting is itself photographic, but cool, elegiac and a good deal more decorous than the original photographs, in which genitals are not only visible but to scale. Henry Scott Tuke prepared for *August Blue*, exhibited at the Royal Academy in 1894, by painting nude boys on the beach at Pietra Santa and Newlyn. Open-air nudity was in fact a male prerogative; all over Europe males could swim naked, while females sat on different beaches covered from top to toe. The ostensible subject of images of naked boys on beaches was healthy, innocent, open-air exercise, but most of the male artists who were still painting it in the mid-twentieth century had their own homoerotic agenda.

In art works over the centuries we have become so used to the convention of clothed females and naked males that we hardly notice it. Nobody comments on the fact that Jesus, whether as a baby or on the Cross, is either nude or all but, or that naked males in the guise of putti frolic around heavily clad princesses and female saints, or even that Psyche is usually dressed and Cupid usually naked. When the unwritten convention surfaces in nineteenth-century depictions of sport, its oddity becomes apparent. In *The Bowlers* exhibited at the Royal Academy in 1870, the youths playing bowls have removed their clothes, but what the narrative pretext for their nudity could possibly be, as distinct from the pictorial necessity of reproducing the types of classical antiquity, is unimaginable. The boys' genitals are carefully hidden from the viewing public but entirely exposed to the clothed women, who appear as uninterested in them as they are in the match.

Above A cameo, carved on onyx in Rome in the first century BCE, shows a male follower of Dionysos, or more correctly Bacchus, dancing over stones and thorns in his drug-fuelled ecstasy. Other versions of such male Maenads or Bacchantes sometimes show them with erections, symbolized by the thyrsus held aloft.

Today's rock star is every bit as close a parallel to Dionysos as Orpheus, Arion and Amphion were. Like the Maenads who danced over the hills of Cithaeron until their feet were torn to pieces by the sharp rocks and thorns, rock fans, high on drink and drugs and their own sense of occasion, think nothing of dancing away a sodden weekend on a windy hillside ankle deep in mud laced with urine. Rock culture is purely Dionysian: just as the Maenads tore apart the cattle that they found in the mountains, and just as Dionysos himself was torn apart by the Titans, rock fans will dismember their god if they can. He cannot move among his screaming Bacchantes unless he is protected against their clutching, grabbing hands. Women have had success as rock stars – Dionysos is the god of women, after all – but in everything, his undying attachment to his mother, his resentment of his father, his dreamy passivity and gratuitous hooliganism, Dionysos is a boy. The vast majority of his would-be avatars, crouched over their twin decks or crooning to their guitars, are boys. If they succeed in the business, like Dionysos they will be boys forever.

Above In *The Bowlers* (1870; detail shown here), William Blake Richmond reduced the pictorial tradition of combining naked men with draped women to unintelligibility; the picture was ridiculed in the public prints at the time. In the twenty-first century what Richmond attempted to present as fraternal love innocently expressed in healthy pastime is interpreted as blatant homoeroticism.

chapter 7

Servant Boys

The streets of pre-industrial towns were and are full of boys. Some are employed, some are looking for work, some are begging, some are thieving, some are prostituting themselves and some are simply playing. All over Africa, Asia and Central and South America, errand boys, delivery boys, beggar boys, rent boys, hordes of boys will gather when any novelty appears. Girls were never free to roam the streets in this fashion; they were at home helping mother, caring for smaller children, fetching water, sweeping and cleaning. Girls might not look for a master but boys could, though the relationship was hardly less risky for them than it was for the girls. A bad master could ill-treat a boy or use him for criminal purposes; a good master could transform his boy's fortunes, setting him on a career that could take him to great eminence. In medieval Europe, the sight of a gentleman unattended brought forth crowds of boys to offer their services as squire or page or footboy, all pleading their case and displaying their usefulness. In the streets of India or Africa today's tourist will find herself similarly besieged by a vociferous horde. The best way to manage the situation is to hire a single boy clever enough to speak English, whose job is to keep all the other boys from underfoot, to guide one through the nameless streets, to share one's meals and to tell his story – a footboy, in short. This is a version of the employment of young urban boys over millennia.

Country boys were set to mind the animals, with only their slingshots and their pan-pipes to while away the interminable hours as they followed their flocks and herds. Even the gods of antiquity had to serve their time in boys' employment. Apollo tamed the horses of the sun, becoming the prototype of centuries of stable-boys and jockeys. He also herded cows (which Hermes stole from him and herded for himself) and the sheep of King Admetus. Hermes made the first shepherd's pipe before leaving his flocks to serve as errand boy to the gods, leaving one son Daphnis to achieve literary immortality as

As Venus is usually depicted in the company of pretty amorini, seventeenth-century great ladies were not only painted with attendant putti, like the cornucopia-bearing child in Huysmans's portrait of Lady Elizabeth Somerset (1665–70), but actually attended by small pages. Having costumed page-boys carry the train of a bride as she walks down the aisle is the only contemporary survival of a practice that was a daily reality in noble households.

the archetypal shepherd reincarnated over and over in bucolic poetry, while another, Pan, never grew up but remained a boy in Arcady forever. Anchises and Paris herded sheep on Mount Ida, Endymion on Mount Latmos. These same country boys are the originals of our pages, for the word 'page' itself is thought, though without any great certainty, to be derived from a generic word for 'peasant boys' in Latin and its medieval derivatives. The *Oxford English Dictionary* gives as the third meaning of the word 'page', 'a boy or lad employed as a servant or attendant; hence a male servant in the lowest grade in his line of service; one whose part it is to assist and learn from an upper or more experienced servant or officer'.

Not much is recorded about the relations between masters and boys. Grown men do not want to remind themselves of the indignities they endured as boys while masters tend to reduce their boys to anonymity, seldom bothering even to name them, let alone give their ages or any kind of description. In this respect the diarist Samuel Pepys is pretty typical. When he found himself going up in the world in 1660, he decided that he needed a footboy to attend

Opposite In the pre-industrial world social status was made visible by the number of a man's retinue and the splendour of their trappings. In his fresco of the *Procession of the Magi* of 1459, Benozzo Gozzoli invented hordes of pages and squires, all beardless, mostly blond and dressed with flamboyant exquisiteness.

Below *The Bird Catcher*, a scene from the Middle Ages as imagined by Dutch history painter Hendrik Leys (1866), contrasts the adult gravity of the working child with the babyishness of other children of the same age. The child's trade, which is the same as Papageno's in *The Magic Flute*, might well have made him the envy of many a small boy shut up in school.

Opposite *The Abduction of Ganymede* is a painting by an unknown Nordic artist from another lost design by Michelangelo. The iconography of Ganymede's rape by Zeus in the form of an eagle can go even further than Michelangelo's suggestive image of the eagle clutching the boy's thighs in his talons, even to portraying the eagle as actually treading him. Ganymede may be shown as anything from a bawling infant to a handsome well-grown boy.

Below The icon of boy with horse is almost as old as human image-making. Despite the passion of little girls for horses, there is no equivalent iconographic tradition, unless we count Lady Godiva. *Pegasus and Bellerophon*, designed in about 1480 by Bertoldo di Giovanni, keeper of antiquities to Lorenzo de' Medici, is actually an allusion to the classic type of man-with-horse known as the Horsetamer.

him whenever he went out of the house, to run his errands and to light the way with a torch or 'link' at night-time. As a footboy came into the family as an extra child, his master and mistress being responsible for his keep, his clothing and his education, it was important that he be of an honest family. The first father Pepys found with a boy for hire was one Jenkins whose son Eliezer he took on as his cabin-boy on a trip to Holland. Back on dry land Pepys went in search of a permanent boy whom he hired from his father as an indentured servant. This boy is known to history simply as 'Will'. Pepys never mentions his age, but he was probably a rather small boy and fairly cheap. Unfortunately within a few weeks Will was discovered to be an incorrigible thief. Though 'he denied all with the greatest subtility and confidence in the world' and the next day was 'in a sad plight over seeming sorrow' Pepys was unimpressed. Will was sent home to his father and his indentures torn up. Pepys then hired Waynman Birch, a country boy, younger brother of one of Pepys's maids.

'This morning I called up the boy to me and find him a pretty well-looked boy, and one that I think will please me.' Looks were important; later Pepys and his wife would have an odd falling-out over Waynman's looks. 'So home, and there my wife and I had an angry word or two upon discourse of our boy compared with Sir W. Penn's boy that he hath now, which I say is much prettier than ours and she the contrary.' The prettiness of a page was part of the general elegance of a gentleman's equipage; a slovenly awkward boy reflected badly upon his master's taste and means. Entries in the accounts of the household of the Duke of Bedford at Woburn show that 'my lady's page' was supplied with two periwigs, while 'Lady Margaret's page' was given 'three pair of stockings, a hat and case, shoebuttons, buttons for his cuffs and a comb'. Another page was taught the flageolet. Pepys dressed Waynman in a fine grey livery trimmed with black and gold lace, taught him to write, took him on pleasure trips and trusted him to carry money.

The archetypal page was Ganymede, the most beautiful boy alive. When Zeus caught sight of him tending his sheep on the Trojan plains he transformed himself into an eagle so that he could carry the boy off to Olympus to be his cup-bearer. Ganymede is usually taken to have been Zeus's catamite as well as his cup-bearer, but a sexual relationship is not always to be assumed. Xenophon tells us that the young Cyrus was anxious to supplant his grandfather's cup-bearer, Sacas, because he resented the way he controlled access to the king's presence. Sacas has been given the job because of his grace and beauty. 'And indeed, these royal cup-bearers are neat-handed at their task,

mixing the bowl with infinite elegance, and pouring the wine into the beakers without spilling a drop, and when they hand the goblet they poise it deftly between thumb and finger for the banqueter to take.'

An exceptionally beautiful and gifted page, who could play and sing to entertain his betters as well as carrying out his menial tasks, could have a brilliant career. He could be passed on from a lesser magnate to a greater one, and so on, until he found himself a member of the most spectacular household of all, the court of the ruler, where every member of the royal family had his or her own complement of pages. As the only way that a grandee could display his wealth and importance before the public was by the number and splendour of his retinue, he might at any one time have scores, even hundreds of young men wearing his livery.

Jack Wilton, eponymous hero of Thomas Nashe's *The Unfortunate Traveller*, written in 1593 and set in the time of Henry VIII, is purportedly the page of Thomas Howard, Earl of Surrey. He is described by a man trying to sell him to an anatomist as 'of stature tall, straight limbed, of as clear a complexion as any painter's fancy can imagine'. Jack describes himself principally in terms of his fetching outfit, from the huge feather in his cap to his wasp-waisted doublet, his ballooning trunk hose and the short cape-cloak that swung from his shoulders. Jack was impressed by the retinue who attended the pope's concubine in the St Peter's day procession: '… before her two and two in order, [went] a hundred pages in suit of white cypress and long horsemen's coats of cloth of silver, who, being all in white, advanced every one of them his picture, enclosed in a white round screen of feathers, such as is carried over great princesses' heads when they ride in summer to keep them from the heat of the sun…'

When the fifteen-year-old Prince of Orange married Princess Mary Stuart in 1641, he was attended by ten pages, all carefully groomed and schooled for the occasion. Sometimes noblemen sent their own sons to court. The first Baron Fitzpatrick of Ossory sent his son to serve as the whipping-boy of Edward VI, so pledging his own loyalty. Robert Carr, who was to have a brilliant career as the favourite of James I, came to court in 1603 as a page in the retinue of the Earl of Peterborough. Endymion Porter was born in Spain in 1587, son of a diplomatic interpreter, and early placed in service to the Count-Duke of Olivares, chief minister of Philip IV. When his family returned to England he was placed in the service of Edward Villiers and soon promoted to the train of his style-setting brother, the royal favourite, George Villiers, eventually the Duke of Buckingham, who in turn secured for Endymion the position of groom of

Opposite In the left panel of Quentin Massys's polyptych of St John of about 1507, the figure of a page struggling to control a naughty dog, while adding nothing to the narrative content of the painting, enlivens an otherwise predictable scene. In life as in art the vitality and beauty of boys in their extravagant liveries added enormously to courtly spectacle.

the bedchamber to the Prince of Wales. For years he was the pin-up of the court, appearing frequently in masques and ballets as himself. He grew up to become a patron and connoisseur of poetry and painting, as well as a shrewd investor who died extremely wealthy. He was painted at least four times by Van Dyck and twice by Dobson – after his looks were gone, alas. Sir William Davenant began his court career as a page to the Duchess of Richmond in whose service he remained until he was in his mid-teens.

If Waynman Birch had profited by the training Pepys was trying to give him he could have done well for himself, but it was not to be. In 1662 the boy had accompanied Elizabeth Pepys to Pepys's father's house at Brampton while Samuel stayed in London. According to Elizabeth, once in the country Waynman had turned 'a very rogue'. Pepys was strangely reticent about just how bad he had been, saying bemusedly, 'strange things he hath been found guilty of, not fit to name'. Before Elizabeth left London for the summer of 1663 the elder Pepys had written to Samuel, instructing him under no circumstances to allow Waynman to return to Brampton. Unfortunately Pepys nowhere tells us how old the boy was, so we cannot judge whether the roguery he displayed at Brampton might have been sexual, but Pepys's reticence suggests something of the sort. Eventually, fed up with his 'staying and playing abroad when he is sent on errands', Pepys decided 'to keep the boy no longer'. He lasted a few more months and then incurred another beating for stopping out to see a bonfire. Pepys was resolved.

> … he is not for my family, he is grown so out
> of order and not to be ruled, and doth himself,
> against his brother's counsel, desire to be gone;
> which I am sorry for, because I love the boy
> and would be glad to bring him to good.

Faced with a flogging rather than the routine canings for failing to comply with Pepys's wishes, Waynman ran away. Pepys caught sight of him 'upon Tower-hill, playing with the rest of the boys'.

> I sent W. Griffen to take him and he did bring him to me; and so
> I said nothing to him, but caused him to be stripped (for he was
> run away with his best suit); and so putting on his other, I sent
> him going, without saying one word more to him – though I am
> troubled for the rogue, though he doth not deserve it.

On 14 November, Pepys wrote in his diary about Waynman for the last time:

> I hear today that my boy Waynman hath behaved himself so
> with Mr. Davis, that they have got him put into a Barbados ship
> to be sent away; and though he sends me to get a release for him,
> I will not, out of love to the boy; for I doubt to keep him here
> were to bring him to the gallows.

The boys Waynman hung out with on Tower Hill picked up work wherever they could. Shakespeare is thought by some to have spent some time as a street boy outside the playhouses, picking up a few pence for holding horses' heads for the play-goers. The stage managers recruited boys to dress in black tights and play imps from among those playing in the streets, among whom was Thomas Killigrew, before he became a page and a functionary in the court of Charles I. Boys in service might well have been jealous of the freedom enjoyed by the street boys who were only too ready to lead them astray, even to plunder them and strip them of their fine livery. In the play *Roister Doister* by Nicholas Udall, headmaster of Eton College from 1534 to 1541, there are two boys, Dobinet Doughtie, who works for Doister, and Tom Truepenie, who works for a wealthy widow. Dobinet finds his work hard:

> Where is the house I go to? before or behind?
> I know not where, nor when, nor how I shall it find.
> If I had ten men's bodies and legs and strength,
> This trotting that I have must needs lame me at length.

He is carrying a ring and a token from his master to the widow, but her servant refuses to take it, leaving him in a quandary. As he hesitates, unsure how to proceed, he is met by Tom, who is accused by passing maidservants of

Opposite In painting *Charles I at the Hunt* (c. 1635) Van Dyck sandwiched two of the king's attendants between the king and his horse, an abstracted boy-page who has dismounted from his own horse to take charge of the king's cloak, and an older equerry who takes charge of the royal mount. Though they are clearly individual portraits, they have never been identified.

flinging and frisking, swinging and whisking and roiling abroad, 'in the street, everywhere'.

When Viola takes employment in the train of the Duke of Orsino in Shakespeare's *Twelfth Night*, she is used by him as the go-between in his wooing of Olivia. Like Dobinet she has to accomplish her mission any way she can; she cannot return to Orsino and tell him that the lady would none of his suit. She is chosen for the job because she is pretty, which will recommend her to the lady, so pretty in fact that the lady falls for her, supposed an adolescent boy.

> Methinks I feel this youth's perfections
> With an invisible and subtle stealth
> To creep in at mine eyes.

In *The Two Gentleman of Verona* Proteus sacks his 'slave', Lance, to take on Sebastian who is none other than his rejected lover, Julia, in disguise. In the Induction to *The Taming of the Shrew*, the lord's page, Bartholomew, dresses up as a lady to play the part of Sly's wife. In *A Midsummer Night's Dream* Puck plays the part of Oberon's footboy, while Titania has a page so ravishing that Oberon is determined to have him, hence the entire plot of the play.

> ... she as her attendant hath
> A lovely boy, stol'n from an Indian king.
> She never had so sweet a changeling;
> And jealous Oberon would have the child
> Knight of his train, to trace the forests wild,
> But she perforce withholds the lovèd boy,
> Crowns him with flowers and makes him all her joy.

Ladies would tumble their little pages on their beds, pinching, tickling and teasing them, while covering them with kisses, much as they did their lapdogs. Titania's behaviour is typical of women's treatment of their small pages, and parallels mothers' treatment of their young sons, while Oberon's attitude reflects the concern both of a father who thinks it time that his son was removed from the boudoir to be introduced to manly and dangerous pursuits and a husband, who thinks his wife's page is getting too old to be allowed such familiarities. We are not here faced with a homosexual desire on Oberon's part, but with a desire to make a man of the lad; it is Titania who would keep him childlike and effeminate. In *Love's Labour's Lost* the Princess of France plays word games with a more or less explicit erotic content with Moth, page to Don Adriano de Armado, a witty child who deserves a better master.

On the stage pages were usually lay figures, nameless and ageless. Their job was, as in life, to answer to the summons 'Boy!', fetching and carrying, bringing messages and information as well as tapers and torches to light the stage, to draw curtains and to play, sing and/or dance on demand. John Marston's *Antonio and Mellida* (1602) written for the Children of St Paul's, features, as well as three nameless pages who play and sing and a heroine who disguises herself as a dancing page, two more pages with obscene names, a small one called Catzo ('cazzo', 'prick' in Italian) and a bigger one called Dildo. Both the boy players and the boys they played were expected to understand the joke of the pages' names; the plays written for them were more rather than less sophisticated than those written for the public theatre. The play the boys fetched and carried in were seldom about them, unless they were not pages at all but ladies in disguise. In Beaumont and Fletcher's play *Philaster* the page Bellario is such a maiden in disguise. The intrigue turns, as usual, on her relationship both with her master and her master's beloved, but we learn much more than usual about the vicissitudes of pages. When Bellario is to be sent away he protests, and his master, Philaster, tells him that this is not a dismissal but a promotion. Bellario argues that his father never promoted a page until he was 'grown too saucy for himself' and promises to reform but, despite his tears, Philaster sends him off to wait on his beloved the Princess Arethusa, musing,

> The love of boys unto their lords is strange;
> I have read wonders of it…

Arethusa is quite taken with the 'pretty sad-talking boy' who is given gold to buy himself clothing that befits a royal servant. Gossip about the princess's 'Hylas', her 'Adonis', whose 'form is angel-like', spreads through the court. Though the boy is described as small, Philaster believes the gossip and comes within an ace of killing Bellario. The impending tragedy is eventually averted.

In Aphra Behn's story *The Fair Jilt*, written in the 1680s and based on actual events, the page's tragedy runs its course. '[The princess Miranda] had a page, called Van Brune, a youth of great address and wit, and one she had long managed for her purpose. This youth was about seventeen years of age, and extremely beautiful, and in the time when [her sister] Alcidiana lived with the princess, she was a little in love with this handsome boy; but 'twas checked in its infancy, and never grew up to a flame. Nevertheless, Alcidiana retained still a sort of tenderness for him, while he burned in good earnest with love for the princess.' Having succumbed to one occupational hazard, Van Brune is easy prey to another. 'The princess one day ordering this page to wait on her in her closet, she shut the door and, after a thousand questions of what he would undertake to serve her, the amorous boy, finding himself alone and caressed by the fair person he adored, with joyful blushes that beautified his face, told her there was nothing on earth he would not do, to obey her least commands. She … treated him more like a lover than a servant, till at last the ravished youth, wholly transported out of himself, fell at her feet and impatiently implored to receive her commands quickly, that he might fly to execute them, for he was not able to endure her charming words, looks and touches, and retain his duty.' Miranda commands him to kill her sister, Alcidiana. He administers poison, is suspected, arrested, imprisoned, tried and condemned. The princess, condemned in her turn to stand under the gibbet as he is hanged, arrives, attended by other pages, 'to see her sad Van Brune approach; fair as an angel, but languishing and pale… He was dressed all in mourning and very fine linen, bare-headed, with his own hair, the fairest that could be seen, hanging in curls on his back and shoulders, very long.'

We will never know how often pages were seduced or sexually harassed by their mistresses. A poem of *c.* 1700 refers to 'smooth young pages' who would not serve their mistresses' lust being 'whipped, cashier'd and of their liveries stripped' and forced to earn their living as link boys (see p. 164), as if it were a common phenomenon. Harder evidence is lacking.

Among the contentious aspects of *Le Mariage de Figaro* that Beaumarchais felt obliged to defend in his preface to the printed play, were the character and behaviour of Chérubin, whose very name designates him as one of the Erotes:

A child of thirteen, with his first flutterings of the heart, searching for everything without excluding anything, worshipping, as one does at that happy age, a for him celestial being whom chance has made his god-mother; can he be the cause of scandal? Loved by everybody in the château, lively, playful, and on fire like all witty children, with his extreme agitation, he upsets ten times, without wanting to, the guilty plans of the Count … perhaps he is no longer a child, but he is not yet a man, and it is that moment I have chosen so that he should be

Opposite All the movement in the three versions of Guido Reni's *Salome Receiving the Head of the Baptist* (1638–9) is supplied by the figure of the page who offers the salver with the Baptist's head on it to a statuesque and immobile Salome. In *The Circumcision* (1635–40) Reni depicts an angel in a similar pose, holding a vessel to receive Jesus's foreskin. His *Rape of Helen* (1631) features in the left foreground a lively blackamoor page with a marmoset on a lead.

interesting without putting anyone to the blush…. But he is a child, nothing more. Haven't I seen the ladies in the boxes all mad about my page? What do they want from him? Alas! Nothing.

Beaumarchais's certainty that no male actor could ever play the part of Chérubin is an interesting illustration of the unbridgeable gulf between the pubescent boy and the man he will become.

> This role can only be played, as it has been, by a young and very pretty woman. We have in our theatres no young man so constituted that he could feel the fine details. Excessively timid before the Countess, otherwise a charming fop, a restless vague desire is at the bottom of his character. He is careering towards puberty but with no plan and no understanding, headfirst into everything; altogether he is what every mother, in her heart of hearts, would want her son to be, however much it made her suffer.

The features of hundreds of servant boys are known to us from the portraiture of their masters but we shall never know their names. The only person to make eye contact with the viewer in Caravaggio's portrait of Alof de Wignacourt is the page who holds his master's plumed helmet. The face of the handsome boy who is delivering a letter to Constantijn Huygens in the portrait painted by Thomas de Keyser in 1627 is unforgettable but commentators do not bother even to guess who he might be. In the portrait of Christina of Sweden on horseback painted by Sebastian Bourdon in 1653, we do not know or apparently care to know the identity of the richly dressed lad walking behind her, holding her falcon on his upraised fist. The servant boys painted by Gerard ter Borch are astonishingly individual: one treads carefully with his tray, his eyes fixed on the glass he is carrying; another looks straight at the painter as if more interested in what he is doing than in serving his mistress.

Of even less concern to us, if possible, are the identities of the hundreds of black pages who begin to make their appearance after Titian placed one beside the beautiful woman known as Laura dei Dianti in the portrait of c. 1524. Black pages are so frequently encountered in the portraiture of the seventeenth century as to appear an indispensable accessory for ladies of fashion; so individual are they, despite their obligatory slave collars and obsequious posture, that one has a nightmare vision of hundreds

Opposite As Grand Master of the Knights of St John, Alof de Wignacourt, whose portrait Caravaggio painted in Malta c. 1608, was attended by numerous pages. It has been suggested that the page in Caravaggio's picture is Nicolas de Paris Boissy, who later became Grand Prior of France. More likely it was Ottavio Costa, young son of one of Caravaggio's Roman patrons. The boy had been summoned to Malta by the Grand Master to serve as a page a few months before the painter's arrival.

Benedetto Gennari, who came to London at about the same time as Hortense Mancini, records that he painted her as Diana the huntress, surrounded not by nymphs but by four 'mori', one sounding a horn, a smaller one astride a big dog, another holding the lead of another dog, and the biggest filling a vessel with water to give to one of the dogs. If such boys were actual members of Mancini's entourage, they have left no trace in history.

Below Gerard ter Borch's images of domestic life have such an air of modest verisimilitude that the crazy elaborateness of the page's outfit in *Lady at her Toilet* (*c.* 1660) seems almost shocking. The lapdog reaching up to the empty chair is an emblem of puppy love which can also be read in the boy's dazzled face.

of small black boys sold into slavery half a world away from home, who never made it to adulthood. When Hortense Mancini arrived in London in 1675 she was attended by a bevy of small black pages. What became of them nobody knows.

Velasquez inherited the slave Juan de Pareja from his aunt. He broke the law by teaching the slave a profession, but de Pareja was so talented that he became the artist's assistant and lifelong companion. Though Velasquez painted his portrait he did not use him as a model so that Pareja escaped being subordinated and feminized by his master's controlling eye. When Joshua Reynolds returned from Italy in 1753 he brought with him an Italian boy called Giuseppe Marchi and painted him as a Rembrandtesque exotic in a brocaded toque (see p. 164). Marchi was to work for Reynolds, setting the colours on his palette each morning, painting drapery and making copies of Reynolds's work, all his life. In 1770 he tried to break away and set up as a portrait painter on his own, but within a year or two he was back working in Reynolds's studio and remained there until Reynolds died. Strangely, perhaps, Reynolds did not mention Marchi in his will. It was left to Mary Palmer, his heiress, to make arrangements for Marchi to continue to receive his salary of £100 per year as he kept on working as a restorer of Reynolds's paintings until his own death in 1808. The portrait of Marchi by Reynolds that is now in the Royal Academy Collection was still in Marchi's possession when he died. At least three more portraits of Marchi have survived, but Reynolds preferred to paint, besides his famous patrons, unnamed urchins whom he was not afraid to portray in suggestive ways.

Opposite To the left of 'Cupid as a Link Boy', painted by Sir Joshua Reynolds in 1774, can be seen a group of cats on a rooftop; the batwing Cupid's gesture and the angle at which he holds his torch are meant to be interpreted as obscene. The child's averted face and blank expression, suggesting that he is not a willing participant in the exchange of innuendoes, make the picture more rather than less offensive.

Below Reynolds met sixteen-year-old Giuseppe Marchi in about 1751 shortly after he arrived in Rome. When he returned to England in 1752 the boy came with him to work as his full-time studio assistant, setting the colours on his palette each morning, painting drapery and occasionally modelling for him.

The model for Reynolds's *Cupid as a Link Boy* is a very young boy who may not have understood that he holds his link as if it were his own giant penis and slaps his hand on his forearm in a familiar obscene gesture. Link boys escorted their clients down dark streets with torches, often towards brothels or the market stalls where the bulkers plied their trade. Some of their clients wanted the boys themselves. In Reynolds's companion piece, *Mercury as a Cut-purse*, a model of the same age, perhaps the same model, holds a wallet-purse that resembles nothing so much as a drained scrotum. Despite their ugly emblematization the two paintings were engraved. The Duke of Dorset, who bought the original of *Cupid as a Link Boy* kept, as well as a dancer as his mistress, a Chinese page called Wang-I-Tong.

Studio assistants have served as models since the beginning of painting. A sketch by Raphael for *The Madonna of the Fish* clearly shows a boy with a piece of cloth thrown over his head posing as the Virgin with a bundle in his arms for the Child. A sketch for Guido Reni's Judith makes of her a long-legged boy. Twentieth-century painters tended to employ their models in the house rather than in the studio. When Glyn Philpot was travelling in Tunisia he picked up 'a tall muscular man with a powerful neck and shoulders and light-coloured skin' who was working on the roads, and took him off to Paris to make a servant and model of him. Dressed in his Arab clothes Ali ben Amor ben M'rad waited at Philpot's table; divested of them he served as a model, until he got into trouble with the police and was returned to Tunisia. Philpot then employed ex-army batman Dick Earle as servant and driver, as well as using him as a

model. George Bridgeman, who served as Philpot's model for more than twenty years, occasionally worked for him as a servant and gardener. Another model, Henry Thomas, who as well as being 'simple, guileless, unsophisticated' was black, 'did household tasks like cooking and gardening', 'lived under Glyn's roof and was drawn in the nude repeatedly'.

It is no easy matter now to recreate the lives of the hundreds of thousands of boys who lived and died in service over the millennia. They had not even the right to a bed of their own, let alone a room. As Pepys's account shows, their masters had the right to chastise them, and even to flog them. In the event that a boy did not survive his punishment, his master was unlikely to be arraigned. Boys who grew to adulthood in service became footmen, or 'Mercuries' as they were sometimes called, or butlers, coachmen and stable-hands. Others became valets and then barbers. Those who eventually achieved autonomy, and even wealth and power, have been by and large unwilling to recount their experiences as dependents in other men's households. Concern for the working boy did not arise until the nineteenth century, along with the determination that his childhood should be spent not at work but at school, where he would be taught to be manly and whipped until he learned. No one would have dreamed of curling his hair and dolling him up in white satin encrusted with silver lace so that he could march through the streets with a hundred others beside the gilded chariot of any courtesan who had a mind to play Venus amid her throng of Erotes.

Opposite John Singer Sargent, *Thomas E. McKellar*, 1917–20. In Sargent's work the tradition of depicting women clothed and men naked is oddly perpetuated. His public career centred on society portraits of upper-class females; his numerous studies of unclothed lower-class men were made for pleasure rather than profit. Despite the evidence, Sargent's sexual orientation has remained unclear, though a generation of homosexual artists followed his example and employed lower-class men as both servants and models.

chapter 8

Soldier Boys

From time immemorial boys who were fitter for love have marched to war, and from the beginnings of literature poets have sung their praises. In the seventh century BCE Tyrtaeus wrote:

> But youth's fair form, though fallen, is ever fair,
> And beautiful in death the boy appears,
> The hero boy, that dies in blooming years.
> In man's regret he lives, and woman's tears,
> More sacred than in life and lovelier far
> For having perished in the front of war.

In the twentieth century Rupert Brooke sang of those who poured 'the red sweet wine of youth' away, and Wilfred Owen of the youth who died like cattle. Untold numbers of the 'men' who died in the Great War were still in their teens. The soldier who figures on thousands of monuments to the fallen is a boy.

The most famous soldier of all time, Alexander the Great, though he was thirty-two when he died, was depicted on coins by his own order as a beardless avatar of Apollo. The iconography of both victory and apotheosis traditionally exaggerates the youth of military heroes as a way of signifying their transcendence of the ills of the flesh and their putting on of immortality. The most portly and bewhiskered general will figure on commemorative medals and plaques as a slender youth. A medal struck for Ferdinand II of Aragon shows the young man's likeness on one side and on the other a composite profile that has been misidentified as 'a bearded and aged male to the left and a younger female

Studio of Adriaen Hanneman, *Portrait of Henry Stuart, Duke of Gloucester, When a Boy*, after 1653. Here painted in military garb, Henry, Duke of Gloucester, was appointed a colonel of the 'Old' English regiment of foot in the Spanish army at the age of sixteen, and fought alongside his brother James, Duke of York, in the Low Countries. He escaped the Fall of Dunkirk by leading a desperate cavalry charge through enemy lines.

Left We do not know which of his young sons C. A. Jensen chose to paint in 1836 wearing his school smock and drawing from its scabbard an officer's sabre that is almost as long as he is tall. The child's face is expressionless, lost perhaps in vague dreams of death or glory.

Right Art historians have long been fascinated by Pontormo's *Halberdier*. Vasari records that during the Siege of Florence in 1528 Pontormo painted a portrait of a young nobleman called Francesco Guardi as a soldier. Guardi may have donned the uniform of a footsoldier during the emergency and he might have signalled his civilian rank by the added accessory of the gold chain. If such is the case, our tall slender halberdier is only fourteen years old.

to the right'. The profile on the right is actually that of a boy, and the whole an emblematic depiction of prudence, or, as we would say, an old head on young shoulders. Such a mistaken inference could only be made within a culture that has become blind to boyhood as a contrast to manhood. Because no one wants to acknowledge the youth, inexperience and vulnerability of soldiers, the commander will always refer proudly to his soldiers as his 'men' but most of the 'men' will refer to themselves as boys.

From the first artists were fascinated by the numinous figure of the combatant, whether preparing for war or sport, beaten or victorious. Greek art provided the types of the Apoxyomenos, the Diadoumenos, the Doryphoros and from there to the Tyrannicides, all represented as naked youths. Greek art provided the precedent for the naked soldier: alongside stockier helmeted figures in the friezes on the Parthenon or the Mausoleum at Halicarnassus, bareheaded beardless nudes wrestle with centaurs, sink to their knees under the blows of fully-clad Amazons, and goad their horses with their bare heels. It would be idle, however, to argue that the nakedness of heroic soldiery is all derived from Greek friezes and metopes, which artists could hardly have studied except as they were translated through Roman copies in different media. It seems rather that the naked boy-soldier is a pre-existing type, related perhaps to the naked gymnasts and athletes who competed in the public festivals, and perhaps also to the immortals. The soldier of the Middle Ages is a knightly figure clad from top to toe in shining armour, even when he is an angel and in need of no such protection (see p. 95). The immediate models for the naked soldiers of the Renaissance were found on Etruscan and Roman sarcophagi and coins where the nakedness of the boy-soldier can be seen to serve two functions, on the one hand to confer upon him heroic qualities and on the other to stress his vulnerability. The subliminal message could be, as it is in Tyrtaeus's poem, that the soldier's duty is not to do *or* die but to do *and* die.

When Mars the god of war is represented as boyish, slender and naked, it is usually in the company of Venus, on whose body according to some authorities he begot Cupid. A much replicated Roman statuary group shows Venus semi-draped apparently restraining the young warrior. Later versions, showing Mars older and with his weight transferred to the other leg, portray Venus not as a lover trying to detain him but as a wife preparing to arm him. This figure gradually assumes more weight, less height and a good deal more drapery, until she is a fully dressed Hausfrau. The earliest versions of the

Opposite Roman married couples were often depicted as Venus and Mars. In less respectable versions of the subject Venus is seen as seducing Mars away from his manly duty. In a militaristic society, as imperial Rome certainly was, the female figure was more likely to be seen arming her husband. In the example illustrated we cannot be sure whether she is sending him off to battle or attempting to restrain him.

group clearly represent the adulterous couple as a typology of duty resisting the blandishments of pleasure. A wall-painting in the House of Venus and Mars at Pompeii shows a young and rather tentative Mars shyly removing Venus's drapery while in a series of suggestive visual puns one amorino plays with his sword and another settles his helmet on his head. This would seem to supply the precedent for Botticelli's unsettling *Venus and Mars*. Botticelli's young Mars is apparently exhausted by his amorous exertions, his body entirely relaxed in a young man's deep sleep, naked except for a cloth flung athwart his loins. Venus, impassive and fully clothed, is as far away from him

as she can get. As the young Mars sleeps, baby fauns play with his helmet and his lance. Only a few years after Botticelli's treatment of the Venus and Mars topos, Piero di Cosimo made his own version of the same subject. Once more Mars lies asleep to the right, under a myrtle tree this time, and Venus once more lies awake on the left, but this time she too is naked. Naughty amorini have carried Mars's armour off into the middle distance, where they play with it against a glimmering still riverine landscape, while turtle doves bill in the foreground. Piero di Cosimo's allegory is of the peace and tranquillity that can exist only while the god of war sleeps, unmanned by womanly love. The

Above The shape of the *Venus and Mars* painted by Botticelli in about 1485 on poplar wood suggests that it was once part of a cassone, a necessary item of furniture in a Renaissance spousal bedchamber. The depiction of conflict overcome by love would in such a case be perfectly appropriate and the coolness of Venus no more than would be expected of a modest wife.

relief is only temporary, for Mars's warhorse is stamping on a hillside in the distance. The same message is appended to Giulio Romano's fresco of Mars and Venus in the bath together in the Sala di Psiche (1528), which is labelled 'Virt[utis] Quieti'. The point was made again much later by Alexis-Simon Belle, whose *Allégorie de la Paix* (1801) gives us Venus sitting on the lap of an all but nude boy-Mars and crowning him with laurel for victory and myrtle for nuptial bliss.

Besides being an exaltation of harmony and peace, the Mars/Venus motif can be interpreted as a cautionary tale, in which Mars stands for all the young men who might be beguiled by women's blandishments into neglecting their martial duty and even deserting their posts. In the Italian *poema cavalleresco*, the Mars-Venus tropos is reworked whenever a young paladin is seduced by an enchantress. In Ariosto's *Orlando Furioso*, it is Ruggiero who falls into the clutches of Alcina, even though he has been warned to keep well away from her. Alcina falls in love with 'this so valiant and so comely knight' and they are soon established lovers:

> And so while sensual life doth bear the sway,
> All discipline is trodden in the dust.
> Thus while Ruggiero here his time misspends,
> He quite forgets his duty and his friends.

When he is found by the good enchantress Melissa, Ruggiero displays 'such wanton womanish behaviour' that he is 'himself in nothing but in name'. No

Above Twenty years or so after Botticelli, *c.* 1505, Piero di Cosimo revisited the topic of Venus and Mars. Though his Venus like Botticelli's is awake while her sated lover sleeps, there is less tension in this relaxed and airy composition with its luminous deep perspective. In the curve of her mother's arm sits Harmonia, Venus's last child by Mars, playing with her pet rabbit.

sooner has the good enchantress shown him Alcina as she really is, 'an old misshapen beast', than he rejects his sloth and sensuality to be masculinized anew.

In the *Gerusalemme Liberata*, published in 1575, Torquato Tasso worked the motif again as the paladin Rinaldo succumbs to the charms of the enchantress Armida. In 1593 Ludovico Carracci painted Rinaldo lolling at Armida's feet holding up a mirror so that she can dress her hair, supposedly for the private apartment of Princess Maddalena Maria Farnese in the Ducal Palace in Parma. Where the Carracci brothers went others followed. In this updated version of the Mars-Venus topos, a moment much favoured by the painters or their patrons or both is when Armida, struck by the beauty of the sleeping paladin whom she had intended to kill, falls in love with him instead. When Poussin limned this moment in 1629, he showed Armida's hand holding the dagger stayed by Cupid, as she leans over the sleeping paladin who lies with

Below There is little to distinguish the iconography of conflict overcome from that of soldiery seduced by pleasure. For his *Rinaldo and Armida* of 1629 Nicolas Poussin chooses the moment when Armida, contemplating the beauty of the sleeping paladin, instead of sinking her dagger in his heart, falls in love with him.

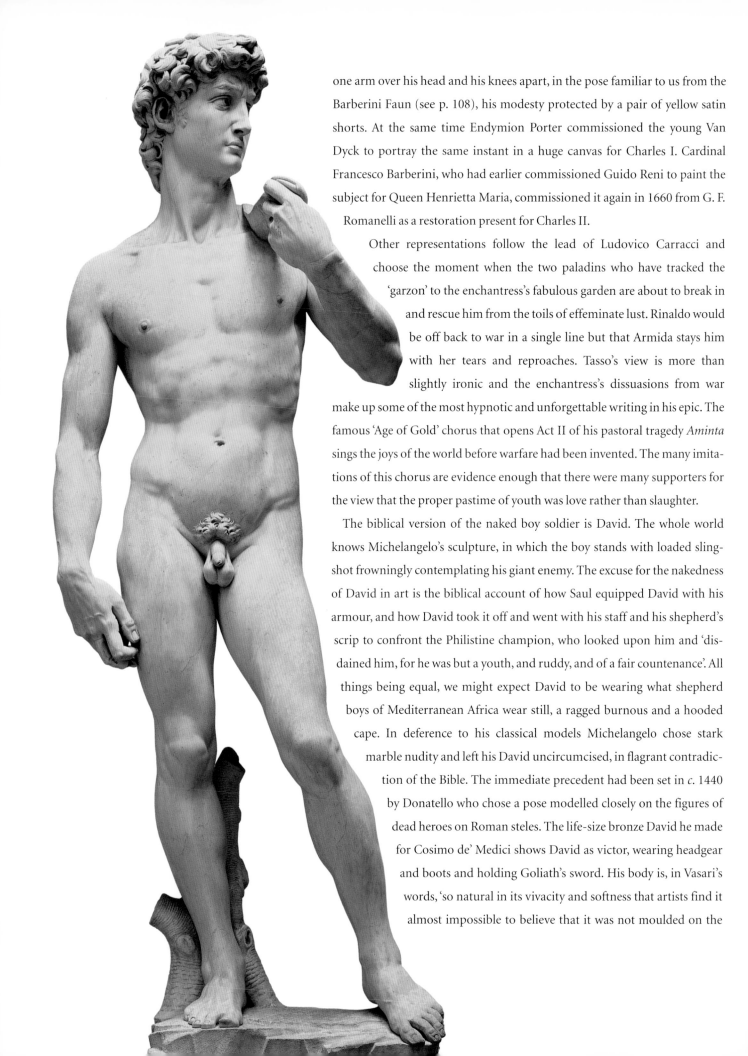

one arm over his head and his knees apart, in the pose familiar to us from the Barberini Faun (see p. 108), his modesty protected by a pair of yellow satin shorts. At the same time Endymion Porter commissioned the young Van Dyck to portray the same instant in a huge canvas for Charles I. Cardinal Francesco Barberini, who had earlier commissioned Guido Reni to paint the subject for Queen Henrietta Maria, commissioned it again in 1660 from G. F. Romanelli as a restoration present for Charles II.

Other representations follow the lead of Ludovico Carracci and choose the moment when the two paladins who have tracked the 'garzon' to the enchantress's fabulous garden are about to break in and rescue him from the toils of effeminate lust. Rinaldo would be off back to war in a single line but that Armida stays him with her tears and reproaches. Tasso's view is more than slightly ironic and the enchantress's dissuasions from war make up some of the most hypnotic and unforgettable writing in his epic. The famous 'Age of Gold' chorus that opens Act II of his pastoral tragedy *Aminta* sings the joys of the world before warfare had been invented. The many imitations of this chorus are evidence enough that there were many supporters for the view that the proper pastime of youth was love rather than slaughter.

The biblical version of the naked boy soldier is David. The whole world knows Michelangelo's sculpture, in which the boy stands with loaded slingshot frowningly contemplating his giant enemy. The excuse for the nakedness of David in art is the biblical account of how Saul equipped David with his armour, and how David took it off and went with his staff and his shepherd's scrip to confront the Philistine champion, who looked upon him and 'disdained him, for he was but a youth, and ruddy, and of a fair countenance'. All things being equal, we might expect David to be wearing what shepherd boys of Mediterranean Africa wear still, a ragged burnous and a hooded cape. In deference to his classical models Michelangelo chose stark marble nudity and left his David uncircumcised, in flagrant contradiction of the Bible. The immediate precedent had been set in *c.* 1440 by Donatello who chose a pose modelled closely on the figures of dead heroes on Roman steles. The life-size bronze David he made for Cosimo de' Medici shows David as victor, wearing headgear and boots and holding Goliath's sword. His body is, in Vasari's words, 'so natural in its vivacity and softness that artists find it almost impossible to believe that it was not moulded on the living form'. This David is small-boned and the contours of his breast and belly are still rounded with puppy fat. Thirty years later, when Verrocchio made another David in bronze for the de' Medici, he chose the same moment as Donatello, with the boy victor standing over the severed head of Goliath with Goliath's sword in his hand, but he deliberately reduced the scale of both head and sword. His David, in contrast to the Praxitelean delicacy of Donatello's, is a young tough, with a hard sinewy body clad in a classical tunic; the face that looks along his jutting arm is sharp and cheeky. Michelangelo returned to the *classicheggiante* practice of Donatello, intending that his Christian David should invite comparison with pagan precedent. At his death he left unfinished a mannerist nude sculpture in sinuous contrapposto that is variously identified as a David or an Apollo.

Opposite Probably the most famous statue in the world, Michelangelo's *David*, 1501–4, does not follow the biblical precedent, in that the figure is stark naked, without headgear or footwear, and has not been circumcised. Rather than follow the convention of posing the figure with the head of Goliath, Michelangelo chooses the moment before he has flung his stone.

Far left Verrocchio's *David*, which dates from thirty years or so before Michelangelo's, makes no attempt to represent ideal masculine beauty. This hero's proportions are still those of a rather nuggetty child, whose lean torso and chunky legs might well be those of a shepherd boy from the Tuscan hills.

Left Donatello's *David* (*c.* 1440), like those of Verrocchio and Michelangelo, stands with left knee bent and right hip shot out in the classic contrapposto. The delicacy of the contours of his rounded limbs and his gracious downward look are those of the Praxitelean ephebe. The contrast of his nakedness with a most unPraxitelean hat garlanded with flowers adds to the fleeting impression of coquetry that clings to his half-smile.

In the centuries that followed, an iconographic battle seems to have waged over whether or not it was correct to show David naked. Interestingly Caravaggio, master of the boy nude, chose to show his Davids dressed, as he would have seen shepherd boys in the Campagna, in shirt and breeches. Guido Reni's Davids come in two varieties, both disconcerting. One, naked except for a swag of drapery about his loins, stands with outflung leg and wrist on hip, looking rather smugly upon Goliath's head, which he holds at the end of his outstretched arm like a rather camp executioner. The other David also gazes languorously at Goliath's head which is now so huge that it has to be propped on a plinth; he is fetchingly draped in a spotted animal skin, presumably that of the 'lion' that he slew in I Samuel, xvii: 33–6, and wears a rakish red toque ornamented with two ostrich feathers. Despite its manifest oddity this picture was so successful that at least a dozen contemporary copies of it are known. David holds his position as the most portrayable of biblical heroes well into our own time. In the development of his iconography we can follow changes and conflicts in the ideology of boyhood itself. In Mercié's remarkable sculpture we see a rangy hard-bodied David, standing with one skinny hip shot out in an angular version of the classical contrapposto, concentrating on sliding Goliath's huge sabre back into its scabbard. When the life-size plaster model was exhibited in 1872, in the immediate aftermath of the Prusso-French war, it caused a sensation. The government acquired the bronze and half-size castings of it sold like hot cakes.

The biblical boy-soldier co-habited with hordes of classical equivalents, all equipped as he was with headgear, footwear, sword and little else. Artists constantly revisited the art of Rome and found in the classical

Opposite Johan Zoffany, *Self-Portrait as David with the Head of Goliath*, 1756. An outrageously pretty version of Zoffany's juvenile self wearing a rakish lambskin hat emerges mostly naked from a mantle of matching lambskin, to triumph over his greatest enemy in the German art establishment.

Below Guido Reni, *David with the Head of Goliath* (detail), *c.* 1605. What seems to us a high-camp image of a languid boy, wearing nothing but a fur stole and a red toque with two huge ostrich feathers, was seen by Reni's contemporaries as an entirely successful depiction of power without force.

nude the correlative of their notion of the rational body politic, regardless of whether it was imperial, revolutionary, republican or fascist. In their smooth impenetrability these monumental nudities are the emblemata of the phallocracy; the whole figure signifies male power. The elision of the vulnerable penis signifies the substitution of masculinity for maleness. The naked soldier of neo-classicism whether he be Canova's Perseus or Thorvaldsen's Jason is the epitome of calm, solidity and balance. When it comes to the elongated bodies of *Achilles Receiving the Ambassadors of Agamemnon* by Ingres, we are witnessing an attempt to achieve greater refinement and subtlety than can be found in the ancient originals, an attempt that signally fails. In trying to invest his history painting with more expressivity Ingres forces his bewhiskered nude soldiers into absurd theatricalities of gesture. The frowning foreheads and outflung arms of Nazi nudes convey a similar sense of overdoneness. The most successful nineteenth-century sculpture of a nude boy-soldier is probably Sir Alfred Gilbert's *Perseus Arming* of 1882. Its combination of sinew and sensibility proved so popular that it was cast in three different sizes for the commercial market. It is no surprise that when Gilbert made the original model in the winter of 1880–81, he was in Italy, reeling under the impact of seeing Donatello's David.

Every single nude soldier, whether depicted before or after battle, is a hero. His erectness of form projects reassurance, regardless of outcome. Depictions of two soldiers in single combat are comparatively rare. The earliest known image of boys fighting, dating back to pre-classical times, was reconstructed from the fragments of a fresco destroyed in a volcanic explosion on the Minoan island of Thera (see p. 184). The boys have long, probably oiled hair and one of them at least is wearing padded mitts. Both wear what appears to be a support but may simply be the sideways view of a breech clout. It has always been assumed that boxing is an ancient sport, and there is some evidence in the survival of classical figures with cauliflower ears, some of them wearing the accoutrements of boxing, principally the protective basket-like coverings called cesti on their hands and forearms. When the sport became popular in England in the late eighteenth century, Roman copies of Greek sculptures of naked athletes were interpreted as effigies of boxers and restored to show them wearing cesti. One of the most famous of these, the Dresden 'Boxer', was transformed into a 'boxer' in the early 1740s. The naked grey marble figure stands, ready accoutred for the encounter, with his eyes cast down, seeming

see p. 184

Opposite The neo-classical sculptors of the late eighteenth century vied with each other to produce new heroic archetypes. While Canova was working on his giant Pericles, the Danish sculptor Bertel Thorvaldsen (1770–1844) adapted the Belvedere Apollo to give us a Jason who strides forward on his right leg while looking past his left shoulder, and has his left arm draped, in this case by the Golden Fleece.

Below Sir Alfred Gilbert's *Perseus Arming* was cast in bronze in 1882 for Henry Doulton. The figure was to be cast many times more, in the original size, 74 cm (29 in.) high, and in reduced versions, 37 cm and 18 cm (14½ and 7 in.). Gilbert's intention for his Perseus was to show him as Michelangelo did David, an adolescent human boy in the anxious moment before he becomes a hero.

Left This late Bronze Age wall-painting from Akrotiri on the island of Thera, now known as Santorini, is the oldest known image of sporting combat. The proportion of head to body suggests that the combatants are quite young and almost certainly male. Each boy appears to be wearing some kind of mitt on the right hand only. Their brows and temples appear to have been shaved, and the rest of their hair allowed to grow in serpentine fashion.

Opposite The laced leather gloves studded with metal that can be seen on the hands and forearms of this Roman pugilist and that justify its identification as such were added in an eighteenth-century restoration. The pose and proportions of the grave marble figure strongly recall the Hellenistic type of the Idolino (see p. 9) and have nothing to do with belligerence of any kind, sporting or otherwise.

more of a victim than a combatant. The Lansdowne Boxer, whose raised arms have been interpreted as some kind of aggressive posture, when actually he would have been holding a strigil to scrape himself clean, is a Roman copy of a Greek type of the fourth century or so BCE. In 1808 twenty artists and collectors arranged to have the pugilist Bob Gregson pose naked so that they could admire his musculature; a week later they repaired to the house of Lord Elgin so that they could compare the heroic proportions of their champion with the Phidian figures on the fragments of the marble frieze stolen from the Parthenon. In a natural progression the pugilist who posed for Benjamin Robert Haydon's heroic nudes left him to fight under Wellington.

In classical iconography single combat is usually represented by the interlocked figures of Hercules and Antaeus, or Hercules and Cacus, none of whom is a boy. The biblical version of classic single combat is Cain's murderous assault on Abel. Ghiberti represented it as the vicious clubbing of an unarmed man, but occasional versions of it as a struggle between two armed men do appear. As the younger brother Abel is usually represented as a boy and Cain as a bigger, usually bearded man.

Soldiers can hardly fight without clothes but in the celebration of battles from the Greeks to the Nazis the moral superiority of the victors, their heroic exposure of what is mortal to all that death and danger dare, is symbolized by their nakedness. Nevertheless we are shocked to find an engraving as gratuitously violent as Antonio Pollaiuolo's *Battle of the Nudes* and the more shocked to find that this multimedia artist's one venture into engraving was a roaring success. The ten male figures, whether wielding bows and arrows or scimitars or daggers or battleaxes, are all beardless. None has any form of protection, though two shields lie abandoned on the ground. One at least appears to be dying. There is no indication of a reason for their murderous onslaught on each other, no standard or insignia; it is as if they had all gone mad. Pollaiuolo modelled his figures on the friezes he had seen on Roman sarcophagi but he did not assemble them in anything like the same harmonious Hellenistic fashion. The lines of the bodies zigzag, criss-crossing from the intersecting ankles of the figures at the centre of the composition, past their reversed mirror images and the asymmetrical interlocked bodies that flank them, to the contorted wood with its writhing branches, against which the furthest four figures dash pointlessly up and down, brandishing their weapons at vacancy. The detail of the bodies' musculature is exaggerated so that their surfaces appear to be rippling non-anatomically, as if in some kind

of fit or unearthly special effect. Pollaiuolo is not so much portraying conflict as the chaos of conflict. There is nothing heroic about the nudity of his figures, convulsed as they are by passion and exertion. The mannerist body too was anything but balanced and solid: the naked bodies in Michelangelo's *Battle of Cascina*, for example, are writhing and swivelling, their attention jerked this way and that.

Images of the fallen boy-soldier are much easier to find than images of the boy fighting. There may be crass reasons for this: it is easier to pose a single youth lying down than for models to hold the difficult poses required for images of grappling. Classical precedents for depictions of the slain were easier to imitate than the interlaced fighting figures to be seen in classical friezes. The Iliad commemorates dozens of mythical fallen soldiers to serve as role models for virgin soldiers through the ages. Sarpedon, son of Zeus, is killed by Patroclus; Zeus, seeing his son lying undistinguished among the common dead, calls Apollo:

Above Antonio del Pollaiuolo, *Battle of the Ten Nudes*, after 1483? Pollaiuolo, said to have been the first artist to dissect bodies to study musculature, was inspired by his study of classical friezes to attempt compositions that would display the nude body in violent action from all angles. Though his intention was didactic the work remains within an iconographic tradition that always showed the warrior, doomed or victorious, as young, beardless and nude.

Descend, my Phoebus! on the Phrygian plain,

And from the fight convey Sarpedon slain:

Then bathe his body in the crystal flood,

With dust dishonoured and deformed with blood:

O'er all his limbs ambrosial odours shed,

And with celestial robes adorn the dead.

Homer is quite clear about the sequence of events: Apollo bathes and dresses the fallen hero before Sleep and Death convey his body back to Lycia. Notwithstanding, red-figure pottery of the sixth century BCE invariably shows Sarpedon carried naked by Sleep and Death; a particularly beautiful fourth-century bronze cista handle consists of the two helmeted figures reverently carrying the virile young body, its head lolling, its arm hanging, its long tresses swinging. Fuseli follows the same precedent. Patroclus is in turn killed by Hector, who strips his body, taking as his trophy the golden armour of Achilles which Patroclus had been wearing. Homer envisioned Patroclus as older than

Left We can only wonder how deliberately Henry Fuseli eroticized the spread-eagled figure of Sarpedon in *Sleep and Death Bear the Corpse of Sarpedon Away to Lycia* (1780). Though the Homeric source says that Sarpedon was washed and clothed before he was transported, from the earliest representations in Greek vase painting he is always shown naked.

Above Though the figure of Barra in Jacques-Louis David's *The Death of Joseph Barra* (1794) is supposed to have been modelled by a boy working in his atelier, its idealized proportions, long legs and short arms, together with the false modesty of the pose, suggest a false consciousness at work. The extreme prettiness of the boy's face is often commented upon, though it is if anything less contrived than the rest of the figure.

Achilles; the pictorial tradition made of him a Jonathan to Achilles's David. The scene beloved of neo-classical painters is naked Achilles's grief for naked Patroclus lying uncovered on a bier. The next hero to die is Hector, and his body too is stripped, dragged behind Achilles's chariot and then held in Achilles's tent until it is ransomed and taken back to Troy where Andromache mourns it. As dead soldiers all of these figures are shown as young, as is Alcibiades though he was in his forties when he was murdered by hirelings of the Thirty Tyrants. Germanicus, nephew and adopted son of Tiberius Caesar, was in his thirties when he was mysteriously done away with in Antioch, but he too is usually shown as a youth.

The image of the naked dead boy-soldier is one of the most numinous in the catalogue. Not only is it charged with pathos, gravitas and beauty, there is often a curious erotic overtone. Elizabeth Barrett Browning began her poetic career writing an epic called 'The Battle of Marathon'. Not long before her death she wrote 'The Forced Recruit: Solferino. 1859'.

> Venetian, fair-featured and slender,
>   He lies shot to death in his youth,
> With a smile on his lips over-tender
>   For any mere soldier's dead mouth.

The strangeness of this mixture of epithets is only partly explained by the fact that the boy sacrificed himself because he had been forced to fight against his own people. Such self-sacrifice cannot have been a common phenomenon and much capital was made when the accidental death of a boy could be parlayed into dazzling exploit and patriotic martyrdom. On 7 December 1793 François-Joseph Barra was killed by brigands who were apparently trying to take from him the horses he was leading. Robespierre seized the opportunity to make a heroic example of him, telling the Assembly that he had been murdered by royalist troops for refusing to cry 'Vive le roi'.

> … seized with indignation, he trembles; he does not answer except with the shout 'Vive la République'. At that instant, pierced by shots, he falls, pressing against his heart the tricolour cockade…. Only the French have heroes thirteen years old!

Jacques-Louis David, charged with staging the solemnities for the boy's interment in the Panthéon in July 1794, took it upon himself to produce a picture for the occasion, using as model one of the boys in his atelier. A good deal has been made of the nakedness of this figure. Some wish to argue that what we have is simply a preparatory oil sketch from the nude and that the finished picture would have dressed the dying boy in the uniform of the Hussars. The figure's degree of finish does not support this hypothesis. The dying Barra, along with David's other heroes, was probably always intended to be a naked boy-soldier. The effeminacy of the face and figure and the fact that the boy's genitals are elided have also been intensively and inconclusively discussed. The re-interment in the Panthéon never happened; within months Robespierre had fallen and David was in prison. David's initiative in depicting the child at the moment of death was followed by the sculptor David d'Angers. At almost the same time as Barra, in July 1793,

Below Alexandre Falguière's *Tarcisius* of 1868 finally allows the boy hero to die decently clothed. Otherwise the tradition of depicting soldiery as young, male and nude remained fundamentally unchanged. Memorials to the dead of two world wars, not to mention Nazi art, often show the generic unknown soldier as a naked boy.

another thirteen-year-old, Joseph-Agricol Viala, crept out under fire to cut the cables joining the pontoons over which royalist troops would have been able to cross the Durance. As he lay dying, he is said to have cried out, 'They didn't miss... I don't care... I die for freedom.' Busts of both boy heroes were modelled in terracotta by Brachard. In 1881 a statue of Barra was erected in his home town of Palaiseau. In 1867 Alexandre Falguière exhibited a life-size plaster model of Tarcisius, a character from Cardinal Wiseman's *Fabiola*, who is supposed to have died protecting the host, which he clutches to his chest in the same way that David's Barra clutches his tricolour cockade. In Tarcisius's case, nakedness was not an issue.

If soldiers actually did fight naked, no boy would ever have joined up. Recruiters from time immemorial devised blandishments that were aimed at the game-cock susceptibilities of boys, offering them a legitimate excuse for spectacular display. In the seventeenth century soldiers had licence to wear huge hats loaded with feathers and could apply as much gold lace to their coats as they could afford. So bedizened they cut a tremendous dash. In her ballad, 'Alcidor', published in 1713, Anne Finch, Countess of Winchilsea, tells how 'a ruffling soldier', a 'man of feather and of lace' came 'in all the pomp of war' and stole the heart of Alcidor's beloved. So spectacular were officers' uniforms in the seventeenth and eighteenth centuries that we might conclude that hostilities were less a matter of actual violence than of bellicose display. If not, there is really no way of explaining the vivid coats, frothing feathers, gold lace, frogging, fringes and tassellings that all ranks but the lowest got to wear. There is not a great deal of evidence about motives for enlisting, but vanity does seem to have been one. On 29 May 1779, when the American War of Independence was at its height, Fanny Burney was chatting with the captain of a company of light infantry who told her that he had been 'cutting off the hair' of all his 'men'.

'And why?'

'Why, the Duke of Richmond ordered that it should be done, and the fellows swore that they would not submit to it — so I was forced to be the operator myself. I told them they would look as smart again when they had got on their caps; but it went much against them; they vowed, at first, they would not bear such usage; some said they would sooner be run through the body, and others, that the duke would as soon have their heads.'

Opposite When Napoleon commissioned a picture of himself commanding the military action at Arcole Bridge from Antoine-Jean Gros in 1796, he was able to give him only one short sitting. The painter completed his preparatory study not so much from memory as by adapting the classic physiognomy of Alexander the Great as represented on Greek coins. Though the finished painting of *Napoleon at the Arcole Bridge* bears no resemblance whatsoever to the actual Bonaparte, it served its purpose. Gros made three versions of it and it was many times engraved.

As a Lieutenant of Artillery, Byron's Don Juan wins the heart of Catherine the Great when she sees him 'sword by side and hat in hand', in his scarlet cloak and form-fitting cashmere breeches, as fetching a figure as an army tailor could make him.

For the major conflicts of the twentieth century boys were usually conscripted from the age of eighteen, which now seems quite young enough. Nobody knows how many boys on both sides lied about their age so that they would be allowed to fight in the Great War of 1914–18; according to the National Service League as many as 15% of recruits may have been underage. Though birth certificates existed the recruiting authorities did not ask to see them. Reports regularly came back from the front of boys as young as fourteen losing their lives. Casualty figures are hard to come by, but the killed and wounded on the allied side number about five and a half million, and of them a disproportionate number would have been boys. Not only are boy-soldiers the least experienced, they are often inadequately trained and equipped, before being exposed to the greatest danger. No matter how young the boy-soldiers in the Great War actually proved to be, if they mutinied or deserted they were executed like men. The War Office and the Ministry of Defence held that if they behaved in such a way as to be found guilty at a court martial they had only themselves to blame, no matter how small, ill, exhausted or terrified they might have been.

After the experience of Vietnam in which the 16% of American soldiers who were draftees provided two-thirds of the casualties, the armies of the rich world have been increasingly professionalized. In a technocratic army bewildered teenagers clutching guns are not seen as an asset. Even so, there are probably a third of a million children under arms in the world, in Afghanistan, Angola, Burma, Cambodia, Chechnya, Colombia, El Salvador, Ethiopia, Guatemala, Honduras, Liberia, Mozambique, Namibia, Nicaragua, Peru, Republic of Congo, Rwanda, Sierra Leone, Sri Lanka, Sudan, Uganda, and God knows where else. Even the UN Convention on the Rights of the Child can only succeed in raising the minimum age of army recruits to fifteen. Nobody knows what the life expectancy of child soldiers in irregular armies might be but, of the 17,000 boys abducted for service in the Sudanese People's Liberation Army, three-quarters are now untraceable and probably lost their lives in 'human wave' attacks. There are ancient reasons for the perennial holocaust of boys, reasons that are and have always been incompatible with civilization. Among them, not so far beneath the surface, is the father's fear

Opposite The year is 1968. Jomo Kenyatta, founder-president of the Republic of Kenya, is opening a hospital built by self-help in his birthplace, Gatundu. His guard of honour is a squad of young mock-soldiers with weapons carved from discarded lumber and caps of painted cardboard. In the ensuing thirty years thousands of child soldiers would be taught to kill with real weapons in Africa and elsewhere.

that his sons will replace him or have already replaced him as the focus of female attention. Old men still send young men to war, and will continue to do so as long as the rest of us let them.

S·QVINTINVS

chapter 9

The Icon of Male Vulnerability

Pontormo depicts Quintinus, or Quentin as he is more often known, after he has been stretched on the rack, flogged, forced to swallow a mixture of vinegar, quicklime and mustard, and then pierced with nails and wires. His recollected stance, despite being transfixed by a huge nail, in an elegantly contrived version of the pillory, is a sign of the direct operation of grace.

Western painters and poets, themselves no longer boys, vie with each other in depicting the untimely deaths of boys. Their public, male and female, apparently takes great delight in beholding such images and hearing such tales, whether of Daphnis, the young Sicilian shepherd who invented the Eclogue and was blinded by the Muses and died for love. Chrysippus, a beautiful Pisan boy, was trained as a charioteer by Laius, who then carried him off to Thebes to be his catamite. (Some historians say that Chrysippus killed himself for shame, others that he was murdered by Laius's wife Hippodameia, who took down her husband's sword as he slept and plunged it into the belly of the boy beside him.) The young shepherd Acis, beloved of Galatea, is killed by the jealous Cyclops, Polyphemus, again and again in poetry, painting and music. The naked body of Icarus, who flew too near the sun so that his home-made wings melted, is shown falling headfirst into the Aegean in all kinds of media great and small. Sometimes the fragility of boys seems extreme: young Elpenor could not fall off the roof of Circe's palace in his sleep without breaking his neck. Artists will even attempt the depiction of Hippolytus being flung from his chariot by his terrified horses (see p. 196) and Orpheus being torn to pieces by women. The list of murdered boys is endless and the manner of their deaths horrifyingly varied. Pelops was killed by his father, dismembered and cooked as a meal for the gods. Athis, an Indian boy, had his face smashed to pulp by Perseus, who alone was unmoved by his youth and beauty. Athis is not to be confused with Attis, the youth beloved of Cybele, who castrated himself. No boy of classical antiquity was more cruelly punished for his impetuosity than Apollo's son, Phaeton, who was killed by Zeus with a thunderbolt when he joy-rode too close to the earth in the chariot of the sun. His divinely perfect young body plummets earthwards on ceilings and walls all over Europe.

When Carle Vernet exhibited a chalk drawing, *The Death of Hippolytus*, at the Salon of 1800, it was much admired and eventually engraved. His usual subjects were horses in action, whether racing, hunting or in battle. The plunging horses and the ideally beautiful young man who is on the point of being dashed to pieces are equally unrealistic.

The more beautiful the boy the less likely he is to survive. According to Homer, Lucian, Apollodorus and Pausanias, the Spartan prince Hyacinthus was so lovely that men departed from a lifetime of heterosexuality to make love to him. He was first pursued by the poet Thamyris, who is said to have invented same sex copulation just for him, and then by Apollo himself. Unfortunately Hyacinthus's beauty also attracted the West Wind whose frustrated love turned to hate. One day, when Apollo was teaching Hyacinthus to throw the discus, the West Wind caught it and flung it full in the boy's face.

> Just as when, in a watered garden, if someone breaks off violets or poppies or lilies, bristling with their yellow stamens, fainting they suddenly drop their withered heads and can no longer stand erect, but gaze, with tops bowed low, upon the earth, so the dying face lies prone, the neck, its strength all gone, cannot sustain its own weight, and falls back on the shoulders.

From Hyacinthus's blood sprang up a flower, not the hyacinth as we know it, but the blue larkspur, which has inscribed on its petals Apollo's cry of grief, 'Ai, ai'.

Hyacinthus and Narcissus are both versions of the spring-flower heroes of pre-classical Crete and, as such, avatars of the Spring Dionysos surnamed '*antheus*' or 'flowering'. The same name is given to the son of Poseidon untimely killed and flayed by Cleomenes, and to Antheus of Halicarnassus who was drowned in a well by Cleobis. The association of untimely death with maleness rather than femaleness, the election of a spring-flower king rather than a queen, can be explained sociobiologically by reference to the obvious fact that, because a single man can pass on his genes through hundreds of women, most of the male population is redundant. Factually, as distinct from theoretically, boys are more fragile than girls. More boys than girls are born but boys are more likely than girls to die of any and all causes between the ages of nought and twenty, by which time the genders have achieved parity. Three times as many boys as girls will commit suicide and twice as many will be accidentally killed.

History tells a terrible story of centuries of ritual slaughter of thousands of young males, beginning in pre-history with the consort of the queen, who could mate with her for a year before being sacrificed to ensure the renewing of the seasons. When his reign began to seem impractically short, it was lengthened to a term of one hundred lunar months, and instead of the king's being killed at the end of each lunar year, a boy-king was killed in his place to supply the blood that would be sprinkled to ensure the return of fertility in spring. 'His ritual death varied greatly in circumstance; he might be torn in pieces by wild women, transfixed with a sting-ray spear, felled with an axe, pricked in the heel with a poisoned arrow, flung over a cliff, burned to death on a pyre, drowned in a pool, or killed in a pre-arranged chariot-crash. But die he must.'

In Ancient Crete the boy chosen to stand in for Minos the Bull-king reigned for a single day, during which he performed an elaborate dance emblematic of the seasons of the year, only to be killed and eaten raw as the Titans devoured Zagreus, the young son of Zeus and Persephone. In Thrace, the *interrex* was married to the queen, reigned for a night and a day, and was then torn apart by women disguised as horses. In Corinth and those cities that followed the same tradition, he was dragged behind a chariot and the horses goaded until he had been battered to pieces. The myth of Acteon rent asunder by hounds appears to be a memory of the stag-kings of the pre-Hellenic era, who reigned for fifty months and were then ripped to shreds. Of the children dedicated to the gods the boys were much more likely than the girls to be slaughtered, as were the boys sacrificed annually to the Cnossian king, and the seven Athenian boys who were sacrificed to the Minotaur. Girls had the option of becoming priestesses and temple prostitutes.

While Adonis, the ultimate flower-hero, was still a child he became the object of the desires of two powerful women, Persephone and Aphrodite. The Muse Calliope, appointed by Zeus to decide between them, declared that Adonis should spend a third of the year with each of them and a third in rest and recuperation, but Aphrodite persuaded the boy to stay with her all the year round. Persephone went to Ares and warned him that Aphrodite was besotted with a mortal boy. The god assumed the form of a boar and, when Adonis and Aphrodite were out together hunting on the slopes of Mount Lebanon, gored the boy to death before the goddess's eyes. Poets of the sixteenth century were irresistibly drawn to the story. In Spain Don Hurtado de Mendoza was writing his *Fabula de Adonis* and Juan de la Cueva de Garoza his *Llanto de Venus en la muerte de Adonis*, in Italy Girolamo Parabosco his *Favola di Adone*, followed close behind by Ronsard with *L'Adonis* in France and Louis de Masure's tragedy *Adonis* in Switzerland. When plague closed the London theatres in 1592, Shakespeare used the time to write a highly visualized erotic burlesque of the subject, which became the favourite bedtime reading of 'wanton housewives'. Shakespeare's Adonis dies when a sex game goes wrong.

> And nuzzling in his flank, the loving swine,
> Sheath'd unaware the tusk in his soft groin.

The clue for this comes from Idyll 30 of (almost certainly not) Theocritus in which Aphrodite commands the Erotes gathered around her to seek out the boar and bring it to her. When she upbraids it for killing her lovely boy, the boar answers:

> Thy lord, thy lovely lover,
> I never willed to wound him;
> I saw him like a statue
> And could not bide the burning,
> Nay, for his thigh was naked,
> And mad was I to kiss it,
> And thus my tusk it harmed him.

Adonis is thought to be a Greek version of the Syrian demi-god Tammuz, who represents the plant-life that completes its life-cycle within the year. Tammuz, like Adonis, was killed by a boar. The rites offered to Adonis by women

Opposite The eighth labour of Hercules (seen as a shadowy figure seated on the wall in the background) was to capture the four mares kept chained up by the Thracian king Diomedes who fed them on human flesh. Hercules knocked Diomedes unconscious with his club and fed him still alive to the mares. In his earliest treatment of a subject to which he returned several times Gustave Moreau renders the event even more horrible by changing the king into a pre-adolescent boy.

include mourning for his death followed by rejoicing at his rebirth. In Theocritus's Idyll 15, Praxinoe sings the praises of Adonis:

> A bridegroom of eighteen or nineteen years is he, his kisses are not rough, the golden down being yet on his lips! And now goodnight to Cypris, in the arms of her lover! But lo, in the morning we will all of us gather with the dew, and carry him forth among the waves that break along the beach, and with locks unloosed and ungirt raiment falling to the ankles, and bosoms bare will we begin our shrill sweet song.... dear to us has thy advent been, Adonis, and dear shall it be when thou comest again.

For the midsummer festival of the Adonia, women made little 'gardens of Adonis' out of containers planted with short-lived annuals, which appear in wall-paintings from the first century BCE. Literary celebration of Adonis is dominated by Bion's famous *Lament for Adonis*; countless painters have since illustrated the scene he describes:

> The lovely one lies wounded in the mountains,
> His white thigh struck with the white tooth; he scarce
> Yet breathes; and Venus hangs in agony there.
> The dark blood wanders o'er his snowy limbs,
> His eyes beneath their lids are lustreless,
> The rose has fled from his wan lips and there
> That kiss is dead that Venus gathers there.

Bion, here translated by Shelley, draws out all the equivocal possibilities of the moment when the living goddess tries to draw a last kiss from her mortal lover. In Shelley's version it runs:

>   the purple blood
> From his struck thigh stains her white navel now,
> Her bosom and her neck like snow.
>
> She claspt him and cried   'Stay, Adonis!
> Stay, dearest one...
>   and mix my lips with thine—
> Wake yet a while—oh, but once,
> That I may kiss thee now for the last time—
> But for as long as one short kiss may live—

Opposite In *Hero and Leander* (*c.* 1626) Nicolas Régnier, a French artist who came under the influence first of Caravaggio and the Neapolitan school, and then of the more refined Carracci, splits his composition diagonally, balancing the outflung arms of the grieving Hero with those of the drowned Leander, whose dramatically foreshortened nakedness is the real subject of the composition. The drapery of his loins may well be a later intervention.

Oh, let thy breath flow from thy dying soul

Even to thy mouth and heart, that I may suck

That…

Shelley translated no farther. When Keats died of consumption in 1821 at the age of twenty-four, Shelley's thoughts turned once more to Bion as the model for 'Adonais', his lament for the poet so untimely dead. Within a year of penning the last of its fifty-four stanzas Shelley himself was dead, drowned in the Gulf of Lerici with a volume of Keats in his pocket.

In his death by drowning Shelley recalls Leander whose story is told by Virgil, Statius, Ovid and, most importantly, by Musaeus in Greek in the fourth or fifth century. In the 1540s poets all over Europe began writing vernacular versions, in Spain Garcilaso de la Vega and Juan Boscán de Almogáver, in Italy Bernardo Tasso, in France Clément Marot, and in Germany Hans Sachs. Fifty years later Christopher Marlowe set about an English version, which opens with a description of Hero elaborately kitted out in green sleeves, blue kirtle

and musical buskins, and goes on to tell of 'Amorous Leander, beautiful and young' – and naked.

> His body was as straight as Circe's wand;
> Jove might have sipped out nectar from his hand.
> Even as delicious meat is to the taste,
> So was his neck in touching, and surpassed
> The white of Pelops' shoulder. I could tell ye
> How smooth his breast was, and how white his belly,
> And whose immortal fingers did imprint
> That heavenly path with many a curious dint
> That runs along his back…

Above Francesco Furini is best known for his paintings from life of fetching boy nudes identified as Isaac, Sebastian, Laurence and the like. In *Hylas and the Naiads* he departs from his usual practice in depicting Hylas fully dressed even to the feathered hat he seems to have borrowed from Reni's famous David (see p. 181), the better to contrast with the rather unconvincing nudity of the nymphs.

Leander becomes the lover of Hero, swimming nightly across the Hellespont to her tower on Abydos, and is eventually drowned. Marlowe did not live to complete his poem; it was left to Chapman to describe Leander's body cast up on the beach and Hero grieving over it. Interest in the story seems never to have flagged: it furnished themes for ballets, musical entertainments, cantatas, oratorios, song cycles, operas, tragedies – and burlesques.

Hylas, Hercules's beloved squire, also perished by water. The thirteenth Idyll of Theocritus tells how, as the two were encamped with the Argonauts on the shores of the Hellespont, Hylas was sent to draw water:

> In the midst of the water the nymphs were arraying their dances,
> the sleepless nymphs, dread goddesses of the country people,
> Eunice and Malis and Nichea with her April eyes. And now the boy
> was holding out the wide-mouthed pitcher to the water, intent on
> dipping it, but the nymphs all clung to his hand, for love of the Argive
> lad had fluttered the hearts of all of them. Then down he sank in
> the black water, headlong all, as when a star shoots flaming out
> of the sky, plumb in the deep it falls…

Hercules refused to sail on with the rest of the Argonauts until he had found the remains of his beloved boy. As he continued to roam ceaselessly searching, they left without him. The iconography of Hylas shows him less often as a drowned boy than as a reluctant sex object being dragged into the water by the lustful nymphs.

The desperate grief of Hercules was later mirrored in the grief of the Emperor Hadrian for his Antinous who drowned in the Nile in 132 CE. Antinous was a Bithynian who entered Hadrian's service when he was eleven or twelve, and travelled with him to Greece in 128 CE as his acknowledged *eroumenos* or favourite. He was gifted not only with beauty but with superior intelligence and sporting prowess. The emperor remained in mourning for Antinous's untimely death for the rest of his life, declaring him a god and ordering the building of a city in Egypt in his memory. Temples dedicated to Antinous sprang up in every community that sought the favour of the emperor and Hellenistic Roman statues of beautiful athletic boys were re-named Antinouses. As the last god to arise in the Roman world Antinous was variously seen as an avatar of Osiris, Apollo, Hermes or Dionysos. What should be clear is that as the emperor's catamite Antinous could never have survived to manhood.

Drowning was a common enough event in real life and there were biblical and other precedents for scenes in which the bodies of drowned youths could be lovingly presented in all their detail. Depictions of the Deluge often appear to present all those drowned as young and male. The most famous depiction of drowned boys is Géricault's masterpiece *The Raft of the Medusa*, which caused a good deal of controversy when it was exhibited at the Salon of 1819

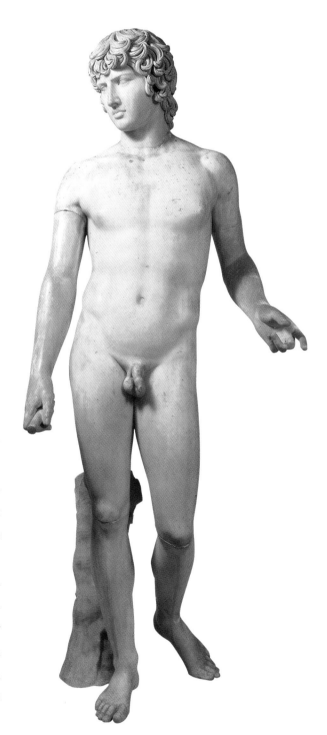

Below The Farnese Antinous, *c.* 130–138 CE. We shall never know what Antinous, the brilliant young athlete beloved of the Emperor Hadrian, actually looked like, because after the emperor had declared the drowned youth a god, all kinds of male effigies were re-christened in his honour. His features have become, like the features of the apotheosed Alexander, stereotypic of ideal beauty as it was perceived in differing cultural contexts.

because of the foregrounding of the two young corpses. The painting illustrates the moment on 17 July 1817 when the fifteen survivors of the wreck of the Medusa believed that their frantic signalling to a passing ship had been in vain. The preparatory sketch for the picture shows only one of the bodies, in rather less detail and without the strange refulgence that in the finished painting spotlights the delicate beauty of both corpses.

The early church might not have been able to turn mortals into gods, but it did have the option of making them immortal and placing them in heaven by the process of canonization. The shortest road to canonization was martyrdom. Much more mysterious in its way than Antinous's translation to godship is the transformation of a middle-aged martyr to an ephebe, as happened in the case of Sebastian, by far the most frequently depicted saint in the Catholic Calendar. *The Golden Legend* relates that, at the time of his martyrdom in *c.* 304 CE, Sebastian had been in the army for nearly twenty years, so he was no stripling. The Emperor Diocletian, not knowing him to be a Christian, had appointed him to a captaincy in the elite Praetorian Guard. When the succeeding emperor, Maximian, set about the suppression of Christianity, he ordered Sebastian's execution. Sebastian was tied to a stake, shot full of arrows and left for dead, but the ministrations of Irene, the saintly widow of another Christian martyr, saved his life. Sebastian actually met his martyrdom many years later by being beaten to death.

In the earliest representations Sebastian stands alone in his niche or on his panel, a full-length upright figure, sometimes armoured, sometimes clad in a mixture of Roman and later armour and civilian dress, holding the arrows that were used in his torture. He is often paired with St Roch, who displays (like Adonis) a wound in his groin. Half-lengths and busts based on the full-length figures were later commissioned for the devotions of private clients. These imaginary portraits show Sebastian as a youth of transcendent beauty, as can be seen in the best known examples by Lorenzo Costa, Boltraffio and Raphael. Benozzo Gozzoli, Andrea Mantegna and Carlo Crivelli show Sebastian stripped to his breech clout and so full of arrows 'as to appear like a hedgehog'. So far the saint's demeanour is one of godly containment; he cannot actually move, being bound hand and foot to his stake or tree or column, but in any case he remains tranquil, simply turning his eyes to heaven. Botticelli's Sebastian and the early examples by Giovanni Bellini are of this kind. Cima da Conegliano dispenses with the stake and with all the arrows but one, presenting us with an apparently uncomplicated image of a

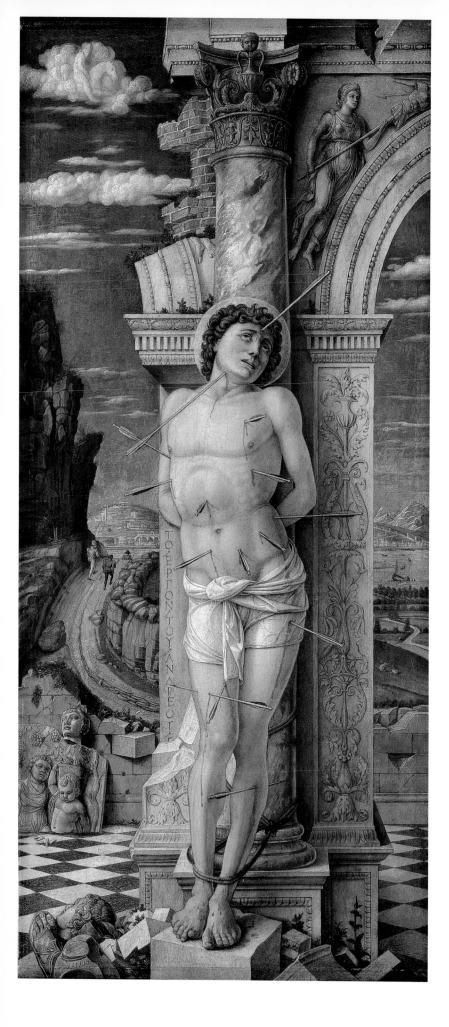

Left Mantegna, *St Sebastian*, 1457–8. Although Mantegna's posing of the figure against an antique Roman background exaggerates the sinuosity of the contrapposto, the hardness of its modelling, combined with the literalness of the depiction of the arrows driven deep into the flesh, drives out any suggestion of sensuality.

beautiful boy with a single arrow piercing his thigh. His colleague Giovanni Bellini adapts the same image for his *Sacred Allegory*, though this time the single arrow is stuck in the saint's breast-bone and his beatified body under its tumbling golden curls is dazzlingly fair.

When Titian pairs St Sebastian with St Roch for the right-hand side of his altarpiece of St Mark Enthroned for the Church of the Salute in Venice in 1510 (see p. 208), he positions Sebastian right on the edge of the picture space looking out and downwards. A single arrow has pierced his ribs while his breech clout has foamed into a sheet, hugely knotted over his genitals and draped behind him like a train. The young man is not only disturbingly human but apparently distracted from the main business of the picture which is the veneration of St Mark, so that he seems to inhabit the same realm as the viewer. Titian must have known that many a woman would come to kneel and pray before this beguilingly sensual picture of a saint and so must the painters of the many other altarpiece groups in which a young, nude Sebastian upstages the line-up of celestial worthies.

In later depictions, Sebastian is no longer collected or composed, but a-thrill with emotion, whether weeping like Sodoma's Sebastian, on whom an angel prepares to bestow the martyr's crown, or convulsed and gasping like Garofalo's Sebastian, or breathing forth his soul like the succession of ecstatic Sebastians by Guido Reni. Reni's Sebastian is a lover whose body is racked less with agony from the arrows of his persecutors than with his soul's longing for the beatific vision that will be his at the moment of death. As exactly the same metaphors of breathing forth the soul are used for orgasm, the erotic content of the image is obvious, but Reni challenged himself to purge such crass associations by sheer painterly control. None of the commentators on the pictures of the transfixed Sebastian sees fit to point out that historically Sebastian was not on the point of death when the arrows entered his body and the whole conceit is gratuitous. Until the seventeenth century Sebastian invariably retained his breech clout, which is as much an identifying attribute as his arrows, but he had long been an excuse for any study of a full-length male nude or nude male torso, especially if the arms were thrown up and the body convulsed in agony or ecstasy.

In another version, rather truer to written history, Sebastian has been taken down from his tree and his wounds are being tended by St Irene. Giordano, Manfredi, Stanzioni, Schedoni, Preti, Cerrini and many other artists of the Baroque period painted versions of this subject. Because the female figure

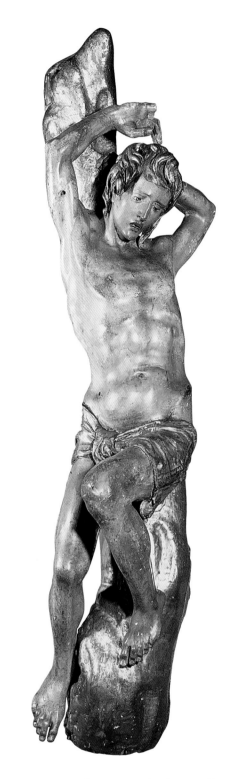

Above This remarkably expressive Sebastian, carved by the Spanish mannerist Alonso Berruguete in about 1530, not long after his return from Italy where he had studied and worked with Michelangelo, enacts the writhing agony rather than the ecstasy of a martyr's death. The saint's body is contorted on its tree in a deliberate reminiscence of the passion of Christ on the cross.

could not be seen in too close contact with the boy's naked body, St Irene is often no more than a head and an arm, gingerly approaching the languishing saint, with none of the two-handed aggression needed actually to extract an embedded arrow from flesh, bone and sinew. Sometimes the problem is solved by presenting Irene as an old woman, with the added benefit that the contrast with her grizzled features makes Sebastian appear yet more beautiful. Another way of solving the problem was to transform Irene into a couple of ministering angels. When these dwindle into cherubs, Sebastian's perforation seems closer to erotic play than ever.

The covert erotic content of the Sebastian-Irene situation becomes explicit in Canto XIX of Ariosto's *Orlando Furioso* when the beauteous princess Angelica tends the Saracen soldier Medoro who, like Sebastian, is so severely injured that:

Opposite In *St Mark Enthroned with Sts Cosmas, Damian, Roch and Sebastian*, c. 1510, Titian mocks the tradition of Sebastian's undress by draping him in a breech clout the size of a sheet. The pointing hands, amid other strong diagonals, all lead the eye to its extravagantly phallic knot.

Above left Were it not for the arrows positioned so as not to be seen piercing his smooth skin, Nicolas Régnier's Sebastian (*c.* 1615) might as well be tied to a bedstead. The emphasis falls not on the physicality of suffering, nor on the bliss of union with God, but on the pathos of the young man's vulnerability.

Above right Gustave Moreau was fascinated by boy victims and returned again and again to the subject of Sebastian, whom he portrayed as a beautiful youth doomed to ecstatic suffering, as if his martyrdom were simply a re-enactment of the Dionysian sparagmos, without doctrinal significance.

Opposite Many pictures of Sebastian, like this one painted by Hendrick ter Brugghen in 1625, are based on studies of the male nude posed in the studio, any additional figures needed to complete the narrative being added afterwards.

Above In this version of *St Sebastian Tended by Irene*, painted in *c.* 1716–18 by Antonio Bellucci, veiled eroticism becomes explicit in the positioning of the women's hands, not to mention the expression on the martyr's face.

the might

Of the faint youth was ebbing with his blood
Which had the ground about so deeply dyed,
Life was nigh wasted with the gushing tide.

Angelica prepares a salve from a potent herb and applies it liberally 'even to his hips, his waist and breast'.

Erotic as Ariosto's account of Angelica's criminal passion certainly is, it pales by comparison with the innocent passion of Erminia for Tancredi in Tasso's *Gerusalemme Liberata*. Erminia finds Tancredi weltering in his blood and apparently lifeless.

And when she saw his face, pale, bloodless, dead,
She lighted, nay, she tumbled from her steed.

She laments the destruction of his beauty in terms that seem fitter for Venus passioning over Adonis:

Though gone, though dead, I love thee still;
Grant me from his pale mouth some kisses cold,
Since death doth love of just reward deprive;
And of thy spoils, sad death, afford me this,
Let me his mouth, pale, cold and bloodless, kiss.

When Tancredi breathes a sigh, Erminia breaks off her lamentation and busies herself about tending him. All she has to staunch his wounds is her veil and the only thing she can bind them with is her golden hair. Giulio Cesare Procaccini (?) and Pietro Ricci both chose to depict Tancredi lying spread-eagled and inert as Erminia mops at his wounds with her hair. Francesco Furini shows her slicing at her hair with a sword, as Tancredi lolls semi-conscious in her lap. Poussin painted the same moment in two very different compositions.

Sebastian is the most popular but by no means the only wounded boy in the religious pictorial tradition, which begins with the very first martyr, Abel, son of Adam and Eve, murdered by his elder brother Cain. Images of Abel's beautiful dead body can be found throughout Christian sculpture, stained glass and manuscript illumination. In Jacopo della Quercia's bas relief of *c.* 1430, a battered Abel raises a helpless hand against his brother's cudgel. Vasari waxed lyrical about Ghiberti's depiction of the clubbing to death of Abel on the third door of the Baptistery in Florence, noticing how 'the very bronze used for the dead limbs of Abel's beautiful body itself falls limp.' Later Renaissance

Above For this elegant altarpiece (*c.* 1610–12), originally commissioned for the Milanese church of Santa Maria in Celso, Giulio Cesare Procaccini eschews the violence and gore of Sebastian's corporeal death, and depicts the saint at the moment when his tortures melt into the ecstasy of union with God, Irene and her servant having been replaced by a playful company of angels.

iconography of the dead Abel is clearly influenced by the Roman copy of a Hellenistic sculpture group of the Niobids that is recorded in the Maffei collection at the end of the fifteenth century, in which one of the boys lies dead, one arm flung up over his head, the other lying at his waist. Drawings of the Roman sculpture by Aspertini, Heemskerck and possibly Perin del Vaga have survived; Aspertini used the figure for the body of a decapitated saint in *The Burial of SS Valerian and Titus*; Raphael also used it for the figure hanging down from the wall in *The Fire in the Borgo*. Giovanni Dupré's neo-classical plaster of 1842 replicates the arch of the young man's body on the uneven ground.

The next Old Testament martyr would have been Isaac, if an angel had not stayed his father Abraham's hand. Rembrandt's 1635 rendition of the subject is one of many, but it is perhaps the most dramatic. The father's large hand pushes down on the face of the boy who has been stripped and his hands bound behind his back, as if to stretch his neck for the cut, arching his smooth white torso upwards to become the fulcrum of the composition.

Below François-Xavier Fabre painted this *Death of Abel* in 1791, when he was studying in Rome. The biblical allusion is clearly merely a pretext for the depiction of a luscious male nude in a posture of abandonment. Fabre later became the companion of Louise de Stolberg, Countess of Albany, widow of the Young Pretender, herself an amateur painter of beautiful young men.

In foregrounding the victim of a father's brutal assault, Rembrandt's treatment is fairly typical of the hundreds of versions of what was a popular subject.

In the Renaissance John the Baptist was gradually transformed from an emaciated ascetic clad in hair and skins to a ravishing boy wearing next to nothing. In 1445 in the predella of an altarpiece Domenico Veneziano portrayed him nude in the desert, but it was probably Raphael's design showing the saint as a beautiful naked boy lounging on a rock, half-draped in a leopard-skin and holding one finger up in the air that started the trend. This figure is a slightly older version of the half-grown St John in Raphael's *Madonna* in the Galleria Palatina. The fashion spread like wildfire, until virtually any male nude could be presented as a 'St John the Baptist in the Desert', the younger the better. In 1673 or so, Jacob Huysmans painted a portrait of Charles II's bastard son James, Duke of Monmouth as St John the Baptist. Sir Joshua Reynolds's *Child Baptist in the Wilderness*, his most successful fancy picture ever, was modelled by a puny and perhaps rather frightened street boy.

Above This shockingly dramatic version of *Abraham's Sacrifice*, in which the boy's trussed body occupies the whole foreground, was painted by Rembrandt in 1635, before he had himself become a father. It is unusual in Rembrandt's work, but by no means out of keeping with the iconographic tradition which focuses on the vulnerable body of the boy.

The Bible furnishes us very few boy martyrs compared to the hordes recorded in the apocryphal history of the early church. St Laurence is supposed to have met his martyrdom in 258 CE by being roasted on a gridiron. In fact he was hardly a boy at the time, having risen so high in the church hierarchy that after Sixtus II met his death, he was effectively in charge. In the decorous Middle Ages and High Renaissance, though Laurence might be seen with his gridiron, it was seldom shown in use. Baroque artists could not resist the opportunity to show an adolescent male body luridly lit from beneath by flames. St Quintin, a Roman patrician, travelled into Gaul to preach the Christian faith. In 287 the Roman prefect of the area caused his body to be pierced with two wires from the neck to the thighs, iron nails to be run into his body, under his nails and through his head. St George defied the orders of the Emperor Diocletian and was beheaded in 303 CE. In 304 CE Diocletian sentenced Florian, an officer in the Roman army, to death by burning for not persecuting the Christians with sufficient vigour. St Florian is said to have threatened to climb to heaven on the flames, so they tied a millstone around his neck and drowned him instead. The legend of St Maurice and the Theban Legion arose in the fifth century. It was believed that 6,600 men, an entire legion of soldiers recruited in Egypt hence 'Theban', was hunted down in the Swiss Alps and killed for failing to carry out orders to persecute their fellow Christians. All these martyrs tend to grow younger and younger in art, until they are all beardless youths; as spiritual beauty can only be expressed in painting as bodily beauty, they are all necessarily ravishing. When Benjamin West was asked to provide an altarpiece for St Stephen Walbrook in London in

Below In *The Martyrdom of St Laurence* (1621–2) Valentin de Boulogne portrays the martyr stripped and about to extend his length on the gridiron where he will be roasted, amid a crowd of realistically observed street people. The saint's figure is the only one illuminated, a reference perhaps to Prudentius's hymn to St Laurence (405 CE) which tells that the faithful only could perceive that light and that the odour of his burnt flesh would smell sweet in their nostrils.

1776, he chose to depict the saint as a half-clad youth of peerless loveliness, totally unmarked by his stoning to death, being carried by two burly bearded men. Another victim who grows younger and younger, at the same time shedding all his clothes, is the battered man found by the wayside by the Good Samaritan. The parable tells us that 'a certain man went down from Jerusalem to Jericho, and fell among thieves, which stripped him of his raiment, and wounded him, and departed, leaving him half dead'. The pretext for yet another glamorous nude male body lying in a posture of total abandonment was too good to resist; in very few of the many paintings of the subject is the hero of the parable, the Good Samaritan, the principal figure.

The suspicion that all these battered boys might really be a single fetishized boy is not entirely unfounded. Felice Ficherelli, surnamed Il Riposo, having posed a dark-eyed, slender, broad-shouldered boy nude but for a breech clout, back leg up, front leg down, leaning on one elbow, hands clasped in prayer, eyes turned heavenward, used the resulting study for paintings of three different subjects, *A Sacrifice of Isaac*, now in the National Gallery of Ireland, a *St Lawrence*, now in the Swedish Nationalmuseum, and a *Sebastian Tended by St Irene*. If each orgasm is a little death, and early modern writers never tired of the parallel, these gasping, fainting, even writhing nudes are all to some extent erotic, yet those who saw them hanging over the altars where they prayed every day may have blinded themselves as efficiently to that eroticism as we have in censoring out the beauty of boys altogether. Otherwise it is hard to imagine how convent after convent could commission painter after painter to provide them with life-size images of Sebastian. The principal icon of male vulnerability is of course the perfect corpse of Christ Himself which, though often enough erotically depicted, could never be erotically viewed. An adequate discussion of that equivocal phenomenon would require a different book.

Opposite In *The Martyrdom of St Florian* (c. 1515) Albrecht Altdorfer shows us the saint with the instrument of his death, the millstone. The complex play of night shadow under the bridge with the cold luminosity of moonlit sky and water reinforces the contrast between the saint's nakedness and the warm clothing of his persecutors, to result in an image of intense vulnerability which is not in the least indulgent or lurid.

chapter 10

The Female Gaze

In 1620 or thereabouts Giovanni Lanfranco painted an oddly suggestive picture of a young man, naked except for a strip of cloth thrown lightly over his loins, lying propped up on his left elbow on a rumpled bed, smiling at the viewer over his right shoulder as his right hand stretches back over his body to caress an adoring black and white cat. The boy is beardless, his body slim, lightly muscled and hairless. The concealing of his genitals suggests that they are unfit to be shown, tumescent perhaps, while the effect of intimacy is heightened by the perspective, which is that of someone looking down into the bed. The boy's knees are slightly drawn up and his back tense and twisted, in a version of the pose of St Laurence reacting to the heat of the gridiron in paintings of his martyrdom, but in this case only cool white sheets lie under the boy's body and all the heat is in his eyes.

Edward Lucie-Smith, writing of this picture in 1972, assumed that the painter was painting someone like himself to be viewed by someone like himself. 'Equally narcissistic in feeling is the painting of a Young Boy on a Bed, by Lanfranco … the boy himself appears to be a self-portrait of the artist, not only because the face resembles other known portraits, but because the picture was fairly obviously painted with the help of a mirror, something which gives a rather different complexion to what might first seem an unusually candid example of a homosexual representation.' The painting certainly suggests a sexual context but, just as Lucie-Smith's hypothetical narcissism depended on a (mistaken) assumption about the painter, the homosexuality hypothesis depends upon an assumption about the viewer. Lucie-Smith may not have known that within thirty years of its being painted this picture was acquired by Christina of Sweden. In 1656 when Christina took up her abode in the Palazzo Farnese in Rome she chose as her private apartment one that opened off the great gallery,

In this famous picture of a naked twenty-four-year-old David Cassidy, Annie Leibovitz captures the elation of narcissistic boyhood at the height of its beauty. David Cassidy became the fave rave of a whole generation of little girls in a TV soap opera; at the age of twenty-one he was the highest paid performer in the world. Issue 108 of *Rolling Stone* in which Leibovitz's picture originally appeared is still the most demanded back number of the magazine.

which the Carracci brothers had sumptuously decorated with a series of paintings of the Triumph of Love featuring such classic tales of female desire as Diana and Endymion and Aurora and Cephalus. Christina brought with her as her secretary Gabriel Gilbert, already the author of a tragedy on Hippolytus, and she had commissioned from him a new tragedy of thwarted female desire, *Les Amours de Diane et d'Endimion,* which had just been performed in Paris. According to some eye-witnesses, she liked to read after

dinner to her guests from Gilbert's 'pastorale heroïque', in particular the speeches in which the goddess declares her love for the shepherd boy. Barred by her poor health from fleshly delights, Christina was an enthusiastic patron of poetry, music, theatre, dance and painting, and greatly embarrassed her staff by insisting on removing the fig leaves from the nude male statues in the Farnese. Thirty years after Gilbert wrote *Les Amours de Diane et d'Endimion* for her she was still so fascinated by the theme that she collaborated with

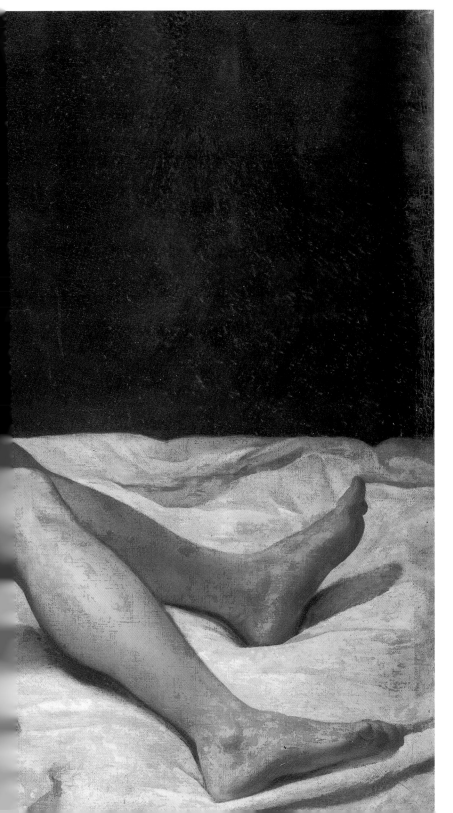

Left Sometimes a cat is just a cat, but perhaps not in this case. Art history is so good at eliding the female viewer that Giovanni Lanfranco's *Young Man with Cat* (1620) has usually been discussed as a 'homo-erotic masterpiece'. The youth's flushed cheeks and shining eyes could be interpreted as a sign that sex has already happened. The cat certainly seems to be purring.

The Female Gaze **221**

Alessandro Guidi on an Italian verse pastoral called *Endimione* that was published after her death as by 'Erilo Cleoneo'. The exposition of her Lanfranco was part and parcel of Christina's conscious and deliberate campaign to reclaim female desire. She also acquired Rubens's opulent and ambiguous rendition of the dying Adonis. Nicodemus Tessin the Younger, who saw the Rubens in situ in the Palazzo Riario during Christina's residence there, also noticed a Ganymede. Michelangelo's famous cartoon of Venus and Cupid was for many years displayed in the Farnese, along with the painting from it that is now in Capodimonte. Garofalo's *Saint Sebastian*, now in Capodimonte, which hung in the second Sala of the Quadreria, may also have been to Christina's taste. Christina also owned the Dürer panels of Adam and Eve that show Adam unusually as an Apollo-type nude. The example of Christina cannot be said to clinch the argument that women are likely to be at least as aware of and as responsive to the charms of boys as men are, but it is important to remember that Christina was one of the very few women who were not obliged to conceal their real feelings under the cloak of modesty. What she could do openly other women may have done privately.

Margaret Walters says in *The Nude Male* that 'up to the nineteenth century men took it for granted that women have a sensuous response to male beauty'. Ovid certainly did. 'Your beauty has captured my heart,' says the hapless Phaedra to her husband's son, Hippolytus. 'To say no more, my eyes delight in whatsoever you do.' Medea was consumed by desire at the very sight of Jason: 'I saw you and I was undone.' Sappho too was betrayed by her eyes:

> You have beauty, and your years are apt for life's delights —
> O beauty that lay in ambush for my eyes!

Helen does not doubt that any woman who saw him would fancy Paris.

> Your beauty, too, I confess, is rare, and a woman might
> well wish to submit to your embrace.

When Phaedra woos her obdurate stepson, she reminds him of goddesses who were seduced by the sight of a boy's beauty, of Aurora leaving her old husband Tithonus to lie with the shepherd-boy Cephalus, of Venus panting for Adonis. The nymph Echo had only to see Narcissus and her fate was sealed. It could be argued that these examples represent nothing more than male fantasies about female arousal, if both men and women had not found the circumstances thoroughly believable.

Above Trained as a portraitist by Bernardino Campi, Sofonisba Anguissola specialized in haunting images of self-possessed children. In her *Portrait of Massimiliano Stampa*, 1557, we see a serious and very dignified mini-man tightly buttoned into formal clothing. His very immobility conveys the impression of intense vulnerability.

Opposite The pastellist Rosalba Carriera is one female artist who encountered no difficulty in rendering male subjects in a convincing manner. Like other young Englishmen on the Grand Tour, when nineteen-year-old Charles Sackville, later second Duke of Dorset, was in Venice in 1730, he sat to Rosalba for two portraits, one in ridotto costume. Rosalba also undertook to make addresses on his behalf to a lady of the city.

There are examples too from Holy Writ; Potiphar's wife had but to cast her eyes upon seventeen-year-old Joseph, who 'was a goodly person, and well favoured', to desire him so ardently that she importuned him daily and ultimately grabbed his garment and tried to drag him into her bed. The hellfire preacher Savonarola persuaded his fifteenth-century Florentine followers that 'in houses where there were young girls it was not right to keep painted figures of naked men and women'. Among the penitents who followed him was the painter Fra Bartolommeo, who brought all his nude studies and paintings to be publicly burned. When it was said of Fra Bartolommeo later that he could not paint the naked human figure, he took up the challenge: '… he did a picture of St Sebastian, naked, very realistic in the colouring of his flesh, who has an air of great charm, and whose body was likewise executed with corresponding beauty. This won him endless praise among the craftsmen. It is said that when this painting was put on show in the church, after the friars had found women in confession who on looking at it had sinned through the captivating and sensuous resemblance of a living figure given to it by Fra Bartolommeo's talent, they removed it from the church…' In 1657 or so the nuns of the Church of Saint Sebastian in Naples commissioned a Sebastian from Mattia Preti only to reject it, ostensibly because the figure was 'without that nobility and beauty that are appropriate to a noble body, and that the face was more like that of a street porter than of a captain of soldiers, as Saint Sebastian was'.

Insights into women's patronage of the arts tend to be fitful and misleading. The fact that Isabella d'Este, the sixteen-year-old bride of Francesco Gonzaga, had no sooner taken possession of her private apartment in the Palazzo Ducale in Mantua in 1490, than she set about commissioning large-scale allegorical paintings by Perugino, Mantegna, Lorenzo Costa and Correggio, all of which showed nudes of both sexes, is usually interpreted as evidence of the influence of her humanist tutors. Yet Isabella was the daughter of one female connoisseur, Eleanora of Aragon, and sister-in-law of another, the Duchess of Urbino, both of whom commissioned secular works from the best painters of their generation for their private apartments. Certainly Isabella was understood to be capable of sophisticated visual pleasure. By the 1620s when Elizabeth de Bourbon wished to visit her husband Philip IV in his summer apartments where the famous Titian *poesie* were hung, she would ask that these fabulously sensual paintings be covered up in advance of her arrival. Catherine the Great accumulated the greatest art collection of any European monarch, but most of it was bought in bulk by agents who had no opportunity to determine her preference. Legend has it that the boudoirs in her palaces were decorated with images of young men that were not so much erotic as pornographic.

More reliable evidence of female response to the beauties of boys may be derived from women's writing. Sylvia, the 'sister' in Aphra Behn's novel *Love-Letters Between a Nobleman and his Sister*, tells her brother-in-law, '… you are beautiful as Heaven itself can render you, a shape exactly formed, not too low nor too tall, but made to beget soft desire and everlasting wishes in all that look on you; but your face! your lovely face! inclining to round, large, piercing black eyes, delicate proportioned nose, charming dimpled mouth, plump red lips, inviting and swelling, white teeth, small and even, fine complexion and a beautiful turn! all which you had an art to order in so engaging a manner that it charmed all the beholders, both sexes were undone with looking on you…' When Sylvia decides to consummate her affair with Philander her justification is that her forces are too weak to withstand his 'shock of beauties', that he has 'charms enough to justify' her yielding, that she is a 'virgin quite disarmed by two fair eyes, an angel's voice and form…'

Behn's women are not simply aware of male beauty but actively seek it. Their gaze will lock on to the charms of young men even when they are hidden. Miranda, the anti-heroine of Behn's story *The Fair Jilt*, loses her heart in church when a young Franciscan friar offers her the collection box. 'She beheld him steadfastly, and saw in his face all the charms of youth, wit and beauty; he wanted no one grace that could form him for love, he appeared all that is adorable to the fair sex, nor could the misshapen habit hide from her the lovely shape it endeavoured to cover, nor those delicate hands that approached her too near with the box…. She gazed upon him, while he bowed before her, and waited for her charity, till she perceived the lovely friar to blush, and cast his eyes on the ground … she … gave him a pistole; but that with so much deliberation and leisure, as easily betrayed the satisfaction she took in looking on him…' Sleepless in bed she fantasizes that the young friar puts off religion and exchanges his habit 'for a thousand dalliances for which his youth was made; for love, for tender embraces, and all the happiness of life'. Every day her passion takes 'new fire from his eyes'. She tries to seduce him, begging, 'Do that which thy youth and beauty were ordained to do.' All ends, as you might expect, in tears.

As a female libertine Aphra Behn might be considered unusually frank in her account of female response to male beauty. Elizabeth Singer was no libertine but the daughter of a non-conformist parson. She probably wrote 'To a very young Gentleman at a Dancing-School' when she was at boarding-school in the 1680s. It is a witty and unusual instance of what is actually a fairly common phenomenon, the reaction of a group of women to the appearance of a solitary gorgeous boy. At first the women gape at him,

Whilst with a lovely pride the graceful boy
Passed all the ladies, like a sultan, by,
Only he looked more absolute and coy.

And then they heave a deep communal sigh of envy as he leads one of them on to the dance-floor.

By the nineteenth century the *bonne bourgeoise* was both required and believed to be free of sexual curiosity or desire. Few respectable women bothered to dispel an illusion so necessary to the peace and good government of the household. A daughter who was found to be masturbating would have been considered in need of medical treatment. If she fantasized about male bodies, nobody was interested in finding out what those fantasies were. Women of the lower orders sleeping in the same room as father and brothers could hardly have been unaware of penises or of erections, but they don't count. Mill girls were suspected of sexual predatoriness and were apparently as ready to accost a good-looking young man as ever girls were, but their sexuality is not written into the record.

In 1978 Margaret Walters argued that women were still estranged from their own visual pleasure: 'But even today, a woman is expected to take a narcissistic pleasure in fulfilling male fantasies rather than in exploring and acting out her own. There is still a rigid distinction between the sex that looks and the sex that is looked at. The dichotomy is bound to breed perversion in both sexes, in the man voyeurism, hostility and envy, and in the woman masochism, exhibitionism and hypocrisy. Both men and women are deprived and impoverished.' Elvis Presley had died the year before, after more than twenty years of driving women into a screaming frenzy mainly by singing, but also by pouting and shaking his hips in a manner beyond suggestive. If women were not allowed to look, we must wonder why it is that Tom Jones, who imitated Presley's pelvic thrusts in a more than convincing manner, was alternately suspected of padding his crotch and credited with an unusually

Above Robert Plant was nineteen years old when Jimmy Page asked him to join The Yardbirds. As the lead singer for Page's next band, Led Zeppelin, with his flying mane of red-gold curls, bare chest and dirty dancing, Plant figured as the embodiment of Dionysian energy for a generation.

bulky form of genital endowment. In 1977 John Travolta had been entirely convincing in his portrayal of a Brooklyn Italian-American boy who lived for Saturday nights when he would ease himself into a tight white suit and dance like a priapic god. Bands like The Doors, Led Zeppelin and Tyrannosaurus Rex were all masters of male display, and in every case the result is not manly but boyish. As trousers were tight and chests were bared, hair could be released in a flowing cloud, eyes darkened and lips reddened, because maleness was beyond doubt. I was once on stage with The Doors and saw James Morrison turn upstage to stimulate himself before turning to show the outline of his engorged member to his shrieking audience. Such things were not meant to happen and they are rarely found in the record. Today's fans cannot know

Below Jim Morrison's band, The Doors, came to fame in 1967. By 1969 his performances had become so exhibitionistic, he was sentenced to eight months' hard labour and a $500 fine for profanity and indecent exposure. In the aftermath he abandoned his snakeskin trousers, grew a beard and put on weight. Among his verse published in 1988 can be found the lines:

Between childhood, boyhood, adolescence
& manhood there should be sharp lines drawn.

He died in his bath in 1971. He was twenty-eight.

how Jimi Hendrix used to rub his guitar against his groin, partly as protest and partly because women were watching. Since those days we have got used to girls wetting the seats at boy-band concerts and grown women throwing their knickers at Tom Jones or tucking banknotes in the G-strings of male strippers. Women have now claimed the right to look and to derive pleasure from looking, but the people who capitulate are not men but boys. A recent television commercial featured a group of female office workers crowding together to get the best sight of the window-cleaner's virile loins in low-slung jeans. The women were salaried employees; the object of their gaze was an inferior, junior to them in age, below them in the social hierarchy, and safely separated from them by the glass wall of the office.

The boy is the missing term in the discussions of the possibility of a female gaze. Women may not frankly evaluate a man's physical attractiveness but a boy is in no position to object. As a junior the boy must defer to his male elders and superiors and may not legitimately assert mastery over anyone. As a subordinate he might be thought to be feminized, if we continue to insist on passivity as a feminine characteristic. To put it another way, biological maleness only takes to itself phallic activity and mastery when it assumes patriarchal power. The boy, being debarred from phallic power, is endowed simply with a responsive penis rather than a dominating phallus and can be sexualized with impunity.

Discussions of visual pleasure as it relates to the depiction of human beings almost invariably assume that the viewer is male; histories of the male nude are all histories of homosexuality in the visual arts. The gaze itself is characterized as male. Laura Mulvey's 'Afterthoughts' to her seminal essay 'Visual Pleasure and Narrative Cinema' argues that though the spectator may not be male in every case, the act of viewing is masculine. The male is the looker-at, and female the to-be-looked-at. The viewer is masterful and empowered; the viewee mastered. Mulvey even describes the woman who views males as objects of erotic interest as a transvestite who has temporarily adopted a masculine habit, or regressed to pre-Oedipal life.

If it is legitimate to assume that the male painter paints the male nude because the male is the object of his desire, we ought surely to be able to interpret the predilection of women painters for female subjects in the same way, but to do so would be absurd. We must consider then whether the initial hypothesis may be wrong. The relationship between artist and model is assumed to be at one level erotic: the luscious female nudes of Picasso and

Matisse are presented as positive proof of the artists' heterosexuality. Such phallic anxiety did not affect the artists of an earlier era who in any case had no access to female models. Their male nudes are sexier and more real than their female figures, not for the most part because they were drawn with pederastic desire, but because they were drawn from life. The female figure was often no more than an inert idealized shape, drawn to a pattern, sometimes even a pattern that reflected the current shape of corsetry, as in the Goya portrait known as *The Naked Maja*. When women begin to paint the figure, they paint women, usually dressed, and children naked and clothed. Even the great Artemisia Gentileschi, who was properly trained and had access to models of both sexes, preferred her nudes female, painting a series of large canvases labelled variously Cleopatra, Danaë, Bathsheba, Susannah and Lucrece. No figure of a nude or semi-draped male has ever been attributed to her. As far as we know she never attempted a Sebastian or a St John or an Apollo.

A few years after Artemisia's death, the Venetian painter Giambattista Piazzetta took as his pupil his cousin, Giulia Lama, who did not shrink from portraying nude figures, usually contorted and so dramatically lit by her own version of Piazzetta's flickering chiaroscuro that they seem burned after-images rather than solid objects. Christ's body hanging on the Crucifix in the altarpiece that may still be seen in the Chiesa di San Vidal in Venice quivers like a reflection on water. Draped across the foreground of her *Judith and Holofernes* in the Venice Accademia lies the man's body, strangely twisted so that his left leg is crossed over his right while his left shoulder has not lifted off the bed. Holofernes is usually shown bearded and bullish but Lama's version is boyish and passive, with slightly tumescent nipples. To her is now attributed a *Martirio di San Giovanni Evangelista*, which shows the saint stripped to the waist and gazing upwards towards the heaven of his approaching death.

Elisabeth Vigée Le Brun painted very few nudes and never a male one until she encountered the young Prince Lubomirsky. At the Salon of 1789 Le Brun exhibited a painting of the enchantingly pretty boy naked but for a red drape,

Above Prince Henri Lubomirski, who posed as Cupid in Paris in 1786 for this painting by Angelika Kauffmann, must have been one of the most beautiful boys who ever lived. Kauffmann and Vigée Le Brun both painted him several times, and Canova too portrayed him as Cupid. All such pieces function both as portraits and as mythological subjects.

bedecked with white wings and holding up a laurel wreath. The picture is variously called *Prince Lubomirsky as the Genius of Fame* and *Prince Lubomirsky as Cupid*, because an arrow-filled quiver lies at the boy's feet, signifying perhaps that love has been given up for the pursuit of glory on the battlefield. Another, *Allegory of the Genius of Alexander I*, seeming to show him slightly older, once more winged and partially draped, looking back over his shoulder as he inscribes on a shield balanced on his knees, was eventually presented by the artist to the imperial collection at the Hermitage. A year or two later Le Brun again posed Prince Lubomirsky as *Amphion jouant de la lyre*, under the adoring gaze of two naiads, one of whom was modelled by her daughter Julie and the other by the young duchesse de Guiche. Prince Lubomirsky also sat more than once to Le Brun's great rival, Angelika Kauffmann; a half-length showing him winged and naked testing the tip of an arrow appeared on the art market in 1923. Better known is the full-length portrait of 'Prince Lubomirski as Cupid' showing rather more of his naked body than Le Brun chose to display, recorded in the possession of the Lubomirski family until after 1900. A contemporary copy hangs in the bathroom of the Zamoyski Palace at Kozlowka. The wholehearted response of two women artists to the beauty of the young prince can be placed in context by a comparison with the full-length sculpture by Canova of Prince Lubomirsky as Eros which shows him entirely naked, free-standing and full-frontal.

As a history painter Kauffmann often painted male figures, usually decently draped and displaying the same proportions of limb and torso that may be seen in her women. In a tondo at Burghley House in Lincolnshire, *Abelard Presents Hymen to Eloise*, the figure of Hymen, naked except for a filmy stole draped over the right arm and held decently covering the genital area by the left hand, is plump and hippy and white. By contrast the

full-length of Prince Lubomirsky presents a recognizably boyish body with flat
square shoulders, slender legs, and serviceable hands and feet. The new type
can also be seen in the oil study for *Cupid and Psyche*; in the finished painting
Cupid has assumed the irrepressible blond curls and patrician profile of the
young prince. In *Diana and Endymion* in the imperial collection at Peterhof,
the flat muscled body of the sleeping shepherd probably indicates Kauffmann's
use of another unclothed male model, but for her *Ganymede* of 1793 she
returns to her earlier practice and takes her model from a Roman intaglio.

No woman could yet permit herself to paint even a juvenile male figure
complete with genitals. When Angélique Mongez undertook large-scale
history pieces in the manner of her master, Jacques-Louis Mongez, she
depicted them high-waisted, long-legged and naked in the heroic manner. In
the foreground of her *Oath of the Seven Theban Chiefs* of 1806 stand two nude
male figures of whom one presents his behind and the other has his sword and
scabbard carefully positioned to conceal his groin. Mongez remains virtually

unique among her female contemporaries in daring to foreground a free-standing nude figure of either sex. If the eighteenth century had seen a growing feminization of the boy figure, by way of suggesting delicacy and virtue, women artists were not about to challenge the trend. The seven sons of St Felicitas as portrayed by Marie Ellenrieder in 1847 might as well be seven daughters. As the pressure of female demand for art training mounted, so did the insistence that women be permitted to draw from the live undraped model. State academies resisted this pressure, but the more enterprising directors of private art schools gave way to it and set up segregated ateliers where women might commune with the nude away from prying male eyes. Marie Bashkirtseff depicted perhaps the most important of these, the

Below Although she was no great admirer of the *peintres pompiers* who taught there, Marie Bashkirtseff entered the women's atelier of the Paris painting academy run by the ex-boxing promoter Rodolphe Julian in 1877. In *Life Class in the Women's Studio at the Académie Julian*, *c.* 1881, she has left a visual record of the crowded conditions under which the women worked. The live model provided for them by Julian was a semi-draped child posing as St John.

women's atelier at the Académie Julian in *c*. 1881. The women students, gowned and hatted, and apparently crowded upon each other, have as their model a woe-begone child partially draped in the skins of St John and holding his banner.

The male nude was feminized apparently as a prelude to its disappearing altogether when the female nude finally replaced it as the principal subject matter of visual art. In bourgeois painting male figures began to play the same role as they do in bourgeois ballet, as the supporters of the exhibitionist female, their beauty seldom emphasized. In painting a St Sebastian the aspiring lady artist in Charles Aubert's *L'Aveugle* (1891) is doing something that almost none of her male contemporaries was interested in doing. In her article 'The Forbidden Gaze', Tamar Garb describes the situation of the model in Aubert's story in the following terms: '... the play-acting of the model requires the adoption of the ethereal abstracted expression of the St Sebastian, traditionally constructed in representation as a feminised male...' This twentieth-century female observer of the tradition does not see in Sebastian a boy-figure but simply a 'feminised male'. To her none of his

Right Anna Lea Merritt's original design for *Love Locked Out*, exhibited at the Royal Academy in 1890, was meant to serve for a bronze relief to be placed at the head of the grave of her husband Henry Lea Merritt who died in 1877 only three months after they were married. Love was modelled for her by a professional child model. The painting is the first by a woman to have been purchased for a British national collection.

contortions, his upturned eyes, his open mouth, suggests the small death of orgasm. Aubert's story has a plot typical of trivial soft porn: the model pretends to be blind, the artist permits herself to shed part of her clothing until she inadvertently reveals a nipple whereupon her model betrays himself by his erection. The story does not deny that there is a desirous female gaze; the artist faints the first time she sees her model's naked body but thereafter she contemplates it unmoved, until the erection calls itself to her attention. Consistency is too much to expect from such writing but it is of a piece with the anxiety of the authorities who feared that the male model might become aroused by the intent scrutiny of so many young women. It seems to have occurred to no one that the ladies might have thrown their knickers at him.

Very few of the women artists who came through the system in the nineteenth century painted the nude and that only occasionally. One, Henrietta Rae, had commercial success as a painter of female nudes, probably because her life-size female figures have no more vitality than shop-window dummies and their genital area is left similarly blank. To the best of my knowledge Rae painted but one undraped male figure, a slender boy crowned with roses and equipped with nacreous moth-wings to impersonate Zephyrus courting Flora, exhibited at the Royal Academy in London in 1888. Zephyrus's lean and handsome young body is clearly drawn from life but when G. F. Watts saw the unfinished painting in Rae's studio he 'drew on the canvas, over the male figure, the complete foreshortened skeleton' so that she could correct the pose. The painting did not find a buyer and remained hanging in Rae's studio until her death.

Rae's contemporary, Dorothy Tennant, learned to paint boys in the studio of Jean-Jacques Henner: *The Death of Love* (1888) is a small-scale adaptation of Henner's *Joseph Bara, Jeune Héros de la Révolution*. In the *Cupid and Psyche* painted by Annie Swynnerton in 1891 (see p. 87) the front of stage is held by the luminous adolescent body of Psyche, as usual bereft of genitals, while Cupid's are decently hidden by plumes from his purple wing. Anna Lea Merritt was so aware of the ways in which her famous picture *Love Locked Out* (1889) might be interpreted that she refused to allow it to be reproduced as an engraving. Their female contemporaries felt less pressure to leave the world of female imagery; men painted women and women painted women too, often themselves. Mary Cassatt, Gwen John, Suzanne Valadon all produced series after series of images of females. Valadon's three-way portrait of her much younger husband André Utter naked, as *Les Lanceurs de Filets*, could hardly be described as a success. We will look in vain for images of the male among the

Opposite The child in Mary Cassatt's *Mother and Child* of 1901 is one of very few male figures ever attempted by the artist. In her many studies of mothers with children, though the children are often nude, their sex is almost always obscured, not only by the pose but also by the title of the work, the real subject being not so much the individual mother with an individual child as the maternal condition.

works of the women of Surrealism. Two images by Léonor Fini may be excepted; in both a sleeping boy occupies the foreground with one knee drawn up in the classically revealing pose of the Barberini Faun (see p. 108). In one he is being watched over by a sphinx-like creature and in another the hands of the sphinx figure are caressing his neck in a manner that is both maternal and threatening. One is reminded of the group of the Sphinx with a Boy Victim, copied by a Roman artist from a detail on the throne sculpted for the Zeus at Olympia by Phidias, in which the sphinx rends the boy with her lion claws.

With the consolidation of second-wave feminism in the 1970s, a small number of women artists, while still preoccupied with questions of female identity and their own corporeality, begin to consider maleness and hetero-sexual desire. In these cases the depiction of the male body is more often confrontational than celebratory. The penis is often the focus of attention as if

Above Sphinx with Boy Victim (reconstruction). The sphinx was a monster with a woman's head and upper torso superimposed on a lioness's body, with a serpent's tail and eagle's wings, who asked every passer-by a riddle. If he could not answer it, she throttled him and ate him on the spot, as she did Jocasta's nephew, Haemon.

Below Léonor Fini is not unusual among female Surrealists in that her principal and virtually only subject is herself. *Sphinx Amalbourga* of 1942 is unusual in that its main subject is the sleeping figure of a sun-tanned boy. The usual stylized version of the artist herself with cat-like features and frothing black hair appears in the head of the high-bosomed sphinx who caresses the boy with human if elongated fingers.

Previous pages In the left-hand panel of this diptych by Deborah Law (1972) we find ourselves once more confronted with the image of the naked man with the clothed female, but instead of supporting the male as in a Madonna and Child or a pietà, the clothed female figure sits on him. The pallor of the figure and its emaciation suggest dependency rather than support. In the right-hand panel it is the female who is nude and the male who is clothed, but the suggestion of female dominance is even more pronounced despite the size of the male hand that clamps her bosom.

Above Sylvia Sleigh's *Philip Golub Reclining* of 1971 is one of the most famous examples of female artists' attempts to treat the male body in the same reifying way as male painters have done the female body. The young man's pose is obviously reminiscent of Velasquez's *Rokeby Venus*, but as well as seeing the young man's face reflected in the mirror we also see the painter, a diminutive distant figure, dwarfed as it were by the tradition she invokes.

it were a failed connection link, as in Eunice Golden's *Cronies*. In some cases, as in that of Sylvia Sleigh's *Philip Golub Reclining* (1971), pictorial revenge was taken for what was perceived as centuries of women's reification as sex objects. Golub's pose might recall the Rokeby Venus but, as his buttocks are compressed and his genitals concealed, he is markedly less sexualized than most of the boys of art history, having turned his back on the tiny figure of the painter reflected in the mirror in which we see his long-suffering face. In her diptych of 1972, in a knowing distortion of the Madonna and Child motif, Deborah Law appears to confront the last taboo, the highly charged relationship between boys and their mothers. In the left panel the mother figure sits on the cowering naked boy's knees and in the right she appears naked on his clothed lap. Both poses are zigzags of attraction and withdrawal; in neither case are the figures in eye-contact. The woman's comforting gesture in the left panel is painfully at odds with the boy's hand splayed across her naked breast in the right.

The development of photography was of immense importance to women artists for whom the role of dominating artist over submissive model was already alien. The degree of control exerted by the camera is hardly less, but it is of a different kind. Nan Goldin photographs her friends behaving spontaneously, without directorial interference, neither lighting the scene nor modifying the image once she has framed it. Most of her subjects are female or gay; it would appear that straight men are loath to co-operate with even this modest assumption of power by a female image-maker. In Goldin's work we may trace survivals of the classic trends in treating the subject of boys; *French Chris on Carhood, NYC* (see pp. 2–3) is a classic example of the sleeping boy motif. Another trend in women's treatment of the boy is to depersonalize him by portraying him in sections; Sarah Kent said of her *Male Nude: California* (1982) that it was a depiction of a well-loved body, a well-loved body that has still undergone the mutilation of circumcision, as none of the male bodies of the earlier tradition have. When Sally Mann published ravishing nude photographs of her own children in 1987, there was an immediate outcry; absurdly enough, her appreciation of her children's physical beauty was seen as both paedophilic and incestuous, as if any mother could be unaware of the tragic loveliness of the bodies she has made within her own and must reconcile herself to losing to time and distance.

Below Artwork featuring the genitalia only is usually to be found only in medical manuals and in pornography. Sarah Kent calls this photograph *Male Nude: California*, 1982, and has described it as 'loving' but Courbet's famous depiction of the female pubis, *L'Origine du Monde*, has not been accepted by feminist critics in the same spirit. What ought also to be obvious is that this is the only image of a circumcised penis in this book, and one of very few in Western art altogether.

Above Sally Mann, *The Last Time Emmett Modeled Nude*, 1987. Mann describes her photographs as gifts to her from her children; she has been denounced as a child pornographer because of her frankly sensuous response to their fleeting beauty. The censoring of a mother's physical delight in her children marks the last stage in the denial of the sensuality of childhood.

Opposite Like most women artists, fashion model turned photographer Ellen von Unwerth, born in Frankfurt in 1954, prefers female subjects. *Ashton Nude with Heart-Shaped Box of Chocolates* is an exception. Whereas Unwerth's pictures of women are very sexy, because her female subjects enjoy playing to her camera, this boy models without enthusiasm, his face studiously expressionless; nor is there any suggestion of the camera's caressing him.

When the female artist contemplates the male body, her attitude is unlikely to be simply and joyously celebratory. If, as I have argued, art is fundamentally narcissistic and elegiac, the female artist could only celebrate herself when young by painting and photographing younger women. Indeed, there is plenty of evidence of female artists doing exactly and exclusively that. When the body a woman artist is contemplating is so obviously other, so obviously not and never hers, because it is male, her approach is necessarily conflicted, even confrontational. Simple sensuality is able to function as a medium through which to see and celebrate the child but not, it seems, the man. The boy is the forgotten middle term. The boy Eros would bring the sexes to a reconciliation, if we would only acknowledge him.

Notes

Proem

p. 8 Idolino Florence, Museo Nazionale Archeologico; **Spinario** a life-size Roman bronze of the first century BCE of a nude boy seated, removing a thorn from his foot, known to collectors since the twelfth century, drawn from every angle and copied by hundreds of artists. Isabella d'Este commissioned a small bronze copy of it from Antico. Tourists returning from Rome brought back commercially produced souvenir copies; **Frederic, Lord Leighton,** *The Sluggard* a life-size bronze figure of a boy stretching, made by Leighton in 1885 in collaboration with the sculptor Henry Brock, now at Tate Britain; **Hamo Thornycroft,** *Teucer* a life-size bronze figure of an archer nude except for a maple leaf, exhibited at the London Royal Academy in 1882, and issued as a limited edition bronze statuette in 1889. It became the trademark of the Tate & Lyle sugar company.

p. 10 A nude boy called Eros In fact, the figure on top of Alfred Gilbert's Shaftesbury Memorial Fountain (1893) was meant to be Eros's alter ego Anteros, interpreted variously as the personification of love, of fame or spiritual love.

1. What is a Boy?

p. 13 rites of passage Bruno Bettelheim, *Symbolic Wounds: Puberty Rites and the Envious Male* (New York, Collier Books, 1955); M. Eliade, *Rites and Symbols of Initiation* (New York, Harper Torchbooks, 1958); Arnold van Gennep, *Rites of Passage*, trans. Monika B. Vizedom and Gabrielle L. Caffe (Chicago IL, University of Chicago Press, 1960); F. W. Young, *Initiation Ceremonies: A Cross-Cultural Study of Status Dramatization* (Indianapolis IN, Bobbs-Merrill, 1965); J. Money and A. Ehrhardt, *Man and Woman, Boy and Girl: Gender Identity from Conception to Maturity* (Baltimore MD, Johns Hopkins University Press, 1972); G. Bleibtreu-Ehrenberg, *Mannbarkeitsriten* (Vienna, Ullstein Materialen, 1980)

p. 16 the Three Ages of Man is the subject of works by Boccaccino (Venice, Accademia), Baccio Bandinelli, Parmigianino, Tobias Stimmer, Baron Gérard (*Les Trois Ages*, Galérie Lithographique de son Altesse Royale Monseigneur le Duc d'Orléans, 1830?, 22), and even Picasso (1942); **Xenophon,** *Cyropedia* I, ii. 4, trans. Walter Miller, *Xenophon in Seven Volumes*, v (London and Cambridge MA, Heinemann and Harvard University Press, 1968)

p. 18 personification of Flora see also Van Dyck, *The Ages of Man*, *c.* 1625 (Vicenza, Museo Storico d' Arte e Storia, Inv. No. A 228), in which an infant, a soldier and an old man are joined by a female figure offering roses. In 1665 this painting was referred to in the inventory of the collection of the Duke of Mantua as 'le quattro età'.

p. 20 Prince Hal Shakespeare, *Henry IV*, Part I, *passim*

p. 21 'shades of the prison-house' from William Wordsworth, 'Ode: Intimations of Immortality from Recollections of Early Childhood', *Poems in Two Volumes*, 1807; **'Danger lies in transitional states'** Mary Douglas, *Purity and Danger: An Analysis of the Concepts of Pollution and Taboo* (London and New York, Routledge, 1988), 96; **R. W. Connell** *Masculinities* (Cambridge, Polity Press, 1995), 93–119

p. 22 Daniel Levinson *The Seasons of a Man's Life* (New York, Knopf, 1978), 21, cf. Y. A. Cohen, *The Transition from Childhood to Adolescence* (Chicago IL, Aldine Publishing Co., 1964), *passim*; **Vasari on Raphael** *Lives of the Artists: A Selection Translated by George Bull* (Harmondsworth, Penguin, 1987), I, 292, 312; **the allegory of prudence** the most famous example is by Titian (London, National Gallery, NG 6376)

p. 27 Van Dyck self-portraits 1613–14 (Vienna, Gemäldegalerie der Akademie der bildenden Künste, Inv. 686), cf. Rubens, *Antonis van Dyck* (Antwerp, Rubenshuis); 1617–18? (Munich, Alte Pinakothek); 1620–21 (New York, Metropolitan Museum of Art); **'While he seeks…'** Ovid, *Metamorphoses*, iii, 415–26, trans. Frank Justus Miller (London and Cambridge MA, Heinemann and Harvard University Press, 1984), i, 153–5

p. 29 Old French metrical romance *Narcisse: Conte ovidien français du XIIe siècle*, ed. Martine Thiry-Stassin and Madeleine Tyssens (Paris, Les Belles Lettres, 1976); *Three Ovidian Tales of Love*, ed. and trans. Raymond Cormier (New York and London, Garland, 1986); **Guillaume de Lorris, Boccaccio, Christine de Pizan, Alamanni, Jean Rus, Ronsard, Gregorio Silvestre Rodriquez de Mesa** see Louise Vinge, *The Narcissus Theme in Western European Literature up to the Early 19th Century* (Lund, Gleerups, 1967); *passim*; **Narcissus images** Boltraffio, 1516 (Florence, Uffizi, inv. 2184; London, National Gallery NG2673), Rosso Fiorentino, 1531–2 (now lost, known only from copies and engravings), Caravaggio, 1598–9 (Rome, Galleria Nazionale d'Arte Antica), Tintoretto (Rome, Galleria Colonna, inv. 70), Bacchiacca (Florence, Palazzo Corsini), Domenichino (Palazzo Farnese, Loggia del Giardino), follower of Rubens, 1636–8 (Madrid, Prado, inv. 1465), François Lemoyne, 1728 (Paris, Louvre, on loan), J. M. W. Turner, 1804 (Petworth House), John Gibson, 1846 (London, Victoria and Albert Museum), Paul Dubois, 1863 (Paris, Musée d'Orsay), Jehan Georges Vibert, 1864 (Bordeaux, Musée des Beaux-Arts), John William Waterhouse, 1903 (Liverpool, Walker Art Gallery, inv. no 2967), Salvador Dalí, Sydney Nolan (Adelaide, Art Gallery of South Australia)

p. 30 sexual experiences with males Judith Stevens-Long and Nancy J. Cobb, *Adolescence and Early Adulthood* (Palo Alto CA, Mayfield Publishing Co., 1983), 111–12; **Emperor Nero** Suetonius, *The Lives of the Caesars*, vi, 12; Tacitus, *Annals*, xiv, xv; **groups in the New Guinea Highlands** Gilbert H. Herdt, *Guardians of the Flutes: Idioms of Masculinity* (New York, McGraw-Hill, 1981), *Sambia Sexual Culture: Essays from the Field* (Chicago IL, University of Chicago Press, 1999); Raymond C. Kelly, 'Witchcraft and Sexual Relations: An Exploration in the Social and Semantic Implications of the Structure of Belief', *Man and Woman in the New Guinea Highlands*, ed. P. Brown and G. Buchbinder (Washington DC, American Anthropological Association, 1976), 16; D. L. Newman and D. Boyd, 'The Making of Men: Ritual and Meaning in Awa Male Initiation', *Rituals of Manhood: Male Initiation in Papua New Guinea*, ed. Gilbert H. Herdt (Berkeley CA, University of California Press, 1982), 283–4

p. 31 'While it is true…' *The Sexuality of Men*, ed. Andy Metcalf and Martin Humphries (London, Pluto Press, 1985)

p. 33 'Males start as FFs…' Joseph H. Pleck, 'The Theory of Male Sex-Role Identity: Its Rise and Fall, 1936 to the Present', *The Making of Masculinities: The New Men's Studies*, ed. Harry Brod (Boston, Allen and Unwin, 1987)

2. The Boy is Beautiful

p. 37 'the far-shooter…' *The Greek Anthology*, ii, 266–70, trans. W. Paton (London and Cambridge MA, Heinemann and Harvard University Press, 1969), i, 79; **'Apollo knoweth…'** ibid., ii, 74–7, i, 65

p. 39 Kenneth Clark *The Nude: A Study of Ideal Art* (London, John Murray, 1956), cf. A. Lawrence, *Greek and Roman Sculpture* (London, Jonathan Cape, 1972) 261

p. 41 Guy Dickins *Hellenistic Sculpture* (Oxford, Clarendon Press, 1920), 70; **A. W. Lawrence** *Greek and Roman Sculpture* (originally published as *Classical Sculpture* in 1929; London, Jonathan Cape, 1972), 261; **Turner drawings of the Belvedere Apollo** Tate Britain, Turner Collection, D00056, D00057, D00058, D40216; **Michelangelo drawing** Paris, Louvre, R. F. 70–1068, recto; **Raphael, Vasari, Sansovino and Dürer** P. P. Bober and R. Rubinstein, *Renaissance Artists and Antique Sculpture: A Handbook of Sources* (London, Harvey Miller, 1986), 71–2; Goethe Propyläen, 11. 11. 1799, Letter v. He remained of this opinion all his life; see his letter of 23 May 1817 to Karl August, Duke of Weimar

p. 43 Winckelmann *Writings on Art*, selected and ed. D. Irwin (London, Phaidon, 1972)

p. 44 Marsyas as man rather than satyr Edith Wyss, *The Myth of Apollo and Marsyas in the Art of the Italian Renaissance: An Inquiry into the Meaning of Images* (Newark NJ, University of Delaware Press, 1996), 25; **Apollo and Marsyas** are depicted also in works by Raphael, 1508 (Vatican, Stanza della Segnatura), Baldassare Peruzzi, 1511–12 (Rome, Villa Farnesina), Michelangelo Anselmi, *c.* 1515 (Washington, National Gallery of Art), Raphael and others, 1519 (Vatican, Loggetta), Giulio Romano, 1527–8 (Mantua, Palazzo del Te), Tintoretto, *c.* 1541 (Modena, Galleria Estense), *c.* 1543 (Padua, Museo Civico, inv. No 2809), *c.* 1544 (Hartford CT, Wadsworth Museum, inv. No. 1950.438), Luca Cambiaso, 1544 (Genoa, Palazzo Doria), Titian, 1570–75 (Kremsier, Archiepiscopal Palace), Palma Giovane, 1610–15 (Brunswick, Herzog Anton Ulrich-Museum), Domenichino, 1616–18 (London, National Gallery, NG 6288), Guercino, 1618 (Florence, Palazzo Pitti), Guido Reni, 1618–19 (Toulouse, Musée des Augustins, much copied), Jacob Jordaens, *c.* 1620 (Antwerp, Huis Osterrieth), Johan Liss, *c.* 1622 (Moscow, Pushkin Museum; another Venice, Accademia), Giovanni di San Giovanni, *c.* 1630 (Florence, Villa del Pozzino), Luca Giordano (Florence, Museo Bardini; Boston CT, Atheneum; Moscow, Pushkin Museum, inv. No. 213), Velasquez, *c.* 1659 (destroyed), Sebastiano Ricci, 1685–7 (Milan, Algranti Collection), Filippo Lauri (Paris, Louvre, inv. 337), Pierre Mignard (Paris, Hôtel d'Armenonville), Tiepolo, 1720–22 (Vicenza, Conte da Schio Collection)

p. 46 'He is supposed to have…' 'Sir Joshua Reynolds, Discourse x', *Discourses on Art*, ed. Robert R. Wark (San Marino CA, Huntington Library, 1959), 179–80; **Sir Joshua Reynolds,** *Commodore the Hon. Augustus Keppel* (London, National Maritime Museum, BHC 2823); **Sir Joshua Reynolds,** *Omai* exhibited at the Royal Academy in 1776, bought for the Castle Howard collection from Reynolds's studio sale, lot 12 in Sotheby's sale of 20 November 2001; **'That it turned out…'** David Mannings, *Reynolds*, ed. Nicholas Penny (London, Weidenfeld and Nicolson, 1986), 181

p. 47 F. G. Stephens *English Children as painted by Sir Joshua Reynolds: an essay on some of the characteristics of Reynolds as a designer, with special reference to his portraiture of children* (London, 1867), 7–8

p. 48 Charles Lawes obituary, *The Times*, 7 October 1911

p. 49 Ben Jonson 'Her Man described by her own Dictamen', first published in *Underwoods consisting of divers Poems* (London, 1640), text modernized by the present author; **Aphra Behn** 'In Imitation of Horace', *Poems on Several Occasions* (London, 1684), text modernized by the present author

p. 50 Lady Mary Wortley Montagu *Poetical Works of the Right Honourable the Lady M——y W———y M———e* (London, 1768), text modernized by the present author

p. 51 Lucian, *Erotes* Lucian with an English Translation by M. D. Macleod (London, Heinemann, 1967), 9

3. Love is a Boy

p. 59 some among the Ancients Robert Graves, *The Greek Myths* (Harmondsworth, Penguin, 1955), i, 58–9; Timothy Gantz, *Early Greek Myth: A Guide to Literary and Artistic Sources* (Baltimore MD and London, Johns Hopkins University Press, 1993), 3–4

p. 62 Vasari *Lives of the Artists: A Selection Translated by George Bull* (Harmondsworth, Penguin, 1987), ii, 194–5; **assumed to be a girl** as for example in the entry on Parmigianino's painting on the website of the Vienna Kunsthistorisches Museum; 'He is a notable lad…' *The Greek Bucolic Poets* (Cambridge MA and London, Harvard University Press and Heinemann, 1960), 423; **'a wild boy…'** Robert Graves, *Greek Myths* (London, Cassell, 1958), 58; **Michelangelo's design for a Venus and Cupid** the cartoon in the Farnese Collection (Naples, Capodimonte) is thought by some to be Michelangelo's original. Besides the Uffizi painting

of the design attributed to Pontormo there is another in the Farnese Collection, which was once thought to be by Bronzino, but has been recently credited to Hendrick van den Broek; another (Rome, Galleria Colonna) is credited to Michele di Ridolfo del Ghirlandaio. Further copies by Salviati, Venusti and Vasari (in the collection of H. M. the Queen) are recorded. See also *Venus and Love: Michelangelo and the New Ideal of Beauty*, ed. Franco Falletti and Jonathan Katz Nelson (Florence, Giunti for Florence Museums, 2002)
p. 63 'The little Cupid has already attacked…' Charles De Tolnay, *Michelangelo III: The Medici Chapel* (Princeton, 1948), 108
p. 64 Cartari Vincenzo Cartari, *Le Imagini, con la Spositione de i Dei degli Antichi* (Venice, 1556), 515; **Ovid** *Metamorphoses*, x, 525–8
p. 69 Lo Scarsellino *Cupid with the Attributes of the Arts* exhibited at the Walpole Gallery in 1991 (*The Cinquecento*); **Riminaldi** *Amor Vincit Omnia* (Dublin, National Gallery of Ireland; Florence, Palazzo Pitti; two at Christie's, 19 March 1965, lot 57, and 9 December 1994, lot 346)
p. 71 Chaucer's squire *The Canterbury Tales*, 'Prologue', ll. 79–100
p. 72 Shakespeare's Rosalind *As You Like It*, III, ii, ll. 397–402; **Elizabeth Sargent** 'A Young Lover', *Love Poems of Elizabeth Sargent* (New York, Signet, 1966), [5]
p. 73 'What is the day for?' '*Für was ist der Tag?*' from Act I of Richard Strauss's opera *Der Rosenkavalier*, libretto by Hugo von Hofmannsthal, first performed in 1911
p. 74 'I gazed at her…' Gustave Flaubert, *Memoirs of a Madman*, trans. Andrew Brown (London, Hesperus Press, 2002), 31
p. 76 'From behind she wrapped me…' Bernhard Schlink, *The Reader*, trans. Carol Brown Janeway (London, Phoenix House, 1997), 23; **'The next night…'** ibid., 25
p. 77 '[T]he diary finishes…' Milan Kundera, *Ignorance: A Novel*, trans. from the French by Linda Asher (London, Faber and Faber, 2002), 87

4. The Castration of Cupid
p. 79 Mournful Erotes Schauenburg and Strocka, *Die Antiken Sarkophagreliefs*, v, 2, *Die Erotensakophage*; **A fragment attributed to Sappho** Fragment 194; **raucous and cruel** *Dionysiaca*, 42, 370; **'She quickly sent…'** Apuleius, *Metamorphoses*, iv, 30, ed. and trans. J. Arthur Hanson (Cambridge MA and London, Harvard University Press, 1989), i, 241
p. 80 Erich Neumann *Amor and Psyche: The Psychic Development of the Feminine; a commentary on the tale by Apuleius* trans. from the German by Ralph Manheim (London, Routledge and Kegan Paul, 1956), 143, 147–8, 153–61
p. 81 'Your womb, still a child's…' Apuleius, *Metamorphoses*, v, 11, ed. and trans. J. Arthur Hanson (Cambridge MA and London, Harvard University Press, 1989), i, 273; **'At your age…'** ibid., iv, 30, i, 305; **Hugh Douglas Hamilton** *Cupid and Psyche in the Nuptial Bower* (Dublin, National Gallery of Ireland, No. 1342); **Romney** cartoon for cycle (Liverpool, Walker Art Gallery); **Bouguereau**, tondo, also *The Abduction of Psyche* (private collection); **Burne-Jones**, illustrations for William Morris, *The Earthly Paradise*, *c.* 1868; **Rodin, *Cupid and Psyche*** plaster model in Paris, Musée Rodin; **Raphael, *Jupiter Kissing Cupid*** drawing, 1517–18 (Paris, Louvre); **Rubens, *Mercury Bearing Psyche to Olympus*** 1625–8 (Mertoun House, Collection of the Duke of Sutherland)
p. 82 Schiavone, *Marriage of Cupid and Psyche* New York, Metropolitan Museum of Art, 1973.116; **Batoni**'s *Venus and Cupid* (Dublin, National Gallery of Ireland, No. 704) shows a Cupid as a plump toddler kissing his mother (if it is his mother and not Psyche) full on the lips
p. 85 growing importance of homosociality see, for example, Abigail Solomon-Godeau, *Male Trouble: A Crisis in Representation* (London, Thames & Hudson, 1997), Chapter 2, 'The Body Politics of Homosociality', *passim*
p. 86 Julia Margaret Cameron see note by Virginia Dodier in *Exposed: The Victorian Nude*, ed. Alison Smith (Tate Britain Exhibition Catalogue, 2001), Cat. No. 86
p. 89 Amor Virtutis Alciati, *Emblems* 110, 111; **Eros and Anteros fighting** Vincenzo Cartari, *Le Imagini, con la Spositione de i Dei degli Antichi* (Venice, 1556)
p. 91 Reni oil sketch Rome, Pinacoteca Capitolina, see Richard E. Spear, *The 'Divine' Guido: Religion, Sex, Money and Art in the World of Guido Reni* (New Haven and London, Yale University Press, 1997), 315; **Hypnos** Ovid, *Metamorphoses*, ix, 592; **Emperor Antoninus Pius** Penelope Davies, *Death and the Emperor: Roman Imperial Funerary Monuments from Augustus to Marcus Aurelius* (Cambridge, Cambridge University Press, 2001)
p. 95 St Michael other well-known examples include Domenico Beccafumi, *c.* 1545 (Siena, Pinacoteca Nazionale) and Luca Giordano, 1666 (Vienna, Kunsthistorisches Museum; also Berlin, Gemäldegalerie, inv. KFMV 261)
p. 96 Piero della Francesca's angels see *The Baptism of Christ* (London, National Gallery), *Madonna del Parto* (Monterchi, Cappella del Cimitero), *Madonna di Senigallia* (Urbino, Galleria Nazionale delle Marche); **Piero's Nativity** London, National Gallery; **Giovanni Bellini, *Dead Christ*, 1460** Venice, Civico Museo Correr, **1470** Rimini, Pinacoteca Comunale; **Bishop Theodore** Arnold Toynbee, *The Crucible of Christianity: Judaism, Hellenism and the Historical Background to the Christian Faith* (New York and Cleveland, World Pub Co, 1969), 188
p. 97 Giovanni Girolamo Savoldo, *Tobias and the Angel* Rome, Galleria Borghese; **Raphael's *Lapidation of Saint Stephen*** the bozzetto has perished; a copy by an unknown seventeenth-century hand is at the Ecole des Beaux-Arts, Paris; **Lo Schiavone** Belluno, Church of San Pietro; **Lot and his daughters** e.g. Alessandro Turchi, *An Angel Leading Lot and his Daughters* (Dublin, National Gallery of Ireland, No. 1653), Veronese; **St Cecilia** e.g. Carlo Saraceni
p. 98 Annibale Carracci, *Angelo Custode* Rome, Galleria Nazionale d'Arte Antica, cf. Filippo Tarchiari (Florence, San Vito a Bellosguardo), Marcantonio Franceschini (London, Dulwich Picture Gallery, Inv. 313), Giambattista Tiepolo, 1737 (Udine, Museo Civico)
p. 102 genii of all kinds e.g. Annibale Carracci, *Il Genio di Fama*, Pompeo Batoni, *Le Arti e il Genio*, *c.* 1740 (Sotheby's, Milan, 2 December 2002), Jean-Baptiste Stouf, Projet d'un Monument à Jean-Jacques Rousseau, 1791 (Paris, Musée des Arts Décoratifs, Inv. 792), Réattu, *Le Triomphe de la République*, 1994 (Arles, Musée Réattu), Pierre Petitot, *Le Génie de la Victoire*, 1799 (Langres, Musées, Inv. 864-4-1), Pierre Peyron, 'Le Génie de l'Histoire' in *Le Temps et Minerve qui n'accordent l'Immortalité qu'à ceux qui ont bien mérité de leur Patrie*, 1799; **genii of Anton Raphael Mengs** e.g. Madrid, Palacio Reale; Rome, Villa Albani; Vatican, Camera dei Papiri; **Jean-Antoine Houdon** Paul Vitry, '*Le Morphée* de Houdon', *Revue de l'Art Ancien et Moderne*, 1907, I, 149–56; Marguerite Charageat, '*Le Sommeil*, étude de Houdon en vue de son morceau de réception a l'Académie', *Musée de France*, June 1950; Louis Réau, *Houdon*, Paris, 1964, I, 42, 43, 99, 148, 155, 156, 178, 220–3, 487, 488 and ii, Plates ix and xi; **Zauner, *Genio Bornii*** Vienna, Belvedere Museum, cf. his Monument to Joseph II; **Canova, tomb of Pope Clement XIII** Vatican City, St Peter's; the tomb he sculpted for Maria Christina (1798–1805) is surmounted by a more woe-begone version of the same naked winged boy; **Regnault, *La Liberté ou la Mort*** Hamburg, Kunsthalle, inv. 510

5. The Passive Love Object
p. 105 Rochester's 'Platonick lady' John Wilmot, 2nd Earl of Rochester, 'The Platonick Lady', first printed from manuscript in John Hayward's edition of 1926 (142), ll. 13–15; **Juan's adventures begin** George, Lord Byron, *Don Juan*, Canto i; **cast up naked…** ibid., Canto ii, *passim*
p. 109 type of Sleeping Cupid e.g. bronze, possibly by Boethus, third century BCE (New York, Metropolitan Museum of Art)
p. 110 Cupid with poppies e.g. Venice, Museo Archeologico, Inv. No. 88; Florence, Uffizi; Corsham Court, Collection of Lord Methuen; **Michelangelo's *Sleeping Cupid*** *Vasari, Lives of the Artists: A Selection Translated by George Bull* (Harmondsworth, Penguin, 1987), i, 334. A sketch of Michelangelo's lost sculpture is in the Royal Collection at Windsor; **Cupid in pose of Barberini Faun** e.g. Sleeping Cupid, marble, Roman, 50–100 CE (Malibu CA, Getty Museum, Inv. 73. AA. 95); Box and Cover with the Sleeping Eros, 4th century, Byzantine (New York, Metropolitan Museum of Art, Inv. 47. 100. 33); **Caravaggio, *Sleeping Cupid*** Florence, Palazzo Pitti; ***Sleeping Cupid on the Island of Cyprus*** variously attributed to Orazio Riminaldi, Sisto Badalocchio and Guido Reni (!)
p. 112 Endymion Ovid, *Heroides*, xviii, 61–5, *Ars Amatoria*, iii, 83; Lucian, *Deorum Dialogi*, xix; Apollodorus Rhodius, *Argonautica*, iv, 54 ff.; Cicero,*Tusculan Disputations*, I, xxxviii, 92; *Natali Conti, Natalis Comitis Mythologiae* (1551), iv, 222; Vincenzo Cartari, *Le Imagini, con la Spositione de i Dei degli Antichi* (Venice, 1556), 84–6
p. 113 Benedetto Cariteo 'Endimione a la Luna', *Libro di Sonetti e Canzone* (Naples, 1506); **Pinturicchio** fresco, 1503–8 (Siena, Duomo, Piccolomini Library); **Cima da Conegliano** *Endymion Asleep*, 1505–10 (Parma, Galleria Nazionale, inv. 370); **Baldassare Peruzzi** fresco, 1511–12 (Rome, Villa Farnesina, Sala delle Prospettive) and painting (Siena, Chigi-Saracini Collection), **Titian** *c.* 1520 (PA, Barnes Collection), **Carpaccio** (formerly London, Sulley Collection), **Parmigianino** (Pittsburgh, Frick Art Museum), **Giulio Romano** (Budapest, Szépmüvészeti Múzeum, inv. 171), **il Garofalo** (Dresden, Gemäldegalerie, inv. 139), **Jacopo Zucchi** 1572 (Florence, Uffizi, Sala delle Carte Geografiche), **Tintoretto** Dublin, National Gallery of Ireland, inv. 768, and Florence, Palazzo Pitti, Contini-Bonaccossi Collection, no. 34
p. 114 'For this boy's love…' *Poems of Michael Drayton*, ed. John Buxton (London, Routledge and Kegan Paul, 1953), 23, ll. 89–92; **Gombauld and Marie de Médicis** Tallemand des Réaux, *Historiettes*, ed. Adam (Paris, 1960), vol. i, pp. 553–6; **Gaspar de Aguilar** *La fabula de Endimeon y la luna*; **Marcelo Díaz Calcerrada** *Endimión*, 1627; **Monteverdi** *Gli amori di Diana e di Endimione*, 1628; **Lully** *Les amours de Diane et d'Endimion*, 1656; **Gaetano Vestris**'s ballet *Endymion* was premiered in Italy in 1773, **Auguste Vestris**'s *Diane et Endymion* in France. In 1949 Serge Lifar premiered his *Endymion* at the Paris Opera; **Annibale Carracci** 1597–1600 (Rome, Palazzo Farnese, Galleria), **Domenichino** and studio, 1609 (Bassano di Sutri, Palazzo Giustiniani-Odescalchi), **lo Scarsellino** (Rome, Galleria Borghese, inv. 214), **Van Dyck** 1622–8 (Madrid, Prado, inv. 1492), **Poussin** *c.* 1630 (Detroit IL, Institute of Arts), **Rubens** 1636–8 (Torre de la Parada, El Pardo, lost), **Guercino** 1644–7 (Rome, Galeria Doria-Pamphili, also Florence, Uffizi, inv. 1461), **Francesco Albani** (Oxford, Ashmolean Museum), **Pietro da Cortona** (Swansea, Glynn Vivian Art Gallery), **Luca Giordano** (Verona, Museo di Castelvecchio, inv. 2679, also New York, R. Manning Collection and Gatchina Castle), **Boucher** three times, 1729 (lost), 1765 (Washington, National Gallery of Art), 1769 (Malibu CA, Getty Museum), **Van Loo** 1731 (Paris, Louvre, inv. 6249 and Brussels, Museé d'Art Ancien, inv. 296), **Mengs** 1758–60 (Rome, Villa Albani). To these may be added Pier Francesco Mola, *c.* 1660 (Rome, Pinacoteca Capitolina), Luca Giordano, 1675–80, Johan Michael Rottmayr, 1690–95 (Chicago, Art Institute, Inv. 1961.38), Gianantonio Pellegrini, 1720 (Paris, Louvre), Charles-Antoine Coypel, 1720s, Jean-Honoré Fragonard, 1753–5, Louis Lagrenée 1768, Angelika Kauffmann (St Petersburg, Peterhof); **Gavin Hamilton** London, British Museum; **Roman relief** Rome, Museo Capitolino; **Keats** D. Robinson, 'A Question of the Imprint of Wedgwood in the Longer Poems of Keats', *Sixth Wedgwood International Seminar*, San Francisco, 1961, 104; **Endymion after Girodet** e.g. Jerome Martin Langlois, 1815 (engraved by C. Muller), Louis Edouard Rioult, 1822, John Wood, 1833 (London, Dulwich Picture Gallery, inv. 453), Sir Noel Paton, *A Dream of Latmos*, 1865, Edward J. Pointer, 1901 (twice, both in Manchester, City Art Gallery), Henri Fantin-Latour, twice, 1903, 1904, Waterhouse, Simeon Solomon, 1887 (Birmingham Museums and Art Gallery)
p. 115 George Frederick Watts 1873 (Glenconner Collection), 1903 (Compton, Watts Gallery); **Anchises** *Homeric Hymn to Aphrodite*, 45–2000; Theocritus, *Idylls*, i. 105–7; Hyginus, *Fabula* 94; Servius on Virgil's *Aeneid*, ii. 649; **'A dainty boy…'** Phineas Fletcher, *Venus and Anchises: Brittain's Ida*, first published in 1633, *Elizabethan Minor Epics*, ed. E. Story Donno (London, Routledge and Kegan Paul, 1963), 309, text modernized by the present author
p. 116 Phrixus Pausanias, i. 44; ix. 34, 4–5 and 23. 3; Apollodorus, i. 7. 3 and iii. 4. 3; Hyginus, *Fabulae* 2 and 4

and *Poetic Astronomy*, ii. 20; Sophocles, fragments of *Athamas*; Nonnus, *Dionysiaca*, x. 1 ff.; Scholiast and Eustathius on Homer's *Iliad*, vii. 86
p. 117 Bellerophon Homer, *Iliad*, vi. 160, xvi. 328 ff.; Eustathius on *Iliad*, vi. 160; Apollodorus, ii. 3. 1; Antonius Liberalis, 9; **Peleus** Pindar, *Nemean Odes*, v. 26 ff. and iv. 59; Scholiast on the above; Zenobius, *Proverbs*, v. 20; Apollodorus, iii. 12. 7; **Tenes** Apollodorus, *Epitome*, iii. 25; Pausanias x. 14. 2; Tzetzes, *On Lycophron*, 232–3
p. 118 'It was then…' Ovid, *Heroides*, iv, 69–74, trans. Grant Showerman, *Ovid: Heroides and Amores* (Cambridge MA and London, Harvard University Press and Heinemann, 1986), 49
p. 119 '… the boy blushed…' Ovid, *Metamorphoses*, iv, 329–36, trans. Frank Justus Miller (London and Cambridge MA, Heinemann and Harvard University Press, 1984), i, 201–3; **'Then quickly, charmed…'** ibid., iv. 344–51, i, 203; **Eos** Apollodorus, i. 4. 4, iii. 12. 4; Homer, *Odyssey*, xv. 250; Hesiod, *Theogony*, 378–82, 984; Scholiast on Apollonius Rhodius, iii. 15; *Homeric Hymn to Aphrodite*, 218–38; Horace, *Odes*, iii. 20; Ovid, *Fasti*, i. 461
p. 120 Rubens projected decoration for the Torre de la Parada, *c.* 1637 (London, National Gallery, NG 2598); **Boucher** 1733 (London, National Gallery); **Francesco Furini** *c.* 1628 (Ponce, Museo de Arte); also Pierre-Narcisse Guérin, 1810 (Paris, Louvre; also studies in Valenciennes, Musée des Beaux-Arts). A year later, Guérin painted a related subject, *The Goddess Iris Gazing on the Beauty of Morpheus Asleep* (St Petersburg, Hermitage). Also Pierre Claude François Delorme, 1822 (Sens, Musée Municipal); **Flaxman** David Irwin, *John Flaxman 1755–1826: Sculptor, Illustrator, Designer* (London, Studio Vista, 1979), 54, fig. 65; **Adonis as willing lover** Hyginus, *Fabulae* 58, 164, 251; Fulgentius, *Mythology*, III, 8; as depicted by Raphael, 1516, Titian, Tintoretto, Veronese, Luca Cambiaso (Naples, Capodimonte), Rubens (New York, Metropolitan Museum of Art), Ludovico Carracci, Joseph Heintz (Vienna, Kunsthistorisches Museum), Abraham Janssens (Vienna, Kunsthistorisches Museum), Francis Le Moyne, 1729, Canova
p. 122 'Thrice fairer than myself…' Shakespeare, *Venus and Adonis*, ll. 7–10, 17–18; **'Over one arm…'** ibid., ll. 25–30
p. 123 'The tender spring…' ibid., ll. 127–8; **'He now obeys…'** ibid., ll. 563–4; **Leighton, *The Fisherman and the Syren*** Alison Smith, *Exposed: The Victorian Nude*, ed. Alison Smith (Tate Britain Exhibition Catalogue, 2001), 67
p. 125 Burne-Jones, *Phyllis and Demophoön* Robert Upstone in *Exposed: The Victorian Nude*, ed. Alison Smith (Tate Britain Exhibition Catalogue, 2001), 142

6. Play Boys
p. 127 Dionysos myths Robert Graves, *The Greek Myths* (Harmondsworth, Penguin, 1955), i, 103–11
p. 128 'from Lydia…' *The Bacchae*, trans. William Arrowsmith, *Euripides V, The Complete Greek Tragedies*, ed. David Grene and Richmond Lattimore (Chicago IL, University of Chicago Press, 1959), 234–9, op. cit.
p. 129 '… the music was now brutally loud…' Bill Buford, *Among the Thugs* (London, Secker and Warburg, 1991), 155
p. 130 'Thousands of boys…' R. Baden-Powell, *Scouting for Boys: A Handbook for Instruction in Good Citizenship* (London, Horace Cox, 1908); **Michelangelo, *Bacchus*** Florence, Bargello
p. 131 Pedro Montoya F. Trinchieri Camiz, 'The Castrato Singer: From Informal to Formal Portraiture', *Artibus et Historiae*, 18, 1988, 171–6; ***The Lute-player*** Caravaggio's autograph original is at present on loan to the Metropolitan Museum of Art, New York; a variant is in the Hermitage
p. 133 Hermes as inventor of the lyre and pan-pipes Robert Graves, *The Greek Myths* (Harmondsworth, Penguin, 1955), i, 64–5; **Pan as re-inventor of pan-pipes** Lucian, *Dialogues of the Gods*, xxii, 4; Ovid, *Metamorphoses*, i, 694–712; **Daphnis** Diodorus Siculus, iv, 84; Servius on Virgil's *Eclogues*, v, 20, viii, 68, x, 26; Aelian, *Varia Historia*, x, 18; **Orpheus** Pindar, *Pythian Odes*, lv, 176; Aeschylus, *Agamemnon* 1629–30; Euripides, *Bacchae*, 561–4; Apollonius Rhodius, i, 28–31, Plato, *Symposium*, Diodorus Siculus, *Biblioteca*, 4. 25. 4, 81–2; Virgil, *Georgics*, iv, 315–558; Ovid, *Metamorphoses*, x, 1–85; Hyginus, *Poetica Astronomica*, ii. 7; **Argonauts saved by Orpheus's music** once from the moving rocks at the entrance to the Bosphorus known as the Symplegades and once from the Sirens; Pausanias ix. 34. 2; Strabo, vi. 1, 1; *Argonautica Orphica*, 1270–97; Hyginus, *Fabula* 164; Diodorus Siculus, iv, 25; Pausanius 9, 30–3; Virgil, *Georgics*, iv; Ovid, *Metamorphoses* x-xi; **moralizing literature** Boethius, *De Consolatione*, III, xii; Fulgentius, *The Mythographer*, 3, x; Dante, *Convivio*, Trattato II, Cap. I, i; Boccaccio, *Geneologie Deorum Gentilium*, v, 12. See *Orpheus: The Metamorphoses of a Myth*, ed. J. Warden (Toronto, University of Toronto Press, 1982) and J. B. Friedman, *Orpheus in the Middle Ages* (Cambridge MA, Harvard University Press, 1970); **Orpheus's head** Odilon Redon, *Head of Orpheus Floating on the Waters*, J. W. Waterhouse, *Nymphs Finding the Head of Orpheus*, Jean Delville
p. 134 Politian *La Fabula d'Orfeo*, different musical entertainments performed in Mantua, 1471–2, 1480, text printed 1494; **Orpheus frescoes: Mantegna** 1468–74 (Mantua, Palazzo Ducale, Camera degli Sposi), **Signorelli** 1499–1503 (Orvieto, Duomo, Capella di San Brizio), **Baldassare Peruzzi** 1510–11 (Rome, Villa Farnesina, Sala di Galatea and Sala del Fregio), **Primaticcio** 1541–7 (Château de Fontainebleau, Galerie d'Ulysse, destroyed); **Orpheus paintings** e.g. Giovanni Bellini, *c.* 1510 (Washington DC, National Gallery of Art, Inv. No. 598), Andrea Schiavone, 1550s (Split, Galleria Unijetnina), Frans Pourbus the Elder, 1570 (Florence, Uffizi, inv. 5409), after Jan Breughel the Elder (Rome, Galleria Borghese; Ipswich, Museum and Art Galleries; Sarasota FL, Ringling Museum, inv. SN231), Leandro or Jacopo Bassano (Verona, Palazzo Canova, much copied, imitated), Gillis Claes de Hondecoeter, 1624 (Utrecht, Centraal Museum, also Otterloo, Rijksmuseum Kroller-Muller and Warsaw, Muzeum Narodowe), Roelandt Savery, 1610–28 (many versions), Rubens workshop, 1636–8 (El Pardo, Torre de la Parada), Il Padovanino (Madrid, Prado, inv. 266), Paulus Potter, 1650 (Amsterdam, Rijksmuseum), Gerrit van Honthorst (Naples, Palazzo Reale), Franz Wouters (St Petersburg, Hermitage), Jean-Baptiste Camille Corot (several times), Eugène Delacroix, 1838–47 (ceiling, Paris, Palais Bourbon, Chambre des Députés), 1845–7 (ceilings, Paris, Palais du Luxembourg, Senate Library), Pierre Puvis de Chavannes, Frans Marc, 1907 (Munich, Städtische Galerie in Lenbachhaus), Lovis Corinth, 1908 (Dresden, Gemäldegalerie), Raoul Dufy (several times), Marc Chagall (several times). This list does not contain the dozens of portraits of now unidentifiable young musicians in undress with their instruments that carry the title 'Orpheus' or 'Allegory of Music'; **Monteverdi, *L'Orfeo*** *Claudio Monteverdi: Orfeo*, ed. John Whenham (Cambridge Opera Handbooks, 1806); **hundreds of composers** including Thomas Campion, Johannes Staden, Antonio Draghi, Reinhard Keiser, François-Joseph de Lagrange-Chancel, Nicolas Racot de Grandval, Thomas Arne, François Lupien Grenet, Friedrich August Werthes, Carl Ditters von Dittersdorf, Vittorio Trento, Prosper-Didier Deshayes, Dmitri Bortnyansky, and so on; **Franz Liszt** *Orfeus. Symphonic Poem*, first performed in Weimar, 16 February 1854; **Kurt Weill** *Der Neue Orpheus, Cantata for soprano, violin and orchestra*, opus 15, first performed in Berlin, 2 March 1927; **Jean Cocteau** *Orphée. Tragedy*, 1925, *La Douleur d'Orphée* (sculpture), *Orphée* (ballet), 1944, lithographs, 1944, *Orphée* (screenplay), 1951, also paintings: mural, 1957–8 (Menton, Hôtel de Ville, Salle des Mariages), *Le Testament d'Orphée* (1959); **Arion** in Mantegna's decorations for the Camera degli Sposi in the ducal palace of Mantua he figures as a bearded older man. A drawing of Arion clinging to his dolphin attributed to Dürer shows him as a comely youth. See Elizabeth B. Welles, 'Orpheus and Arion as symbols of music in Mantegna's Camera degli Sposi', *Studies in Iconography*; **boy on a dolphin** denarii, L. Lucretius Trio (?) 300–225 BCE; the badge of Augustan Rome?
p. 136 Verrocchio (?) bronze *c.* 1470; **boys and dolphins** at the Human Dolphin Therapy Center in Miami, ailing humans are greatly helped, we are told, by swimming with dolphins; **Amphion** Homer, *Odyssey*, ii, 260–64; Pausanias, *Description of Greece*, 6. 20. 18, 9. 5. 7–8; Hesiod, fr. 182; Palaiphatos, fr. 41; Propertius, 1. 9.10; Horace, *Odes*, iii, 11.2; *Ars Poetica*, 394–6; Ovid, *Ars Amatoria*, iii, 323–4; Philostratus, *Imagines*, i. 10; Lucian, *Imagines*, 14; Apollodorus, *Biblioteca*, iii, 5. 5–6; *Scholium in Apollonium Rhodium vetera*, i, 740–41; Hyginus, *Fabulae* 7, 8, 9, 69. Amphion is the subject of musical works by Carlo Grossi, Jean-Claude Gillier, Paolo Magni, François Lupien Grenet, Jean-Benjamin de la Borde, Johann Gottlieb Naumann, Baldassare Galuppi, Friedrich Weis, Etienne Méhul, Claude Debussy, Arthur Somervell, Charles Ives, Pascual de Rogatis, Athur Honegger and Ian Hamilton
p. 137 dance see, for example, Peter Brinson, *Background to European Ballet: A Notebook from its Archives* (Leyden, A. W. Sijthoff, 1966)
p. 142 athletes Michael Messner, 'The Meaning of Success: The Athletic Experience and the Development of Male Identity', *The Making of Masculinities: The New Men's Studies*, ed. Harry Brod (Boston, Allen and Unwin, 1987), 199–202
p. 144 Michelangelo, *Bathers* depicts nude Florentine soldiers struggling into their armour after a swim: central section of a cartoon, *c.* 1504, now destroyed, for a fresco depicting the Battle of Cascina commissioned by the Signoria of Florence for the Sala del Gran Consiglio, Palazzo Vecchio; **Antonio Carracci, *Landscape with Bathers*** *c.* 1616 (oil version, Boston, Museum of Fine Arts; tempera, Florence, Galleria Palatina, Palazzo Pitti); **Frederick Walker, *The Bathers*** Port Sunlight, Lady Lever Art Gallery; **Seurat, *Bathers at Asnières*** 1884 (London, National Gallery, NG3908); **Henry Scott Tuke** *Studio*, 1895; *Artists of the Newlyn School 1880–1900* (Exhibition Catalogue, Newlyn Art Gallery, 1979), 132. Many of Tuke's studies are preserved in the Tuke Collection of the Royal Cornwall Polytechnic Society

7. Servant Boys
p. 147 Apollo and the horses of the sun Giulio Romano, stucco relief (Mantua, Palazzo Te, Camera delle Cariatidi) and drawing (Collection of the Duke of Devonshire, Chatsworth, 122)
p. 150 Pepys's first footboy, Will *Diary*, 28 and 30 August, 1 and 5 September, 1660; **'This morning…'** ibid., 22 September, 1660; **'So home and there…'** ibid., 7 June 1663; **pages of the Duke of Bedford** Gladys Scott Thomson, *Life in a Noble Household 1641–1700* (London, Jonathan Cape, 1950), 119; **Ganymede** Homer, *Iliad*, XX, 231–5; Apollodorus, III, 12:2; Virgil, *Aeneid*, v. 252 ff. The rape of Ganymede has been depicted by Berlin Painter, red-figure Attic krater, early 5th century BCE (Paris, Louvre), Correggio, *c.* 1530 *int. al.* (Vienna, Kunsthistorisches Museum), Michelangelo, design known only from copies, Giulio Romano, stucco relief (Mantua, Palazzo Te, Camera dei Cavalli) and drawing (New York, Pierpont Morgan Library) *int. al.*, Girolamo da Carpi (Dresden, Staatliche Kunstsammlung, inv. 145), Damiano Mazza, *c.* 1573 (London, National Gallery), Nicholas van Helt Stockade (Dublin, National Gallery of Ireland, inv. 1046), Annibale Carracci, fresco, 1597–1600 (Rome, Palazzo Farnese), Rembrandt, 1635 (Dresden, Gemäldegalerie), Rubens, 1611 (Madrid, Prado, inv. 1679), Paulus Bril (Antwerp, Koninklijk Museum voor schone Kunsten), Nicolaes Maes, nine portraits of children as Ganymede, Antonio Verrio, *c.* 1699 (ceiling, Ham House, Queen's Closet), Anton Domenico Gabbiani, *c.* 1700 (Florence, Uffizi), Charles-Joseph Natoire, *c.* 1731 (Château de la Chapelle-Godefroy), Giovanni Battista Tiepolo, 1753 (ceiling, Wurzburg, Residenz, Grand Staircase), Bertel Thorvaldsen (several times), Gustave Moreau (more than several times). A remarkable painting attributed to Guido Reni (*c.* 1603), apparently based on a design by Raphael, shows St John the Evangelist, traditionally depicted as a beautiful young man, being transported on the back of an eagle (Berlin, Bode Museum); **Xenophon** *Cyropedia* I, iii, 8, trans. Walter Miller, *Xenophon in Seven Volumes*, v (London and Cambridge MA, Heinemann and Harvard University Press, 1968)
p. 152 'of stature tall…' Thomas Nashe, *The Unfortunate Traveller*, end Pt IX, text modernized by the present author; **'… before her two and two…'** ibid., Pt II, text modernized by the present author; **Prince of Orange and Mary Stuart** married 12 May 1641 in the Chapel Royal at Whitehall; **Baron Fitzpatrick** Robert Fuller, *Church History* (1655) vii, 47; **Robert Carr** *DNB*, White Kennett, *Compleat History of England* (1719), ii, 686
p. 153 Endymion Porter as performer presenter of William Drummond of Hawthornden's 'Horoscopal Pageant' in *The Entertainment of the High and Mighty Monarch, Prince Charles* (Edinburgh, 1633); see also Sir William Davenant, 'Song:

Endymion Porter and Olivia', *Metaphysical Lyrics and Poems of the Seventeenth Century*, ed. H. J. C. Grierson (Oxford, 1921), No. 43; **portraits of Endymion Porter: Van Dyck** 1632, *Endymion and Olivia Porter with their Three Eldest Sons* (private collection, England); 1635, *Endymion Porter with the Artist* (Madrid, Prado); **William Dobson** 1642–5 (London, Tate Britain); **'strange things…'** Pepys, *Diary*, 28 September 1662; **'… he is not for my family…'** ibid., 27 April 1663
p. 154 'I sent W. Griffen…' ibid., 7 July 1663; **'I hear today…'** ibid., 14 November 1663; **Thomas Killigrew** A. Harbage, *Thomas Killigrew Cavalier Dramatist 1612–83* (Philadelphia, 1930); **'Where is the house…'** Nicholas Udall, *Roister Doister*, II. i. 1–4, text modernized by the present author
p. 156 'Methinks I feel…' Shakespeare, *Twelfth Night, or what you will*, I. v. 300–2; **'… she as her attendant hath…'** Shakespeare, *A Midsummer Night's Dream*, II. i. 21–7
p. 157 'The love of boys…' Beaumont and Fletcher, *Philaster* II, i; **'[The princess Miranda] had a page…'** Aphra Behn, *The Fair Jilt*, 1689, text modernized by the present author
p. 158 A poem of *c.* 1700 George Stepney (1663–1707), 'Imitated from the Latin of Horace, Odes, Book III, 7'; **'A child of thirteen…'** Pierre Augustin Caron de Beaumarchais, Preface to the second printing of *Le Mariage de Figaro*, 1775, *Théâtre* (Paris, Editions Garnier, 1980), 154
p. 161 'This role can only be played…' ibid., 155; **Thomas de Keyser** *Constantijn Huygens*, 1627 (London, National Gallery, NG212); **Sebastian Bourdon** *Christina of Sweden*, 1653 (Madrid, Prado); **ter Borch servant boys** *The Concert*, *c.* 1657 (Paris, Louvre), *The Letter* (Royal Collection); **Titian** *Portrait of Laura Dianti*, *c.* 1523–5 (Heinz Kisters Collection); see P. H. D. Kaplan, 'Titian's Laura Dianti and the Origin of the Motif of the Black Page in Portraiture', *Antichità Viva*, xxi: 1 (1982), 1118 and xxi: 4, 10–18; *The Image of the Black in Western Art*, ed. Ladislas Bugner (Cambridge MA, Harvard University Press, 2002), Vol II, Part ii, *passim*
p. 162 Velasquez and Juan de Pareja Antonio Palomino, *Lives of the Eminent Spanish Painters and Sculptors*, trans. Nina Ayala Mallory (Cambridge, Cambridge University Press, 1987), 159, 208–9; **Giuseppe Marchi** W. T. Whitley, *Artists and their Friends in England 1700–1799* (Medici Society, 1928), ii, 159
p. 164 Reynolds, *Cupid as a Link Boy* *Reynolds*, ed. Nicholas Penny (London, Royal Academy and Weidenfeld and Nicolson, 1986), 264–5, entry on Catalogue nos. 92 and 93 by David Mannings; **Raphael, sketch for *The Madonna of the Fish*** Florence, Uffizi, Gabinetto Disegni, inv. 524E; **Guido Reni** Judith (or Salome?)1640–42 (London, Wallace Collection); **Glyn Philpot** J. G. P. Delaney, *Glyn Philpot: His Life and Art* (Aldershot, Ashgate Publishing Ltd, 1999), 52–3, 94–6

8. Soldier Boys
p. 169 Tyrtaeus as translated by Thomas Campbell (1777–1844); **medal of Ferdinando II** Washington, National Gallery of Art; Raymond B. Waddington, 'The Bisexual Portrait of Francis I: Fontainebleau, Castiglione and the Tone of Courtly Mythology', *Playing with Gender: A Renaissance Pursuit*, ed. J. R. Brink, M. C. Horowitz and A. P. Coudert (Urbana and Chicago, University of Illinois Press, 1991), 102–3
p. 172 Venus and Mars statuary group Rome, Museo Nazionale delle Terme, cf. Rome, Capitoline Museum, cf. 'Sabina and Hadrian', Paris, Louvre
p. 174 Pompeii wall-painting the motif reappears in a wall-painting from the house of the cithara-player at Pompeii (Naples, Museo Nazionale)
p. 176 Sala di Psiche Mantua, Palazzo Te; **Alexis-Simon Belle, *Allégorie de la Paix*** Rouen, Musée des Beaux-Arts; **'And so while sensual life…'** Ariosto, *Orlando Furioso*, Canto vii, stanza 29, trans. Sir John Harington
p. 177 Ludovico Carracci *Rinaldo and Armida* (Naples, Museo Nazionale di Capodimonte); **other painters of *Rinaldo and Armida*** Annibale Carracci, *c.* 1600 (Naples, Museo Nazionale di Capodimonte), Marcantonio Franceschini, 1708 (Turin, Galleria dell'Accademia Albertina)
p. 178 Van Dyck *Rinaldo and Armida* (Baltimore Museum of Art); another version is in the Louvre; **G. F. Romanelli** *Rinaldo and Armida* (Edinburgh, Holyroodhouse); **two paladins** Boucher chose the subject for his *morceau de réception* to the Académie Royale in 1734 (Paris, Louvre); Tiepolo painted a mural of it in the Residenz at Wurzburg in 1752; **David** I Samuel, xvii: 38–43; **Roman steles** e.g. Treviso, Museo Civico; **Vasari on Donatello's *David*** *Lives of the Artists: A Selection Translated by George Bull* (Harmondsworth, Penguin, 1987), i. 179
p. 179 Michelangelo, *Apollo/David* 1525–30 (Florence, Bargello)
p. 181 Caravaggio, *David* 1605–6 (Rome, Galeria Borghese); **Guido Reni, *David*** *c.* 1605, illustrated (Paris, Louvre, cf. Florence, Uffizi, Dresden, Gemäldegalerie, Munich, Alte Pinakothek, and Vienna, Kunsthistorisches Museum; cf. variant in Sarasota, Ringling Museum)
p. 183 Canova, *Perseus* New York, Metropolitan Museum of Art, cf. Anton Raphael Mengs, *Perseus and Andromeda*, 1777 (St Petersburg, Hermitage); **Ingres, *Achilles Receiving the Ambassadors of Agamemnon*** 1801 (Paris, Ecole Nationale Supérieure des Beaux-Arts); **Nazi nudes** e.g. Arno Breker, *Comradeship*, *Warrior's Departure*, *Readiness*, *Prometheus*, *The Party*, etc., cf. Willy Meller, *Torchbearer*; **restored boxers** Seymour Howard, 'Some Eighteenth Century "Restored" Boxers', *Journal of the Warburg and Courtauld Institutes*, 56, 1993, 238–55
p. 185 Bob Gregson Joseph Farington, *Diary*, 20 and 30 June, 1808, and Benjamin Robert Haydon, *Diary*, 2 March 1816; **Cain's attack on Abel** Jacopo della Quercia (Bologna, San Petronio), Orazio Riminaldi (La Valletta, Museo and Dublin, National Gallery of Ireland, inv. 1667), Titian, 1576, Tintoretto (Venice, Accademia), Pietro Novelli, Il Monrealese (Rome, Galleria Nazionale de Arte Antica); **the dead Abel** has been depicted by artists as different as William Blake and the French sculptor Giovanni Dupré, 1842 (Paris, Louvre)
p. 186 Michelangelo, *Battle of Cascina* *c.* 1504, cartoon, now destroyed, for an unexecuted fresco in the Sala del Gran Consiglio, Palazzo Vecchio, Florence
p. 187 'Descend, my Phoebus!…' Homer, *Iliad*, trans. Alexander Pope; ***Sarpedon Borne by Sleep and Death*** see also Joseph-Marie Vien, 1770 (Langres, Musée Didier, inv. 863-11), Gavin Hamilton (Edinburgh, National Gallery of Scotland), William Blake Richmond, 1875–6 (Vancouver, Vancouver City Art Gallery); **fourth-century bronze cista handle** Etruscan (Cleveland, Cleveland Museum of Art); ***Achilles Mourning Patroclus*** Benjamin West (Edinburgh, National Gallery of Scotland); Nicolai Gay, 1855 (Minsk, Art Museum of Belarus)
p. 188 Alcibiades e.g. Roman mosaic portrait found at Sparta; marble tondo found at Aphrodisias; **Germanicus** Thomas Banks, *The Death of Germanicus*, 1773–4, marble relief (Holkham Hall, Collection of the Earl of Leicester)
p. 189 Joseph Barra G. Bord, 'Deux légendes républicaines: Barra et Viala', *Revue des Questions Historiques*, 32, 1882, 233–57; J. C. Sloane, 'David, Robespierre and the Death of Bara', *Gazette des Beaux-Arts*, September 1969, 143–40. Henner, *Bara, Jeune Héros de la Révolution*; **David d'Angers** *Death of Bara*, plaster, Musée d'Angers
p. 191 Joseph-Agricol Viala *La Mort de Viala*; Pierre-Paul Prud'hon (att.), Lyon, Musée des Beaux-Arts, inv. 1966–13; **Brachard, Viala bust** Sèvres, Musée National de la Céramique, Inv. MNC 23456, 23458; **Alexandre Falguière, *Death of Tarcisius*** the government bought the plaster and commissioned its execution in marble (Paris, Louvre); **Anne Finch, 'Alcidor'** *Miscellany Poems with a Tragedy by a Lady* (London, 1713), 184; **'cutting off the hair'** *The Diary of Fanny Burney*, ed. Lewis Gibbs (London and New York, Dent and Dutton, 1966), 31
p. 192 Don Juan and Catherine the Great Byron, *Don Juan*, Canto ix, stanzas 44–5

9. The Icon of Male Vulnerability
p. 195 Daphnis Diodorus Siculus, iv. 84; Servius on Virgil's *Eclogues*, v. 20, viii, 68, x. 26; Philargyrius on Virgil's *Eclogues*, v. 20; Aelian, *q*, x. 18 For an account of the much-copied Hellenistic sculpture group of Pan teaching Daphnis, see P. P. Bober and R. Rubinstein, *Renaissance Artists and Antique Sculpture: A Handbook of Sources* (London, Harvey Miller, 1986), fig 74, 109; **Chrysippus** Apollodorus, iii. v. 5; Hyginus, *Fabulae* 85 and 271; Athenaeus, XIII. 79; Plutarch, *Parallel Stories*, 33; **Acis** Ovid, *Metamorphoses*, xiii, 750–968; **Icarus** Ovid, *Metamorphoses*, viii, 182–235; Hyginus, *Fabula* 40; **Elpenor** Homer, *Odyssey*, xi; **Hippolytus** Euripides, *Hippolytus*; Plutarch, *Parallel Stories*, 34; Seneca, *Hippolytus*, Ovid, *Heroides*, iv, *Metamorphoses*, xv; Pausanias, ii; ***The Death of Orpheus*** see notes for pp. 133–4; **Pelops** Hyginus, *Fabulae* 82, 83; Tzetzes, *On Lycophron*, 152; **Attis** Ovid, *Fasti*, iv, 221 ff., Servius on Virgil, *Aeneid*, ix, 116; **Phaeton** Scholiast on Pindar's Olympian Odes, VI, 78; Tzetzes, *Chiliads*, IV, 137; Hyginus, *Fabulae* 52, 125 and 154; Euripides, *Hippolytus*, 137; Apollonius Rhodius, IV, 598 ff.; Lucian, *Dialogues of the Gods*, 25; Ovid, *Metamorphoses* i, 755 ff.; Virgil, *Eclogues* VI, 62; Diodorus Siculus, V, 3; Apollodorus, I, iv, 5; Homer, *Iliad*, ii, 595–600; Lucian, *Dialogues of the Gods*, 14; Apollodorus, *Biblioteca*, I. iii. 3; III. x. 3; Pausanias, *Description of Greece*, IV. xix. 3–5; ***Fall of Phaeton*** Guido Reni, 1596–8 (Bologna, Palazzo Rossi)
p. 196 Hyacinthus Homer, *Iliad*, ii, 595–600; Lucian, *Dialogues of the Gods*, 14; Apollodorus 1. 3. 3; Pausanias, iii, 1, 3; **'Just as when…'** Ovid, *Metamorphoses*, x, 183–95, trans. Frank Justus Miller (London and Cambridge MA, Heinemann and Harvard University Press, 1984), ii, 77–9
p. 197 Spring Dionysos Robert Graves, *The Greek Myths* (Harmondsworth, Penguin, 1955), i, 108–10; **son of Poseidon** Philostephanus, Fragment 8; **Antheus of Halicarnassus** Parthenius, *Narrations*, 14; **suicide, accidental death** Steve Jones, *Y: the Descent of Men* (London, Little, Brown, 2002), 244; **'His ritual death…'** Robert Graves, *The Greek Myths* (Harmondsworth, Penguin, 1955), i, 18; **Zagreus** Diodorus Siculus, v.75.4; Nonnus, *Dionysiaca*, vi. 269 and xxvii. 228; Tzetzes, *On Lycophron*, 355; Eustathius on *Iliad*, ii. 735; Firmicus Maternus, *Concerning the Errors of Profane Religions*, vi; Euripides, *The Cretans*, fragment 475; Orphic Fragments (Kern, 34); **Acteon** Hyginus, *Fabula* 181; Pausanias, ix, 2, 3
p. 198 Adonis Apollodorus, iii.14.3–4; Hyginus, *Poetic Astronomy* 11.7; Hyginus, *Fabulae* 58, 64, 251; Fulgentius, *Mythology*, iii.8; **death of Adonis** Servius on Virgil's *Eclogues*, x. 18; Orphic Hymn, lv.10; Ptolemy Hephaestionos, i. 306; **Hurtado de Mendoza, *Fabula de Adonis*** written *c.* 1553, published in *Obras* in 1610; **Juan de la Cueva, *Llanto de Venus*** published in *Obras* (Seville, A. Pescioni for F. Rodriguez, 1582); **Girolamo Parabosco, *Favola di Adone*** written before 1557 (the year of his death); **Ronsard, *L'Adonis*** published in *Les trois livres du receuil des nouvelles poésies* (Paris, Buon, 1563); **Louis de Masure, *Adonis*** published in 1586, twelve years after his death; ***The Appearance of the Boar before Venus*** Niccolo dell'Abbate, *c.* 1570; **'And nuzzling in his flank…'** Shakespeare, *Venus and Adonis*
p. 200 'gardens of Adonis' depicted on Greek pottery, e.g. Lekythos, 425–375 BCE (Karlsruhe, Badisches Landesmuseum, Inv. B39); ***The Death of Adonis*** painted by *int. al.* Giorgione (formerly Venice, Palazzo Widman), Baldassare Peruzzi, 1511–12 (for the Sala delle Prospettive in the Farnesina), Sebastiano del Piombo? (Florence, Uffizi, inv. 916), Primaticcio or Niccolo dell'Abbate, 1533–5 (for the Chambre du Roi, Fontainebleau, destroyed), Rosso Fiorentino, 1535–40 (for the Galerie François I at Fontainebleau), Tintoretto, more than once (1543–4, Padua, Museo Civico, inv. 2812, and Paris, Louvre, inv. 1759), Domenico Tintoretto (Tucson, University of Arizona, Inv. K2135), Perin del Vaga? (Florence, Uffizi, Inv. SmeC 119), Luca Cambiaso (many times), Veronese, 1580–82 (Stockholm, Nationalmuseum, inv. 4414), Hendrik Goltzius, 1603 (Amsterdam, Rijksmuseum, inv. A1284 and Blois, Musée de l'Art Ancien, no. 183), Domenichino, 1603–4 (Rome, Palazzo Farnese), Lo Scarsellino (Rome, Galleria Borghese), Poussin, *c.* 1625 (Caen, Musée des Beaux-Arts), Ribera, 1637 (Rome, Galleria Corsini), Alessandro Turchi (Dresden, Gemäldegalerie, no. 521), Luca Giordano, 1682 (fresco, Florence, Palazzo Medici), Constantijn Netscher (Paris, Louvre, inv. 1608), Francis Le Moyne, 1729 (Stockholm, Nationalmuseum, inv. 854), Benjamin West (several times, Pittsburgh, Carnegie Institute Museum of Art, also New Brunswick, Rutgers University Art Gallery), Goya, *c.* 1771 (Zurich, private collection), James Barry, *c.* 1775 (Dublin, National Gallery of Ireland, no. 1393); **'The lovely one…'** P. B. Shelley, 'Fragment of the Elegy on the Death of Adonis from the Greek of Bion', *Shelley: Poetical Works*, ed. Thomas Hutchinson (Oxford, Oxford University Press, 1967), 721–2

p. 201 Leander: Virgil, *Georgics*, iii, 258–263; **Statius**, *Thebaid*, vi, 542–7; **Ovid**, *Heroides*, xviii, 9; **Musaeus**, *Hero and Leander*; **Garcilaso de la Vega** 'Pasando el mar Leandro el animoso…', *Obras* (Madrid, Garcia, 1570); **Juan Boscán de Almogáver** 'Hero y Leandro', *Obras de Boscan y algunas de Garcilaso de la Vega* (Barcelona, 1543); **Bernardo Tasso** 'Favola di Leandro e d'Hero', *Gli Amori di Bernardo Tasso* (Venice, Stagnino, 1534–7); **Clément Marot** *Histoire de Léandre et Héro* (Paris, 1541); **Hans Sachs** *Historia die unglückhafft lieb Leandri mit Frau Ehron* (1541)
p. 202 'His body was as straight…' Christopher Marlowe, *Hero and Leander* (London, Felix Kingston for Paul Linley, 1598), ll. 51–69; ***Hero Grieving over the Drowned Leander*** depicted by Annibale Carracci (Rome, Palazzo Farnese), Rubens, *c.* 1605 (New Haven, Yale University Art Gallery), Domenico Feti, 1610–12 (Vienna, Kunsthistorisches Museum), Jan van den Hoecke, 1635–7 (Vienna, Kunsthistorisches Museum), Giacinto Gimignani (Florence, Uffizi, inv. 2131), Gillis Backereel (Vienna, Kunsthistorisches Museum, inv. 1711), Nicolas Régnier, *c.* 1650 (Melbourne, National Gallery of Victoria, inv. 3262-4), William Etty, 1829, on loan to New York City Art Gallery; **ballets, etc.** Harriet (1796), Briant, De Fabre, Taillasson (1798, Louvre), Debucourt (1801), Monsiau (1806), Ducis (1808), Palliere (1817), Delorme (1841)
p. 203 *Hylas Dragged into the Water by Nymphs* depicted by Francesco Primaticcio (Fontainebleau, Galerie d'Ulysse, destroyed), Francesco Furini (Dublin, National Gallery of Ireland, inv. 1658), Pierre-Jerôme Lordon, 1812 (Gray, Musée Baron Martin), Thorvaldsen, 1833 (Copenhagen, Thorvaldsen Museum, inv. A482), François-Pascal-Simon Gérard, 1826 (Bayeux, Musée Baron Gerard), William Etty, 1833, Joseph Anton Koch (Frankfurt, Städelsches Kunstinstitut), Jules-Etienne Lenepveu, 1865 (Angers, Musée des Beaux-Arts), Jean-François Millet (Otterloo, Rijksmuseum Kröller-Müller, inv. 508), John William Waterhouse, 1896–7 (Manchester, City Art Gallery), Arthur B. Davies, 1910 (New York, Stephen C. Clark Collection); **Antinous** Athens, National Archaeological Museum; Paris, Louvre; Cambridge, Fitzwilliam Museum (inv. GR.100.1937); Rome, Vatican Museum; Port Sunlight, Lady Lever Art Gallery; Delphi, Archaeological Museum (inv. 1718); Eleusis, Archaeological Museum; Olympia, Museum (inv. Lambda 104 and 208); ***The Deluge*** Raphael (Vatican, la Loggia), Michelangelo (Rome, Sistine Chapel), Joachim Antonisz Wtewael (Nuremberg, Germanisches Nationalmuseum); **Géricault, *The Raft of the Medusa*** Paris, Louvre, Inv. 488
p. 204 *Sebastian* Lorenzo Costa 1490–91 (Florence, Uffizi), **Boltraffio** 1490s (Moscow, Pushkin Museum), **Raphael** 1503 (Bergamo, Accademia Carrara), **Benozzo Gozzoli** San Gimignano, Duomo, **Andrea Mantegna** 1456–9 (Paris, Louvre), 1457–8 (Vienna, Kunsthistorisches Museum), 1490 (Venice, Ca d'Oro), **Carlo Crivelli** 1490–91 (Milan, Museo Poldi Pezzoli), **Botticelli** 1473 (Berlin-Dahlem, Staatliche Museen), **Giovanni Bellini** 1460–64 (Venice, Accademia), after 1464 (Basilica di SS. Giovanni e Paolo), **Cima da Conegliano** 1480s (Strasbourg, Musée des Beaux-Arts)
p. 205 Van Dyck John Rupert Martin, 'Van Dyck's Early Paintings of Saint Sebastian', *Art, the Ape of Nature: Studies in Honor of H. W. Janson* (New York, Harry N. Abrams Inc., 1985), 393–400; also Del Cairo, Modena, Campori Collection, Rome, Villa Albani, Tours
p. 207 Giovanni Bellini *Sacred Allegory*, cf. 1480s (Paris, Louvre and Pala di San Giobbe), 1487 (Venice, Accademia); **Titian** Averoldi Polyptych, 1522 (Brescia, SS. Nazario e Celso), 1570 (St Petersburg, Hermitage), **Sodoma** 1525 (Florence, Pitti), **Garofalo** *c.* 1526 (Naples, Capodimonte, inv. Q 80), **Guido Reni** 1615–16 (Genoa, Palazzo Rosso, also Voltaggio, Cappuccini; Madrid, Prado; Paris, Louvre; Auckland, City Art Gallery; Ponce, Museo de Arte), 1640–42 (Bologna, Pinacoteca Nazionale); ***Sebastian and Irene* Giordano** (Melbourne, National Gallery of Victoria), **Schedoni** 1615 (Naples, Capodimonte), **Preti** 1657 (Naples, Capodimonte), **Cerrini** Geneva, Musée d'Art et d'Histoire, cf. Marcantonio Bassetti (Marseille, Musée des Beaux-Arts)
p. 212 'the might of the faint youth…' Ariosto, *Orlando Furioso*, Canto xix, trans. Sir John Harington; **Angelica caring for the wounded Medoro** Peterzano Simone, 1570 (Bergamo, Accademia Carrara), Giovan Francesco Romanelli, Lorenzo Lippi, 1747 (Dublin, National Gallery of Ireland, no. 1747), Poussin, 1625–6 (Moscow, Pushkin Museum); **'And when she saw his face…'** Tasso, *Gerusalemme Liberata,* Canto xix. 104 in Fairfax's translation; **'Though gone, though dead…'** ibid.; ***Erminia and Tancredi* Giulio Cesare Procaccini** (?) Sotheby's New York, 28 May 1999, lot 101, **Francesco Furini** (Budapest, Szépmüvészeti Múzeum), **Poussin** 1630s (St Petersburg, Hermitage), 1634 (Birmingham, Barber Institute of Fine Arts); also Ludovico Lana (Modena, Museo Civico d'Arte, no. 36), Guercino, 1621–3 (Rome, Galleria Doria-Pamphili), Pier Francesco Mola (Houston, Sara Campbell Foundation); **Abel: Jacopo della Quercia** Bologna, San Petronio; **Vasari on Ghiberti's Abel** *Lives of the Artists: A Selection Translated by George Bull* (Harmondsworth, Penguin, 1987), 117
p. 213 *Dead Niobid* P. P. Bober and R. Rubinstein, *Renaissance Artists and Antique Sculpture: A Handbook of Sources* (London, Harvey Miller, 1986), fig 109, 140; **Giovanni Dupré** *The Dead Abel*, 1842 (Paris, Louvre); **Abraham's intended sacrifice of Isaac** is the subject of works by Giotto (Naples?), Ghiberti (Florence, Baptistery), Donatello, 1418, Mantegna, 1490–95 (Vienna Kunsthistorisches Museum), Andrea del Sarto, 1529, two examples (Madrid, Prado, No. 336, and Brescia), Caravaggio, 1601–2 (Florence, Uffizi, also att.), Procaccini, *c.* 1615 (art market), Domenichino (Madrid, Prado), Pieter Lastman, 1616 (Paris, Louvre), Orazio Riminaldi, *c.* 1625 (Rome, Galleria d'Arte Antica; a superior version, also considered to be autograph, was recently on the art market in Switzerland), Laurent de La Hyre, 1650 (Reims, Musée Saint-Denis), Valentin de Boulogne, *c.* 1630 (Quebec, Montreal Museum of Fine Arts Inv. 1927.446). The mood of Rembrandt's later engraving of the same subject is very different; Abraham looks simply distraught and bewildered, and hides his boy's head in the skirt of his robe.
p. 214 Domenico Veneziano *St John the Baptist in the Desert, c.* 1445 (Washington DC, National Gallery of Art); **Raphael** *St John the Baptist in the Desert,* 1518–20. The Uffizi painting of Raphael's design (inv. 1890, no. 1446) is believed to be autograph. Zoffany's painting of the Tribuna or Wunderkammer of the Uffizi in 1772 shows Raphael's picture hung in pride of place; ***St John the Baptist in the Desert*** Leonardo da Vinci, Andrea del Sarto (Florence, Palazzo Pitti, also Corsham Court, Methuen Collection and Vaduz, Liechtenstein Collection), Alessandro Allori, *c.* 1580s (Dublin, National Gallery of Ireland, Inv.1088), Bronzino, 1550–55 (Rome, Galleria Borghese), Anton Raphael Mengs (Collection of the Duke of Wellington), Daniele da Volterra, Simone Cantarini (Dublin, National Gallery of Ireland, Inv. 71), Valentin de Boulogne, 1628–30 (Camerino, Santa Maria in Via), Nicolas Régnier, 1615–20 (St Petersburg, Hermitage), Guido Reni, in various versions (e.g. Turin, Galleria Sabauda; London, Dulwich Picture Gallery), Baciccio, *c.* 1676 (Manchester, Manchester City Art Gallery). Caravaggio produced half-a-dozen versions, all posed by different models (1605–10, Rome, Galleria Nazionale d'Arte Antica; 1609–10, Rome, Galleria Borghese; Basel, Offentliche Kunstsammlung; Rome, Galleria Doria Pamphili); **Jacob Huysmans** *Duke of Monmouth as John the Baptist* (Selkirk, Bowhill); **Sir Joshua Reynolds, *Child Baptist in the Wilderness*** the first version to be exhibited was sold to the Duke of Rutland for £100. It is not clear how many more Reynolds painted and sold, but there remain one in the Wallace Collection, catalogued as *Master Wynn as the Child St John*, and an unfinished version in the Minneapolis Institute of Art; there were six in posthumous estate sales and autograph versions periodically appear on the art market. The subject was twice engraved (see D. Mannings and M. Postle, *Sir Joshua Reynolds: A Complete Catalogue of his Paintings*, No. 2041); ***St Laurence on the Gridiron*** Titian, 1567 (Escorial), Carlo Dolci, altarpiece, Chapel of St Laurence, Prato, Duomo, Valentin de Boulogne, 1621–2 (Madrid, Prado), Belluno, Duomo, Bartolommeo Bandinelli, Massimo Stanzione, 1625 (Indianapolis, Ball State University Museum of Art)
p. 215 St Maurice and the Theban Legion Pontormo, 1529–30 (Florence, Pitti), and Pontormo and Bronzino (Florence, Uffizi). See also Dürer's compendium painting of ten thousand assorted martyrs, all male, and El Greco, 1582 (El Escorial, Monasterio di San Lorenzo)
p. 217 the Good Samaritan tends a naked, swooning man in works by a follower of Jan Scorel (Amsterdam, Rijksmuseum), Maarten van Heemskerk, Met de Bles, Luca Giordano (Rouen, Musée des Beaux-Arts), Antonio de Bellis (Milan, private collection)

10. The Female Gaze
p. 219 'Equally narcissistic in feeling…' Edward Lucie-Smith, *Eroticism in Western Art* (London, Thames & Hudson, 1972), 207; **Christina of Sweden** Baron de Bildt, *Christine de Suède et le Cardinal Azzolino* (Paris, 1899); Christina owned too a copy of the Parmigianino, *Cupid Carving a Bow* (see p. 60). Ellis Waterhouse, 'Queen Christina's Pictures in England'
p. 220 Gabriel Gilbert Eleanor J. Pellet, *A Forgotten French Dramatist, Gabriel Gilbert (1620?–1680?)* (Baltimore/Paris, 1931)
p. 223 Rubens, *Dying Adonis* Jaffe no. 25 ill.; **Dürer, *Adam and Eve*** Christina presented the panels to Philip IV of Spain and they are now in the Prado; **Margaret Walters** *The Nude Male: A New Perspective* (Harmondsworth, Penguin, 1978), 15; **Phaedra** Ovid, *Heroides*, iv, 64; **Medea** ibid., xii, 33; **Sappho** ibid., xv, 21–2; **Helen** ibid., xvii, 93–4
p. 224 Potiphar's wife Genesis xxxix: 7–12; **Savonarola** Vasari, *Lives of the Artists*, ii, 123; **nuns on Preti's *St Sebastian*** De Dominici, 1742–45, iii, 348; **studiolo of Isabella d'Este** J. Cartwright, *Isabella d'Este, Marchioness of Mantua, 1474–1539: A Study of the Renaissance* (New York, 1903); C. M. Brown, *Isabella d'Este and Lorenzo da Pavia* (Paris, 1982); Keith Christiansen, 'The Studiolo and Late Themes', *Andrea Mantegna*, ed. Jane Martineau (Milan, Electa, 1992), 418–26; **Elizabeth de Bourbon** Cassiano del Pozzo
p. 225 '… you are beautiful…' Aphra Behn, *Love-Letters between a Nobleman and his Sister*, text modernized by the present author; **'She beheld him steadfastly…'** Aphra Behn, *The Fair Jilt*, text modernized by the present author
p. 226 Elizabeth Singer, 'To a very young Gentleman…' *Poems on Several Occasions, by Philomela* (1696); **'But even today…'** Margaret Walters, *The Nude Male: A New Perspective* (Harmondsworth, Penguin, 1978), 15
p. 228 Laura Mulvey, 'Visual Pleasure and Narrative Cinema', *Screen*, 16: 3, 6
p. 230 Goya, *The Naked Maja* *c.* 1798–1805 (Madrid, Prado); **Giulia Lama, *Martirio di San Giovanni Evangelista*** 1730 (Quimper, Musée Municipal des Beaux-Arts)
p. 231 Elisabeth Vigée Le Brun *Prince Lubomirsky as the Genius of Fame* (Berlin, Gemäldegalerie), ***Allegory of the Genius of Alexander I*** 1788 (St Petersburg, Hermitage), ***Amphion Playing the Lyre*** 1793–5; **Angelika Kauffmann *Portrait of Prince Henry Lubomirski as Cupid*** (Berlin, Gemäldegalerie, copy in Kozlowka, Zamoyski Museum); **Canova, *Prince Henry Lubomirsky as Eros*** commissioned by Princess Izabella Lubomirska in 1786, gesso at Possagno, marble at Lancut Castle, marble copy for English patron, now at Anglesey Abbey, another in Dublin (*Canova*, Marsilio, 1992, No. 124, 250–53); **Kauffmann, *Abelard Presents Hymen to Eloise*** London, Burghley House, Inv. no. 291
p. 232 Kauffmann, *Diana and Endymion* St Petersburg, Peterhof; **Kauffmann, *Ganymede and the Eagle*** 1793 (Bregenz, Vorarlberger Landesmuseum, inv. No. Gem. 6); **Angélique Mongez, *Oath of the Seven Theban Chiefs*** 1806 (Angers, Musée d'Angers)
p. 234 Charles Aubert, *L'Aveugle* (Paris, 1891); **Tamar Garb** 'The Forbidden Gaze: Women Artists and the Male Nude in Late Nineteenth Century France', *The Body Imaged: The Human Form and Visual Culture since the Renaissance*, ed. K. Alder and M. Pointon (Cambridge, Cambridge University Press, 1993)
p. 236 Henrietta Rae Arthur Fish, *Henrietta Rae (Mrs. Ernest Normand)* (London, Cassell, 1905), *Zephyrus Wooing Flora* (plate facing p. 48), 49–51, and plate facing p. 92, 'The Studio at Norwood'
p. 238 Léonor Fini, *Sphinx Amalbourga*, 1942, *Chthonian Divinity Watching over the Sleep of a Young Man*, 1947
p. 243 well-loved body Sarah Kent, 'The Erotic Male Nude', *Women's Images of Men*, ed. S. Kent and J. Morreau (London, Writers and Readers Co-operative Society, 1985), 102

Picture Credits

Measurements are given in centimetres, followed by inches, unless otherwise stated.

p. 1 Pinturicchio (1454–1513), *Portrait of a Boy*, 1480–85. Tempera on panel, 50 x 35.5 (19⅝ x 14). Gemäldegalerie, Dresden
pp. 2–3 Nan Goldin (b. 1953), *French Chris on Carhood, NYC*, 1979. Type-C print, 40.6 x 50.8 (16 x 20). Courtesy of the artist and Matthew Marks Gallery, New York
pp. 4–5 Francesco Albani (1578–1660), *Salmacis and Hermaphroditus*, *c.* 1633. Oil on canvas, 184 x 231 (72½ x 91). Galleria Sabauda, Turin
p. 6 Will McBride (b. 1931), *Markus in Casoli*, 1978. Gelatin silver print, 40 x 24 (15¾ x 9½). Courtesy the artist
p. 8 Antonin Mercié (1845–1916), David, 1872. Bronze, 184.1 x 76.8 (72½ x 30¼). Musée du Louvre, Paris. Photo © RMN – Jean Schormans
p. 9 Idolino, Hellenistic. Bronze, H. 149 (58⅝). Museo Nazionale Archeologico, Florence. Photo Scala.
p. 10 Caravaggio (1573–1610), *St John the Baptist*, 1602. Oil on canvas, 129 x 94 (50¾ x 37). Museo Capitolino, Rome. Photo Scala
p. 12 Titian (*c.* 1485–1576), *Ranuccio Farnese*, 1542. Oil on canvas, 89.7 x 73.6 (35¼ x 29). National Gallery of Art, Washington, D.C, Samuel H. Kress Collection
p. 14 Hans Holbein the Younger (*c.* 1497–1543), *Edward, Prince of Wales*, *c.* 1539. Oil on panel, 56.8 x 44 (22⅜ x 17⅜). National Gallery of Art, Washington, Andrew W. Mellon Collection
p. 15 left Flemish School, *Edward VI* (detail), *c.* 1544–6. Oil on panel, 107.2 x 82 (42¼ x 32¼). The Royal Collection © 2003, Her Majesty Queen Elizabeth II. Photo Stephen Chapman
p. 15 right Studio of William Scrots, *King Edward VI*, *c.* 1546. Oil on panel, 47.3 x 27.9 (18⅝ x 11). By courtesy of the National Portrait Gallery, London
p. 17 Girolamo Bedoli (*c.* 1500–69), *Parma Embracing Alessandro Farnese*, 1555. Oil on canvas, 149.7 x 117.2 (58⅞ x 46⅛). Su concessone del Ministero per I Beni e le Attività Culturali, Parma e Piacenza
p. 18 Valentin de Boulogne (1591–1632), *The Four Ages of Man*, *c.* 1629. Oil on canvas, 96 x 134 (37¾ x 52¾). National Gallery, London
p. 19 Titian (*c.* 1485–1576), *The Three Ages of Man*, 1512–14. Oil on canvas, 90 x 150.7 (35⅜ x 59⅜). Duke of Sutherland Collection, on loan to the National Gallery of Scotland, Edinburgh
p. 20 Louis-Léopold Boilly (1761–1845), *Three Young Artists in a Studio*, *c.* 1820. Black chalk with white chalk heightening and stumping on beige paper, 29.8 x 36.5 (11¾ x 14⅜). The J. Paul Getty Museum, Los Angeles
p. 21 Collier Schorr (b. 1963), *Upper Bunk*, 2001. Colour photograph, 40.6 x 50.8 (16 x 20). Art & Commerce
p. 22 Raphael (1483–1520), *Portrait of Bindo Altoviti*, *c.* 1515. Oil on panel, 60 x 44 (23½ x 17¼). National Gallery of Art, Washington, D.C., Samuel H. Kress Collection
p. 23 Titian (*c.* 1485–1576), *Portrait of a Man in a Red Cap*, *c.* 1516. Oil on canvas, 82.3 x 71.1 (32⅜ x 28). The Frick Collection, New York
p. 24 above Alessandro Allori (1535–1607), *Portrait of a Young Man*, 1590. Oil on panel, 133 x 104 (52⅜ x 41). Private Collection
p. 24 below left Anonymous artist after Rembrandt, *Portrait of Rembrandt with Gorget*, date unknown. Panel, 37.9 x 28.9 (14⅞ x 11⅜). Royal Cabinet of Paintings, Mauritshuis, The Hague
p. 24 below right Rembrandt (1606–1669), *Self-Portrait*, 1629. Oil on canvas, 15.5 x 12.7 (6⅛ x 5). Alte Pinakothek, Munich/Artothek
p. 25 above left Albrecht Dürer (1471–1528), *Self-Portrait at the Age of Thirteen*, 1484. Silverpoint on paper, 27.5 x 19.6 (10⅞ x 16⅛). Graphische Sammlung Albertina, Vienna
p. 25 above right Albrecht Dürer (1471–1528), *Self-Portrait, aged Twenty-One* (detail), 1492. Black pen drawing, beige paper, 20.4 x 20.8 (8 x 8¼). University Library, Erlangen
p. 25 below left Albrecht Dürer (1471–1528), *Self-Portrait at Age Twenty-Two* (detail), 1493. Pen and brown ink, 27.6 x 20.2 (10⅞ x 8). Metropolitan Museum of Art, New York. Robert Lehman Collection, 1975 (1975.1.862)
p. 25 below right Albrecht Dürer (1471–1528), *Self-Portrait with a Spray of Eryngium*, 1493. Parchment on panel, 56.5 x 44.5 (22¼ x 17½). Musée du Louvre, Paris
p. 26 Anthony Van Dyck (1599–1691), *Self-Portrait*, 1620–21. Oil on canvas, 116.5 x 93.5 (45⅞ x 36½). © The State Hermitage Museum, St Petersburg
p. 27 Anthony Van Dyck (1599–1691), *Lord John and Lord Bernard Stuart*, 1637. Oil on canvas, 237.5 x 146.1 (93½ x 57½). National Gallery, London
p. 28 Larry Clark (b. 1943), *Oklahoma City*, 1975. Black and white photograph, 35.6 x 27.9 (14 x 11). Courtesy of the artist and Luhring Augustine, New York
p. 29 above *Narcissus*, wall-painting. Pompeii, House of Marcus Lucretius Fronto
p. 29 below Benvenuto Cellini (1500–1571), *Narcissus*, 1548. Marble, H. 149 (58⅝). Bargello, Florence. Photo Scala
p. 30 above Thomas Gainsborough (1727–1788), *Master John Heathcote*, *c.* 1770–74. Oil on canvas, 127 x 101.2 (50 x 39¾). National Gallery of Art, Washington, D.C., given in memory of Governor Alvan T. Fuller by the Fuller Foundation
p. 30 below Sir Joshua Reynolds (1723–1792), *Alexander, 10th Duke of Hamilton*, 1782. Oil on canvas, 68.5 x 55 (27 x 21⅝). National Gallery of Scotland, Edinburgh
p. 31 Sir Joshua Reynolds (1723–1792), *Francis George Hare*, 1788. Oil on canvas, 76 x 63.5 (29⅞ x 25). Private Collection
p. 32 Sir Thomas Lawrence (1769–1830), *Lydia, Lady Acland, with her two sons, Thomas and Arthur*, 1818. Oil on canvas, 155 x 121.4 (61 x 47¾). National Trust Photographic Library/John Hammond
p. 34 Kurt Cobain, 1994. Rex Features Ltd/SIPA/James Road
p. 35 James Dean, film still from *Rebel Without a Cause*, 1955. Rex Features Ltd.
p. 36 Katoey. National Geographic Society Image Collection. Photo Jodi Cobb
p. 38 left Kritios Boy, 490–480 BCE. Marble, 84 (33). Acropolis Museum, Athens. Photo Scala
p. 38 right Piraeus Apollo, 530–520 BCE. Bronze, life-size. National Museum, Athens. Photo Scala
p. 39 Kouros from Melos, 550–540 BCE. Marble, H. 214 (84⅜). National Museum, Athens. Photo Scala
p. 40 Belvedere Apollo. Roman copy of Greek 4th century bronze original. Marble, H. 224 (88¼). Vatican Museums and Galleries, Vatican City. Photo Scala
p. 41 Apollo Sauroktonos. Roman copy after an original by Praxiteles, third quarter of 4th century BCE. Marble, H. 149 (58⅝). Photo © RMN – H. Lewandowski
p. 42 Andrea Sacchi (1599–1661), *Marcantonio Pasqualini Crowned by Apollo*, 1641. Oil on canvas, 243.8 x 194.3 (96 x 76½). Metropolitan Museum of Art, New York. Purchase, Enid A. Haupt Gift, Gwynne Andrews Fund and Purchase, 1871, by exchange, 1981 (1981.317)
p. 43 Apollo of Veio. Etruscan, *c.* 500 BCE. Painted terracotta, H *c.* 180 (70). Museo Nazionale di Villa Giulia, Rome. Photo Scala
p. 44 Jusepe de Ribera (1588–1656), *Apollo Flaying Marsyas*, 1637. Oil on canvas, 202 x 255 (79½ x 100⅜). Musées Royaux des Beaux-Arts de Belgique, Brussels
p. 45 left Circle of Michael Sweerts, *Interior of a Sculptor's Studio* (detail), *c.* 1655–1700. Oil on canvas, 50.5 x 43.8 (19⅞ x 17¼). Hunterian Art Gallery, University of Glasgow, Glasgow. Photo Bridgeman Art Library
p. 45 right Rubens (1577–1640), *Council of the Gods*, 1622–4. Oil on canvas, 394 x 702 (155 x 276½). Musée du Louvre, Paris
p. 47 Sir Joshua Reynolds (1723–1792), *Frederick Howard, 5th Earl of Carlisle*, 1769. Oil on canvas, 254 x 173 with frame (100 x 68⅛). From the Castle Howard Collection
p. 48 Taddeo Zuccari (1529–1566), *Seated Youth Surprised by Two Soldiers*, date unknown. Sepia pen, wash, 26.3 (10⅜). Auckland Art Gallery Toi o Tamaki, purchased 1955
p. 51 Frank Sinatra, 1945. Rex Features Ltd/SIPA
p. 52 Elvis Presley, Rex Features Ltd
p. 53 Boy George, 1988. Rex Features Ltd
p. 54 Preparing for Geerewol. Robert Estall Photo Library © Carol Beckwith
p. 55 Surma body painting. Robert Estall Photo Library © Angela Fisher/Carol Beckwith
p. 56 Trobriand Islander, 1990. Aurora. Photo Peter Essick
p. 57 Corsetted Dinka men tending their cattle, Sudan. Robert Estall Photo Library © Fabby Nielsen
p. 58 Canova (1757–1822), *Cupid and Psyche* (side view), 1796. Marble, H 137 (53⅞). The State Hermitage Museum, St Petersburg, Bridgeman Art Library
p. 60 left Eros Stringing a Bow. Roman copy of 4th century Lysippian statue. Marble, H. 123 (43⅜). Museo Capitolino, Rome. Photo Alinari
p. 60 right Francesco Mazzola Parmigianino (1503–1540), *Cupid Carving a Bow*, 1533–4. Oil on canvas, 135 x 65.3 (53⅛ x 25¾). Kunsthistorisches Museum, Vienna
p. 61 Eros. Roman copy after Praxiteles. Marble, H. 164 (64⅝). Museo Nazionale, Naples. Photo Alinari, Florence
p. 62 Gherardo di Giovanni del Fora (*c.* 1432–1497), *The Combat of Love and Chastity*, 1475–1500. Tempera on wood, 42.5 x 34.9 (16¾ x 13¾). National Gallery, London
p. 63 Pontormo (1494–1556/57), *Venus and Cupid*, 1532–3. Oil on canvas, 128 x 197 (50⅜ x 77½). Galleria dell' Accademia, Florence. Photo Scala
p. 64 Alessandro Allori (1535–1607), *The Disarming of Cupid*, 16th century. Oil on panel, 150 x 124 (59 x 48⅞). Musée Fabre, Montpellier. Photo Frédéric Jaulmes
p. 65 Correggio (*c.* 1489/94–1534), *Danaë*, *c.* 1531. Oil on panel, 161 x 193 (63⅜ x 76). Galleria Borghese, Rome
p. 66 Bronzino (1503–1572), *An Allegory with Venus and Cupid*, *c.* 1540–50. Oil on wood, 146.1 x 116.8 (57⅝ x 46). National Gallery, London
p. 67 Bartholomäus Spranger (1546–1611), *Venus and Cupid*. Pen and brown ink, with brown wash, heightened with white (oxidized) over black chalk. 19.4 x 19.3 (7⅝ x 7⅝). British Museum, London
p. 68 Lorenzo Lotto (1480–1556), *Venus and Cupid*, *c.* 1540. Oil on canvas, 92 x 111 (36¼ x 43¾). Metropolitan Museum of Art, New York. Purchase, Mrs Charles Wrightsman Gift, in honor of Marietta Treet, 1986
p. 69 Caravaggio (1573–1610), *Love Triumphant*, *c.* 1599. Oil on canvas, 156 x 113 (61⅜ x 44½). Gemäldegalerie, Berlin
p. 70 Bartolomeo Manfredi (*c.* 1580–*c.* 1620), *The Chastisement of Love*, 1605–10. Oil on canvas, 175.3 x 130.5 (69 x 51⅜). Courtesy of The Art Institute of Chicago, Charles H. & Mary F. S. Worcester Collection 47.58
p. 71 Giovanni Baglione (1571–1644), *The Triumph of Sacred Love over Profane Love*, *c.* 1602–03. Oil on canvas, 183.4 x 121.4 (72¼ x 47¾). Gemäldegalerie, Berlin
p. 73 Pierre-Paul Prud' hon (1758–1823), *Love Seduces Innocence*. Graphite, heightened with white, 37 x 25 (14⅝ x 9⅞). Musée du Louvre, Paris. Photo © RMN – Michèle Bellot
p. 74 Egon Schiele (1890–1918), *Schiele's Wife with her Little Nephew*, 1915. Charcoal, opaque and transparent watercolour on paper, 48.2 x 31.7 (19 x 12½). Museum of Fine Arts, Boston, Edwin E. Jack Fund 65.1322
p. 75 Benjamin West (1738–1820), *Venus Consoling Cupid Stung by a Bee*, *c.* 1786–1802. Oil on canvas, 77 x 64 (30¼ x 25¼). © The State Hermitage Museum, St Petersburg
p. 78 Luis Gonzáles Palma (b. 1957), *Corazon I (Winged Man with Heart)* (detail), 1989. Sensitized watercolour on paper

with ink and dyes, 44.4 x 44.4 (17½ x 17½). Luis Gonzáles Palma/Spencer Museum of Art, University of Kansas
p. 81 Pompeo Batoni (1708–1787), *The Marriage of Cupid and Psyche*, 1756. Oil on canvas, 85 x 119 (33½ x 46⅞). Staatliche Museen zu Berlin – Preussischer Kulturbesitz, Gemäldegalerie/bpk. Photo Jorg P. Anders
p. 82 Jean-Baptiste Greuze (1762–1842), *Psyche Crowning Love* (detail), *c.* 1785–90. Oil on canvas, 89.5 x 64 (35¼ x 25¼). Musée des Beaux-Arts, Lille. Photo © RMN – H. Lewandowski
p. 83 left Gérard (1770–1837), *Psyche Receiving Cupid's First Kiss*, 1798. Oil on canvas, 186 x 132 (73¼ x 52). Musée du Louvre, Paris. Photo © RMN – Gérard Blot
p. 83 right Angelika Kauffmann (1740–1807), *The Plymouth Children as Cupid and Psyche*, 1795. Oil and canvas, 139 x 110 (54¾ x 43¼). Bündner Kunstmuseum, Chur
p. 84 Jacques-Louis David (1788–1856), *Cupid and Psyche*, 1817. Oil on canvas, 184.2 x 241.6 (72½ x 95⅛). Cleveland Museum of Art, Ohio (Purchase, Leonard C. Hanna, Jr., Bequest)
p. 85 François-Edouard Picot (1786–1868), *Cupid and Psyche*, 1817. Oil on canvas, 233 x 291 (91¾ x 114⅝). Musée du Louvre, Paris. Photo © RMN
p. 86 left Antoine-Denis Chaudet (1763–1810), *Cupid Trapping a Butterfly*, 1802. Marble, 89.5 x 64 (35¼ x 25¼). Musée du Louvre, Paris. Photo © RMN
p. 86 right Adolphe-William Bouguereau (1825–1905), *Cupidon*, 1875. Oil on canvas. Roy Miles Fine Paintings/ Bridgeman Art Library
p. 87 Annie Swynnerton (1844–1933), *Cupid and Psyche*, 1891. Oil on canvas, 145 x 89 (57⅛ x 35). Oldham Art Gallery, Lancashire, Bridgeman Art Library
p. 88 Julia Margaret Cameron (1815–1879), *Venus Chiding Cupid and Removing his Wings*, 1872. Albumen, 32.4 x 24.3 (12¾ x 10¼). John Paul Getty Museum JPGM 84.XM.443.4
p. 89 Guido Reni (1575–1642), *The Triumph of Sacred Love over Profane Love*, 1622–3. Oil on canvas, 131 x 163 (51⅝ x 64⅛). Galleria Nazionale di Palazzo Spinola, Genoa
p. 90 Guido Reni (1575–1642), *Amor Divino*, 1640–42. Oil on canvas, 252 x 153 (99¼ x 60¼). Pinacoteca Capitolina, Rome
p. 93 Antonio del Pollaiuolo (*c.* 1433–1498), *Tobias and the Angel*, 1465. Oil on canvas, 188 x 119 (74 x 46⅞). Galleria Sabauda, Turin. Photo Scala
p. 94 left Raphael (1483–1520), *St Michael Victorious*, 1518. Oil on canvas, 268 x 160 (105½ x 63). Musée du Louvre, Paris. Photo Scala
p. 94 right Guido Reni (1575–1642), *St Michael*, *c.* 1633–5. Oil on silk, 293 x 202 (115⅜ x 79½). S. Maria della Concezione, Rome
p. 95 Francesco Botticini (1446–1497), *The Three Archangels and Tobias*, *c.* 1467–71. Tempera on wood, 153 x 154 (60¼ x 60⅝). Galleria degli Uffizi, Florence. Photo Scala
p. 97 Giambattista Tiepolo (1696–1770), *Sarah and the Angel*, 1727. Palazza Patriarcale, Udine
p. 98 Caravaggio (1573–1610), *Rest on the Flight into Egypt* (detail), 1596–7. Oil on canvas, 135.7 x 166 (53⅜ x 65⅜). Galleria Doria-Pamphili, Rome. Photo Scala
p. 99 Hendrick ter Brugghen (1588–1629), *The Deliverance of St Peter*, 1624. Oil on canvas, 105 x 85 (41⅜ x 33½). Royal Cabinet of Paintings, Mauritshuis, The Hague
p. 100 Giovanni Lanfranco (1582–1647), *Hagar in the Wilderness*, date unknown. Oil on canvas, 138 x 159 (54⅜ x 62⅝). Chateaux de Versailles et de Trianon. Photo © RMN – Arnaudet/J. Schormans
p. 101 Domenichino (1581–1641), *The Vision of St Jerome*, *c.* 1602. Oil on canvas, 51.1 x 39.8 (20⅛ x 15⅝). National Gallery, London
p. 103 A. A. Dumont (1801–1884), *The Genius of Liberty*, 1833. Bronze patiné, 235.5 x 112 (92¾ x 44⅛). Musée du Louvre, Paris. Photo © RMN – H. Lewandowski
p. 104 Bartholomäus Spranger (1546–1611), *Hermaphroditus and the Nymph Salmacis*, *c.* 1585. 110 x 81 (43¼ x 31⅞). Kunsthistorisches Museum, Vienna
p. 106 Ford Madox Brown (1821–1893), *The Finding of Don Juan by Haidée*, 1878. Oil on canvas, 115 x 142 (45¼ x 55⅞). Musée d'Orsay, Paris/Bridgeman Art Library
p. 107 Louis Lagrenée (1725–1805), *Psyche Surprising the Sleeping Eros*, 1769. Oil on canvas, 121 (47⅝). Musée du Louvre, Paris. Photo © RMN – J. G. Berizzi
p. 108 The Barberini Faun, early 2nd century BCE. Marble, H. 213.4 (84). Staatliche Antikensammlungen, Munich. Photo Hirmer
p. 109 Michelangelo (1475–1564), The Dying Slave, 1513–16. Marble, H. 229 (90⅛). Musée du Louvre, Paris. Photo © RMN – R. G. Ojeda
p. 110 Guido Cagnacci (1601–1681), *Sleeping Christ with John the Baptist*, 17th century. Oil on canvas, 94 x 131 (37 x 51⅝). Musée Condé, Chantilly/Bridgeman Art Library
p. 111 Ludovico Carracci (1555–1619), *Study of a Nude Boy Sleeping*, date unknown. Red chalk on cream paper, 23.7 x 22.3 (9⅜ x 8¾). Ashmolean Museum, University of Oxford
p. 112 Giovanni Battista Caracciolo called Battistello (*c.* 1570–1637), *Sleeping Cupid*, date unknown. Oil on canvas, 75 x 140 (29½ x 55). Whitfield Fine Art, London
p. 113 Henry Fuseli (1741–1825), *Selene and Endymion*, 1810. Pen, pencil and watercolour, 37.3 x 30.2 (14⅝ x 11⅞). Auckland Art Gallery, Toi o Tamaki, purchased 1965
p. 114 Canova (1757–1822), *Sleeping Endymion*, 1819–22. Marble, 93 x 185 (36⅝ x 72⅞). Devonshire Collection, Chatsworth. By permission of the Duke of Devonshire and the Chatsworth Settlement Trustees
p. 115 Girodet (1767–1824), *The Sleep of Endymion*, 1791. Oil on canvas, 198 x 261 (78 x 103). Musée du Louvre, Paris
p. 118 Francesco Albani (1578–1660), *Salmacis and Hermaphroditus*, *c.* 1633. Oil on canvas, 184 x 231 (72½ x 91). Galleria Sabauda, Turin
p. 119 Rodin (1840–1917), *Aurora and Tithonus*, before 1906. Plaster, H. 26.7 (10½). National Gallery of Art, Washington, D.C. Gift of Mrs John N. Simpson, 1942
p. 120 Pietro Ricchi (1605–1675), *Tancredi Succoured by Erminia*, *c.* 1650. Oil on canvas, 121 x 180.5 (47⅝ x 71⅛). Residenzgalerie, Salzburg
p. 121 Rubens (1577–1640), *Venus Lamenting over the Dead Adonis*, date unknown. Pen and brown ink, with brown wash, heightened with white, 20.6 x 15.1 (8⅛ x 6). British Museum, London
p. 122 Rubens (1577–1640), *Venus Mourning Adonis*, *c.* 1614. Oil on panel, 48.5 x 66.5 (19⅛ x 26⅛). By permission of the trustees of Dulwich Picture Gallery, London
p. 124 Frederic Leighton (1830–1896), *The Fisherman and the Siren*, 1856–8. Oil on canvas, 66 x 48.8 (26 x 19¼). Bristol City Museum and Art Gallery/Bridgeman Art Library
p. 125 Edward Burne-Jones (1833–1898), *Phyllis and Demophoön*, 1870. Watercolour and bodycolour, 91.5 x 45.8 (36 x 18). Birmingham City Museums and Art Gallery
p. 126 Head of the Young Bacchus. Roman, 1–50 CE. Bronze with silver inlays, H. 21.6 (8½). The J. Paul Getty Museum, Los Angeles
p. 128 Dionysos, 460–450 BCE. Bronze, 24 (9½). Musée du Louvre, Paris. Photo © RMN – Chuzeville
p. 129 Dionysos with kantharos. Hellenistic. Archaeological Museum, Eleusis. Photo Alinari, Florence
p. 130 Caravaggio (1573–1610), *Bacchus*, 1595–7. Oil on canvas, 95 x 85 (37⅜ x 33¾). Galleria degli Uffizi, Florence. Photo Scala
p. 131 Caravaggio (1573–1610), *The Musicians*, 1595–6. Oil on canvas, 92 x 118.4 (36¼ x 46⅝). Metropolitan Museum of Art, New York. Rogers Fund, 1952 (52.81).
p. 132 Melozzo da Forlì (1438–1494), *An Angel Playing the Viol*. Fragment of detached fresco, 113 x 91 (44½ x 35⅞). Vatican, Rome
p. 133 Erigbaagtsa boy with pan pipe. Photo Harald Schultz
p. 135 Agnolo Bronzino (1503–1572), *Portrait of Cosimo I as Orpheus*, *c.* 1539. Oil on wood, 93 x 67 (36⅝ x 26⅜). Philadelphia Museum of Art
p. 138 Nijinsky, *L'Après-Midi d'un Faune*, 1912. Photo Private Collection
p. 139 Tutsi dancing. National Geographic Society Image Collection. Photo George F. Mobley
p. 140 Rudolf Nureyev, 1962. Photo Zoë Dominic
p. 141 Grace Lau (b. 1939), *Untitled*, 1993. Black and white photograph. Courtesy the artist
p. 142 Thomas Eakins (1844–1916), *Swimming*, *c.* 1889. Oil on canvas, 69.5 x 92.2 (27⅜ x 36⅜). Purchased by the Friends of Art, Fort Worth Art Association, 1925; acquired by the Amon Carter Museum, 1990, from the Modern Art Museum of Fort Worth through grants and donations from the Amon G. Carter Foundation, the Sid W. Richardson Foundation, the Anne Burnett and Charles Tandy Foundation, Capital Cities/ABC Foundation, Fort Worth Star-Telegram, the R. D. and Joan Dale Hubbard Foundation and the people of Fort Worth
p. 143 Henry Scott Tuke (1858–1929), *August Blue*, 1893–4. Oil on canvas, 121.9 x 182.9 (48 x 72). © Tate, London 2003. Presented by the Trustees of the Chantrey Bequest 1894
p. 144 Dancing Maenad. Roman, 1st century BCE. Carved onyx, 4.5 x 3.3 (1¾ x 1¼). British Museum, London
p. 145 William Blake Richmond (1842–1874), *The Bowlers* (detail), 1870. Oil on canvas, 65 x 273 (25⅝ x 107½). The Master, Fellows and Scholars of Downing College in the University of Cambridge
p. 146 Jacob Huysmans (*c.* 1633–1680/96), *Lady Elizabeth Somerset, Countess later Marchioness Powis*, 1665–70. Oil on canvas, 238 x 147.3 (93¾ x 58). National Trust Photographic Library/Powis Estate Trustees/John Hammond
p. 148 Benozzo Gozzoli (1420–1497), *Procession of the Magi* (detail), 1459. Fresco. Palazzo Medici Riccardi, Florence
p. 149 Hendrik Leys (1815–1869), *The Bird Catcher*, 1866. Oil on canvas, 61 x 92 (24 x 36¼). Koninklijk Museum voor Schone Kunsten, Antwerp
p. 150 Bertoldo di Giovanni (*c.* 1420–1491), *Pegasus and Bellerophon*, before 1486. Bronze, H. 32.5 (12⅞). Kunsthistorisches Museum, Vienna
p. 151 Unknown Nordic artist, *The Abduction of Ganymede*, *c.* 1550–1600. Oil on canvas, stuck onto poplar board, 89 x 75 (35 x 29½). Bildergalerie von Sanssouci, Stiftung Preussische Schlosser und Garten Berlin-Brandenburg, Potsdam
p. 153 Quentin Massys (*c.* 1465–1530), *St John Altarpiece* (left panel), 1507–8. Oil on canvas, 260 x 120 (102⅜ x 47¼). Koninklijk Museum voor Schone Kunsten, Antwerp
p. 155 Anthony Van Dyck (1599–1691), *Charles I at the Hunt*, *c.* 1635. Oil on canvas, 272 x 212 (107⅛ x 83½). Musée du Louvre, Paris
p. 159 Guido Reni (1575–1642), *Salome Receiving the Head of the Baptist*, 1638–9. Oil on canvas, 248 x 174 (97¾ x 68½). The Art Institute of Chicago
p. 160 Caravaggio (1573–1610), *Alof de Wignacourt, Grand Master of the Order of Malta from 1601–22 with his page* (detail), *c.* 1608. Oil on canvas, 194 x 134 (76⅜ x 52¾). Musée du Louvre, Paris. Photo © RMN – R. G. Ojeda
p. 162 Gerard ter Borch (1617–1681), *Lady at her Toilet*, *c.* 1660. Oil on canvas, 76.2 x 59.7 (30 x 23½). The Detroit Institute of Arts, Founders Society Purchase, Eleanor Clay Ford Fund, General Membership Fund, Endowment Income Fund, and Special Activities Fund no. 65.10
p. 163 Benedetto Gennari (*c.* 1633–1715), *Portrait of Hortense Mancini, Duchess of Mazarin* (detail), undated. Oil on canvas, 228.5 x 178 (90 x 70). Photo Sotheby's, London
p. 164 Sir Joshua Reynolds (1723–1792), *Giuseppe Marchi*, *c.* 1753. Oil on canvas, 73.5 x 62.3 (28⅞ x 24½). The Royal Academy of Arts, London
p. 165 Sir Joshua Reynolds (1723–1792), *Cupid as a Link Boy*, 1774. Oil on canvas, 76 x 63.5 (30 x 25). Albright-Knox Art Gallery, Buffalo, New York. Seymour H. Knox Fund, through special gifts to the fund by Mrs Majorie Knox Campbell, Mrs Dorothy Knox Rogers and Mr Seymour H. Knox, Jr, 1945
p. 166 John Singer Sargent (1856–1925), *Thomas E. McKellar*, 1917–20. Oil on canvas, 125.7 x 84.5 (49½ x 33¼). Courtesy of the Museum of Fine Arts, Boston. Henry H. and Zoe Oliver Sherman Fund
p. 168 Studio of Adriaen Hanneman, *Portrait of Henry Stuart, Duke of Gloucester When a Boy*, after 1653. Oil on canvas, 67.5 x 53.5 (26½ x 21). Photo Sotheby's, London
p. 170 C. A. Jensen (1792–1870), *A Son of the Artist*, 1836. Oil on canvas, 31.5 x 23 (12⅜ x 9). Statens Museum for Kunst, Copenhagen

p. 171 Pontormo (1494–1556/57), *Portrait of a Halberdier (possibly Francesco Guardi)*, *c.* 1528–30. Oil on panel, 92 x 72 (36¼ x 28⅜). The J. Paul Getty Museum, Los Angeles. © The J. Paul Getty Museum

p. 173 Venus and Mars. Marble, H. 215 (84⅝). Uffizi, Florence. Photo Alinari, Florence

pp. 174–5 Botticelli (1444/45–1510), *Venus and Mars*, *c.* 1485. Egg tempera and oil on poplar, 69.2 x 173.4 (27¼ x 68¼). National Gallery, London

p. 176 Piero di Cosimo (1462–1521), *Venus and Mars*, *c.* 1505. Oil on wood, 72 x 182 (28⅜ x 71⅝). Staatliche Museen zu Berlin – Preussischer Kulturbesitz, Gemaeldegalerie/bpk. Photo Jorg P. Anders

p. 177 Nicolas Poussin (1594–1665), *Rinaldo and Armida*, 1629. Oil on canvas, 82.2 x 109.2 (32⅜ x 43). By permission of the Trustees of the Dulwich Picture Gallery, London

p. 178 Michelangelo (1475–1564), David, 1501–4. Marble, H. 409 (161). Accademia, Florence. Photo Scala

p. 179 left Verrocchio (1435–1488), David, before 1476. Bronze, H. 125 (49¼). Bargello, Florence. Photo Scala

p. 179 right Donatello (*c.* 1386–1466), David, *c.* 1440. Bronze, H. 158.2 (62¼). Bargello, Florence/Bridgeman Art Library

p. 180 Johan Zoffany (1733–1810), *Self-Portrait as David with the Head of Goliath*, 1756. Oil on canvas, 92.2 x 74.7 (36¼ x 29⅜). Purchased by The Art Foundation of Victoria, in conjunction with the Isabella Mary Curnick Bequest, 1994. National Gallery of Victoria, Melbourne

p. 181 Guido Reni (1575–1642), *David with the Head of Goliath* (detail), *c.* 1605. Oil on canvas, 220 x 145 (86⅝ x 57⅛). Musée du Louvre, Paris. Photo © RMN – Gérard Blot

p. 182 Bertel Thorvaldsen (1768/70–1844), *Jason with the Golden Fleece*, 1828. Marble, H. 242 (95¼). Thorvaldsens Museum, Copenhagen

p. 183 Sir Alfred Gilbert (1854–1934), *Perseus Arming*, 1882. Bronze, H. 73.7 (29). Private Collection

p. 184 Late Bronze Age boxers, Akrotiri, Thera. National Archaeological Museum, Naples. Photo Scala

p. 185 Pugilist, Roman. Marble, H. 174 (68½). Musée du Louvre, Départment des Antiquités Grècques/Romaines, Paris. Photo Erich Lessing, AKG, London

p. 186 Antonio del Pollaiuolo (1433/32–1498), *Battle of the Ten Nudes*, after 1483. Engraving, 40.4 x 59 (15⅞ x 23¼). Private Collection

p. 187 Henry Fuseli (1741–1825), *Sleep and Death Bear the Corpse of Sarpedon away to Lycia*, 1780. Oil on canvas, 91.4 x 71 (36 x 28). Courtesy of Canton of Zurich

p. 188 Jacques-Louis David (1748–1825), *The Death of Joseph Barra* (detail), 1794. Oil on canvas, 118 x 155 (46½ x 61). Musée Calvet, Avignon/Bridgeman Art Library

p. 189 Alexandre Falguière (1831–1900), *Tarcisius*, 1868. Marble, 64 x 59.9 (25¼ x 23⅝). Musée du Louvre, Paris. Photo © RMN – R. G. Ojeda

p. 190 Antoine-Jean Gros (1771–1835), *Napoleon at the Arcole Bridge*, 1796–7. Oil on canvas, 130 x 94 (51⅛ x 37). © State Hermitage Museum, St Petersburg

p. 193 Mock warrior snaps a salute during patriotic festivities at the opening of the hospital in Gatundu, Kenya, 1968. National Geographic Society Image Collection. Photo Bruce Dale

p. 194 Pontormo (1494–1556/57), *St Quentin*, 1517–18. Oil on canvas, 150 x 100 (59 x 39⅜). Museo Civico, Sansepolcro

p. 196 Carle Vernet (1758–1836), *The Death of Hippolytus*, 1800. Black chalk stumped and heightened with white, framing line in light brown ink, black chalk and incised, 64.8 x 99.1 (25½ x 38⅞). The J. Paul Getty Museum, Los Angeles

p. 199 Gustave Moreau (1826–1898), *Diomedes Devoured by Horses*, 1851. Watercolour, 21.6 x 19.7 (8½ x 7¾). The J. Paul Getty Museum, Los Angeles

p. 201 Nicolas Régnier (*c.* 1590–1667), *Hero and Leander*, *c.* 1625–6. Oil on canvas, 155.3 x 209.5 (61⅛ x 82½). Felton Bequest, 1955. National Gallery of Victoria, Melbourne

p. 202 Francesco Furini (1604–1646), *Hylas and the Naiads*, 17th century. Oil on canvas, 230 x 261 (90½ x 102¾). Galleria Palatini, Florence. Photo Scala

p. 203 The Farnese Antinous, *c.* 130–138 CE. Marble, H. 180 (70⅞). Museo Archeologico Nazionale, Naples. Photo Scala

p. 205 Anthony Van Dyck (1599–1691), *The Martyrdom of St Sebastian*, after 1621. Oil on canvas, 199.9 x 150.6 (78¾ x 59¼). Alte Pinakothek, Munich. Photo Artothek

p. 206 Andrea Mantegna (1431–1506), *St Sebastian*, 1457–8. Poplar, 68 x 30 (26¾ x 11¾). Kunsthistorisches Museum, Vienna

p. 207 Alonso Berruguete (*c.* 1486–1561), *St Sebastian*, 1526–32. Wood, 111 x 33 (46¾ x 13). © Museo Nacional de Escultura, Valladolid

p. 208 Titian (*c.* 1485–1576), *St Mark Enthroned with Saints Cosmas, Damian, Roch and Sebastian*, *c.* 1510. Oil on panel, 230 x 149 (90½ x 50⅝). S. Maria della Salute, Venice. Photo Scala

p. 209 left Nicolas Régnier (*c.* 1590–1667), *St Sebastian*, *c.* 1600–10. Oil on canvas, 130 x 100 (51 x 39). © State Hermitage Museum, St Petersburg

p. 209 right Gustave Moreau (1826–1898), *St Sebastian and the Angel* (detail), 1876. Oil on panel, 69.5 x 39.7 (27⅜ x 15⅝). Fogg Art Museum, Harvard University Art Museums. Bequest of Grenville L. Winthrop/Bridgeman Art Library

p. 210 Hendrick ter Brugghen (1588–1629), *St Sebastian*, 1625. Oil on canvas 150.2 x 120 (59⅛ x 47¼). Collection of the Allen Memorial Art Museum, Oberlin College, R. T. Miller Jr. Fund 1953

p. 211 Antonio Bellucci (1654–1726), *St Sebastian Tended by Irene*, *c.* 1716–18. Oil on canvas, 144.7 x 134.3 (57 x 52⅞). By permission of the Trustees of Dulwich Picture Gallery, London

p. 212 Giulio Cesare Procaccini (*c.* 1570–1625), *St Sebastian Tended by Angels*, *c.* 1610–12. Oil on panel, 285 x 139 (112¼ x 54¾). Musées Royaux des Beaux-Arts, Brussels

p. 213 François-Xavier Fabre (1766–1837), *The Death of Abel*, 1791. Oil on canvas, 146.6 x 198 (57¾ x 78). Musée Fabre, Montpellier. Photo Frédéric Jaulmes

p. 214 Rembrandt (1606–1669), *Abraham's Sacrifice*, 1635. Oil on canvas, 193.5 x 132.8 (76⅛ x 52¼). © The State Hermitage Museum, St Petersburg

p. 215 Valentin de Boulogne (1591–1632), *The Martyrdom of St Laurence*, 1621–2. Oil on canvas, 195 x 261 (76¾ x 102¾). Museo del Prado, Madrid

p. 216 Albrecht Altdorfer (*c.* 1480–1538), *The Martyrdom of St Florian*, *c.* 1515. Oil on panel, 76.4 x 67.2 (30⅛ x 26½). Galleria degli Uffizi, Florence/Bridgeman Art Library

p. 218 Annie Leibovitz (b. 1949), *David Cassidy*, 1972. Gelatin silver print. © Annie Leibovitz (Contact Press Images). Courtesy of the artist

pp. 220–21 Giovanni Lanfranco (1582–1647), *Young Man with Cat*, 1620. Oil on canvas, 113 x 160 (44½ x 63). Christie's Images, London/Bridgeman Art Library

p. 222 Rosalba Carriera (1675–1757), *Portrait of Charles Sackville, 2nd Duke of Dorset* (detail), 1731–2. Pastel, 55.9 x 44.5 (22 x 17½). Private Collection. National Trust Photographic Library/John Hammond

p. 223 Sofonisba Anguissola (*c.* 1527–1625), *Portrait of Marchese Massimiliano Stampa*, 1557. Oil on canvas, 136.8 x 71.5 (53⅞ x 28⅛). Walters Art Gallery, Baltimore

p. 226 Robert Plant, 1971. Retna © Michael Putland

p. 227 Jim Morrison, 1968. Joel Yale/Time Life Pictures/Getty Images

p. 229 Jan Steen (1626–1679), *The Drawing Lesson*, *c.* 1665. Oil on panel, 49.3 x 41 (19⅜ x 16¼). The J. Paul Getty Museum, Los Angeles

p. 230 Angelika Kauffmann (1740–1807), *Prince Henri Lubomirski as Cupid*, 1786. Oil on canvas, 155 x 115 (61 x 45¼). Liviv State Picture Gallery, Ukraine/Bridgeman Art Library

p. 231 Angelika Kauffmann (1740–1807), *Cupid and Psyche*, 1792. Oil sketch, 29.9 x 23.8 (11¾ x 9⅜). Vorarlberger Landesmuseum, Bregenz

p. 232 Marie Ellenrieder (1791–1863), *St Felicitas and her Seven Sons*, 1847. Oil on canvas, 107.2 x 159.1 (42¼ x 62⅝). The Royal Collection © 2003, Her Majesty Queen Elizabeth II

p. 233 Marie Bashkirtseff (1860–1884), *Life Class in the Women's Studio at the Académie Julian*, *c.* 1881. Engraving. Samuel Courtauld Trust, © Courtauld Gallery. Courtauld Institute, London

p. 234 Dorothy Tennant (1855–1926), *The Death of Love*, 1888. Oil on canvas, 22.9 x 33.3 (9 x 13⅛). Robert Coale, Chicago

p. 235 Anna Lea Merritt (1844–1930), *Love Locked Out*, 1889. Oil on canvas, 115.6 x 64.1 (45½ x 25¼). Tate, London

p. 237 Mary Cassatt (1844–1926), *Mother and Child*, 1901. Oil on canvas, 81.6 x 65.7 (32⅛ x 25⅞). Metropolitan Museum of Art, New York

p. 238 Sphinx with Boy Victim (reconstruction). Black painted plaster, H. 79 (31⅛). Kunsthistorisches Museum, Vienna

p. 239 Léonor Fini (1908–1996), *Sphinx Amalbourga*, 1942. Oil on canvas, 38 x 55 (15 x 21⅝). © ADAGP, Paris and DACS, London 2003

pp. 240-41 Deborah Law, *Untitled*, 1972. Tempera on board, 182.9 x 121.9 (72 x 48). Courtesy of the artist

p. 242 Sylvia Sleigh (b. 1925), *Philip Golub Reclining*, 1971. Oil on canvas, 106.7 x 152.4 (42 x 60). Courtesy of the artist

p. 243 Sarah Kent, *Male Nude: California*, 1982. Black and white photograph, 25.4 x 20.3 (10 x 8). Courtesy Sarah Kent

p. 244 Sally Mann (b. 1951), *The Last Time Emmett Modeled Nude*, 1987. Gelatin silver enlargement print, 50.8 x 61 (20 x 24). © Sally Mann. Courtesy Edwynn Houk Gallery, New York

p. 245 Ellen von Unwerth (b. 1954), *Ashton Nude with Heart-Shaped Box of Chocolates*. Art & Commerce

Index

Figures in *italic* refer to illustrations.